Woodworking Techniques and Projects

Anthony Bailey

First published 2003 by
Guild of Master Craftsman Publications Ltd,
166 High Street, Lewes,
East Sussex BN7 1XU

ISBN 1 86108 356 4

A catalogue record of this book is available from the British Library.

Cover design by Oliver Prentice
Colour origination by Universal Graphics (Singapore)
Printed and bound by CT Printing Ltd (Hong Kong)

Contents

makita
3612C
CLEAR

Introduction

When I was asked by the GMC Book people whether I thought a book based on the work I have done for woodworking magazines was a good idea, I was frankly bemused. Surely no one really wants to read a book about me? However, taking a mental step back and looking objectively at the many articles, tests and projects I have done over the years, it does seem that if you take me as a 'personality' out of the equation, there is a vast body of quite readable, usable material for the aspiring woodworker. Wiser minds than I have put together a goodly mixture of projects, techniques and ideas from my vast back catalogue.

I am particularly pleased to see the inclusion of a whole set of biscuit jointer articles first published in New Woodworking magazine. So little has been written about the biscuit jointer and yet it is surely one of the easiest and most effective powertools to master. I have taken its basic jointmaking function and proved that it can adapt to other techniques, including decorative effects. It will never equal the router at this latter task but it shows what a bit of imagination can produce.

Talking of the router, there are a number of router-based projects which are useful around the home or in the workshop. I know many router owners like workshop projects as they extend the uses of this versatile machine at little cost.

In addition, there is my series on the mechanics of making which discusses the problems attached to making a piece of furniture and how to overcome them.

We haven't put in any of the many tests I have done; these date fairly rapidly as models are changed or improved. As someone who cut his teeth, so to speak, on hand tools, this rate of progress and change is quite noticeable. To a large extent, traditional tools such as bench planes and Sheffield steel handsaws are gone, but in exchange we have cheap, lethally sharp hardpoint saws and power planers. At the time of writing, new designs of router from the Far East have appeared and even a cordless model from North America. The biscuit jointer has proliferated into a large number of models from all parts of the planet.

This ease of access to labour-saving tools is such a good thing. There is no need to bemoan the past when woodworking has never been so easy! I hope this book will make a good accompaniment on your journey through this exciting world of working wood.

Anthony Bailey

Introduction to the biscuit jointer

PART I: BISCUIT JOINTER BASICS

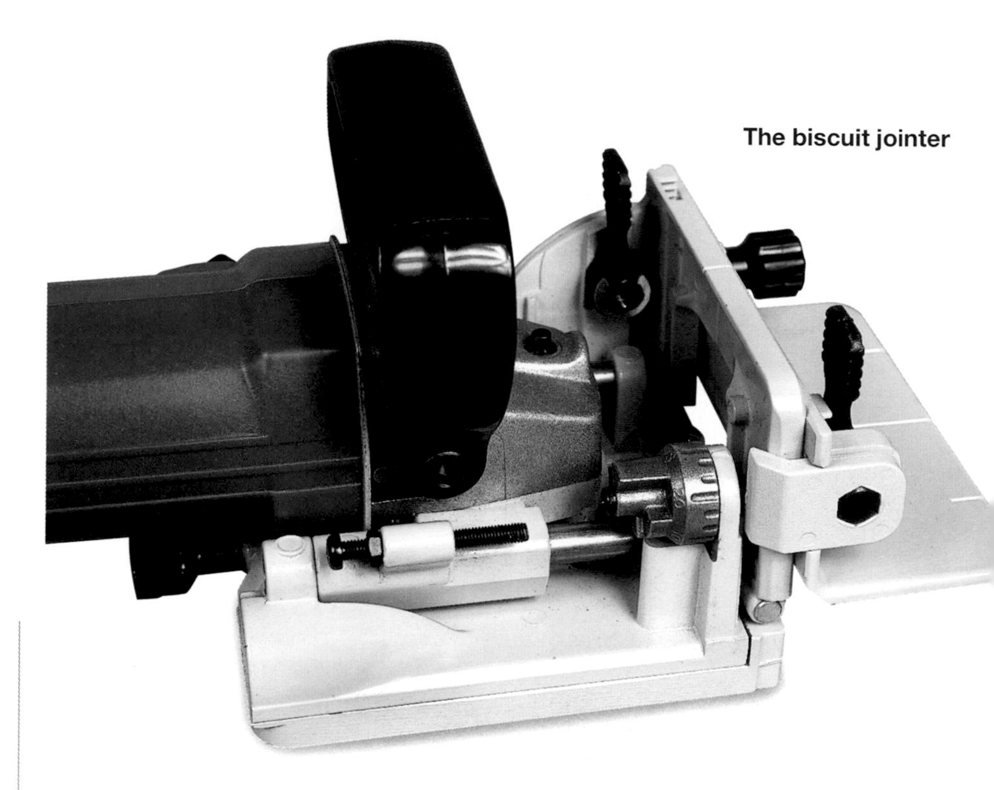
The biscuit jointer

There are many exciting possibilities with this wonder tool

For many people, the biscuit jointer is still a largely unexplored power tool whose true advantages have yet to be appreciated. In essence, you have a motor of between 550–750W input power, right angle gearing (like an angle grinder), a mini-saw blade of 100mm (4in) diameter, a housing to cover the blade, a means of pushing the blade out of the housing, safely retracting after the cut is made and a means of setting the depth of cut. Finally, some kind of adjustable fence is fitted on for guidance.

Standard beech biscuits come in three sizes: 0, 10 and 20. These are stamped out of fine-grained beech wood and are 4mm (5⁄32in) thick, the same as the jointer blade. The beech biscuits are compressed during the stamping, so that they will swell once wet with glue inside the joint and have a hatched pattern which makes them grip the sides of each slot when they do swell; the grain runs at 45°. Once the joint is closed the biscuits are so strong they cannot snap as would happen if the grain ran along the direction of the joint.

Plunge and swing-down body types

The basic pattern for the jointer is the plunge type, that is to say that you grip the motor body and push the running blade straight into the workpiece.

The alternative swing-down type is just that: the motor hinges on a pivot thus the blade swings into the workpiece in an arc. This sort is more suited to board sawing since the motor body can be swung down behind the blade allowing it to be pushed along easily. The plunge type has the motor above the blade and the workpiece and is therefore less suitable for this operation.

Machine safety

Take a suitable piece of board, cramp it down and set the fence so the blade is roughly centred on the edge of the board and plug in. Hold the machine in place with the fence and faceplate pressed firmly and squarely on the board without the blade being plunged, switch on and then plunge. Allow the blade to

Standard beech biscuits come in a variety of sizes

The basic pattern is the plunge type

The alternative pattern is the 'swing-down' type

retract by slackening arm pressure and switch off.

Don't work with both the jointer and the workpiece loose; either the work or the machine must be firmly fixed.

Biscuits

For most applications beech biscuits are best. I would suggest you buy a mixed pack of 500 or 1,000 biscuits in the three standard sizes 0, 10 and 20. As you get used to using them I think you will find that 20s invariably get used much more than the smaller sizes, so re-stock with 20s to reflect your general usage. Use the biggest practical size because it will obviously hold the work together better; 0s in particular tend to break easily or have pieces missing, whereas 10s and 20s have a bit more structural integrity.

Manufacturers normally sell biscuits in boxes made of corrugated cardboard which doesn't keep moisture out, but does absorb some, thus helping to keep the biscuits dry. A better move is to transfer your biscuits into polythene ice cream boxes or similar food containers or into sealed plastic bags (keeping the different sizes apart). That way you can prevent the biscuits swelling up when in storage.

It's OK to tap biscuits gently into their slots with a hammer if you have a lot to fit or if they are a little tight. You can place biscuits as close as you like, but it makes economic sense to make the gaps between 150–250mm (approx 6–9 3/4in), 200mm (8in) being a good average.

Triton biscuits

Triton supply biscuits designed for their biscuit jointing accessory to the Series 2000 Workcentre that will appeal to a lot of users. These are 4mm (5/32in) thick, as usual, but are shorter and fatter as they have to fit into slots created by a router cutter. The unique feature of the Triton system is that having got a Workcentre, you then fit the optional router table.

On to that, the biscuit jointing fence is fitted thus giving a static set-up. A router is installed with the special Triton biscuit cutter fitted; the fence sits over the cutter. Then you mark your biscuit slots and adjust the stop on the fence and apply the component forming one half of the joint to the fence and push.

The fence swings across, exposing the cutter which slots the wood. Do the same with the matching component against the other side of the fence and your joint is cut. The result is precise, quick jointing using this swinging fence system, and by adjusting the fence stop all your slots can be cut in the same way.

Assembly biscuits

For 'try outs' and awkward assembly situations there are special assembly biscuits available from Lamello. These are bright red plastic and have ridges or barbs making non-cramp assembly theoretically possible. Other makes such as Knapp produce biscuits with similar features. However, these are not one piece like the Lamello biscuits, but are demountable two-part biscuits which are proper joint forming biscuits.

A mixed pack of biscuits will be very useful

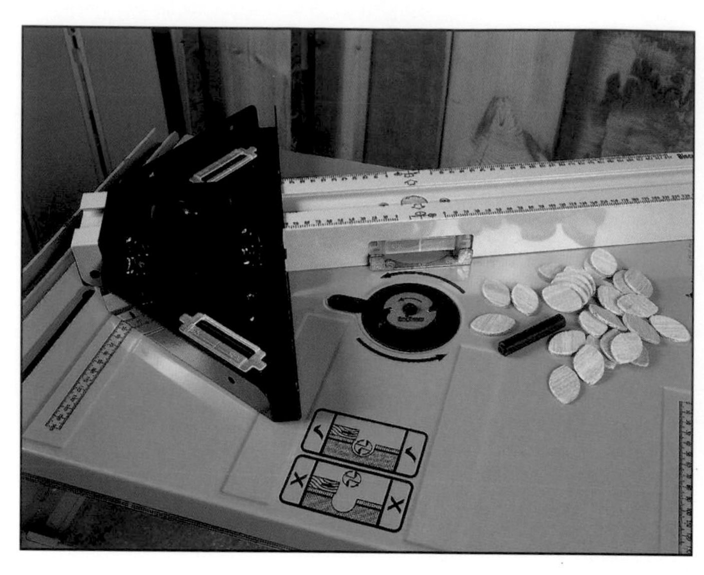

Triton supply biscuits designed for their biscuit jointing accessory to the Series 2000 Workcentre

I have my doubts as to whether assembly biscuits designed to be fully removable are really useful, as they damage the sides of the slots when pulled out. However, as a means of attaching parts such as mouldings – permanently and invisibly – they are extremely useful especially on-site where no adequate means of cramping is available.

Glues and applicators

For most situations PVA will do for all your needs. It remains usable under most conditions except in winter when it gets thick when cold. It dries fairly quickly too, providing it is used in reasonably warm conditions. Used washing-up liquid bottles are good dispensers, though you may need to cut out the star moulding under the nozzle to prevent it blocking up.

You could use a Dosicol-type dispenser designed for biscuit slots, however they are expensive and are not meant for placing glue between slot positions. Axminster Power Tools sell a complete glue dispenser kit with a variety of nozzles, though these need to be kept clean and unblocked.

There is also aliphatic resin glue with a pale yellow colour and a sharp smell. It has a fast grab which will make it difficult to use on a complicated glue-up as one part may start to set before you have cramped the entire workpiece. However, it does remain runny during cold weather making it preferable to PVA which thickens.

There are special assembly biscuits for awkward situations

Biscuit glue joining accessories from Lamello

Planning joints, marking out

Placing all the un-jointed parts in their correct positions and lightly cramping them allows you to mark each joint carefully. A useful degree of tolerance is possible because each joint has some lateral movement once assembled. Where T-joints are needed, as in bookcase shelves for example, you need to use a decent, large marking square to draw across the board where each shelf will go. You also need to mark clearly whether the shelf goes above or below each line.

When machining slots in board edges make sure you get the board the right way up in relation to the jointer. In other words, if you mark the joint on one face, the jointer fence will sit on that face as it is the 'reference' face of the machine as well as the workpiece. If you do the same operation with the jointer sitting on another board without using the fence, the workpiece is inverted so the reference face is underneath. This time the underside of the jointer acts as the reference face of the machine. Not unsurprisingly, this kind of mental juggling makes a lot of woodworkers opt for the freehand method whenever possible, but this isn't always a good idea.

Sometimes a lot of components have joint positions that are effectively the same from piece to piece. It is possible to make up a simple indexing stick with the correct number of 'strike marks' on it. This can be used to mark quickly all similar joints with repeatable accuracy.

You can dry-assemble with some biscuits to see how the piece goes together. A pair of pincers are useful for removing these afterwards. Narrow components can be slotted

Jobs for the biscuit jointer

- Join solid timber and manufactured boards
- Create entire furniture carcasses
- Make joints that substitute for many of the conventional woodworking joints
- Saw boards to size
- Make knock-down furniture
- Add various functional features to your furniture such as sliding doors or drawer pulls
- Add decorative detail, even repair old or antique table tops

Make up a simple indexing stick with the correct number of 'strike marks' on it

Spacing is generally 150-250mm (6-9¾in)

To hold the jointer, use a combination of handgrip and the rear of the body

on the end, but the strike marks need to be centred so the biscuit slot does not break out at one side. This is best done in a static set-up.

The spacing between biscuits isn't critical, generally 150–250mm (6–9¾in) spacing is OK. Narrow components need two No. 20 biscuits close together for proper strength. You end up with a semi-continuous tongue-and-groove joint.

Freehand

The most obvious way to hold a jointer is to use a combination of handgrip and the rear of the body, though you can sometimes hold the top of the blade housing front face once the machine is sitting on the workpiece. This assumes that you have cramped the workpiece and are operating freehand.

If you are trying to joint into narrow edges this may not be satisfactory. It can be difficult to offer the machine dead square onto such a narrow surface ready to cut, especially as you cannot observe the position of the fence and body face vis-à-vis the workpiece.

The sprung pins or rubber pads used to prevent the machine slipping sideways may not help in judging how square the jointer is to the wood as these devices project slightly from the blade housing faceplate. So, for narrower work it may be better to work by sitting both the jointer and workpiece on a flat surface.

Wider workpieces can be jointed freehand more successfully because they contact with more of the fence or front face of the jointer with greater accuracy.

When biscuit jointing smallish moulding sections onto a carcass, a safe static set-up is needed. It is possible to work freehand quickly if you are confident that all your joint marking is correct. A carcass or a succession of parts can be dealt with at a speed that no other machine can match, though you need to keep an eye on the standard of accuracy with such repetitious working.

Next we will look at working on a reference board and the different kinds of biscuit joints.

Introduction to the biscuit jointer

PART II: JOINTING TECHNIQUES

Having covered the basics of biscuit jointing, move onto static set-ups, joints and more!

For working on a flat reference surface, a 19mm+ thick piece of MDF, ply or blockboard with a smoothish surface is best. This in turn should be lying on a flat bench top or similar so that it cannot bow causing any slot misalignment.

The reason for working on a board is that the face and baseplate of the biscuit jointer blade housing have been machined true to the blade and at 90° to each other thus giving greater accuracy of working than using the fence and freehand method when slotting board edges.

It may be necessary to pack the jointer or the workpiece so one is raised in relation to the other so that the slot is correctly aligned in the board edge. Therefore, a selection of thin packing pieces such as Formica offcuts, thin ply or hardboard allow suitable adjustment though this mustn't allow either the machine or the workpiece to 'float' on the packers. Also, a little downward pressure may be needed to ensure accuracy, or it may be better to glue or pin the packers in position. With this method always cramp the workpiece down anyway, as with any hand or machine operation, either the tool or the wood must stay fixed – in this case it is the wood. The jointer fence can be pushed down and locked; this will act as a 'hold-down' to keep the workpiece flat so long as it is carefully set.

The jointer fence holds the workpiece down tightly onto the reference board

Assembly technique

With complicated pieces you need to be organised and work out the correct assembly order or whether it is possible to make up several sub-assemblies first, before bringing these together once the glue is dry.

Gluing technique is important. Run a thin line of glue along one edge so it trickles into the biscuit slots, then apply glue to the slots only on the other joint half. Push the biscuits into this second lot of slot. This will help hold the glue in while you lift it over the other half to assemble the joint, then close the joint, ensure the strike marks line up and that edges and ends also align properly.

Components with a gluing surface wider than say 25mm need a zig-zag pattern of glue laid down. The larger the area, the bigger the zig-zag pattern. Have plenty of cramps of suitable

Apply a thin, even line of glue

Once both of the joint halves are cramped together, the glue will spread out fairly evenly

sizes for the job in hand and apply these carefully using pads to prevent marking the work, so that pressure is put on the joints without distorting the carcass or pushing it out of square. Use a square (preferably an engineer's square) to check all corners and a steel tape rule for diagonal corner-to-corner checking, to ensure that the measurements agree and the carcass is truly square.

You only need cramps on alternate biscuit positions; these should be moved after a while so that other biscuit joints also close properly. Once you are satisfied, the glue can be removed with a 'second best' chisel and a damp cloth, though it may be easier to leave this until it has started to set.

Pieces of French-polished walnut veneer solid are joined edge to edge

Different ways of using the biscuit

Edge to edge joint

This is easy to achieve either freehand or on a reference board. Use it to increase the width of a board or to put together solid wood and veneered board.

Veneered board can be joined along, not across, the grain if the pattern and colour of the grain is well matched. When used to joint solid wood boards to make door panels which are 'raised and fielded' (i.e. with the panel edges machined down for moulded effect), take care with biscuit positions as it is easy to have biscuits in their slots 'grinning' through where the panel cutter has sliced straight through the middle of a biscuit.

The second option for jointing different materials is useful if you want a centre panel of man-made board with a solid wood frame for strength and appearance. There is no difference in technique, though the timber may be a bit tougher to machine than the board if the blade is starting to go blunt. If you want the panel recessed (set back) then obviously the fence will need to be set further from the blade when slotting the frame.

Corner joint

This can be done freehand, or for more control, a simple L-jig set-up will make the face slotting easy, while the edge slotting can be done flat down on your reference board. As always, remember to mark the biscuit positions on the outside faces, but transfer them to the inside faces as these are the ones that you will see when machining. Use an index stick to simplify the marking out.

T-joint

Suppose you have two sides of a bookcase – you know the spaces needed for the books and you know the thickness and number of shelves. Mark all shelf positions on one bookcase side showing the shelf locations clearly and transfer these positions accurately to the other half by lying them side by side. Now nominate the top or bottom face of the shelves as the reference for the jointer base. The jointer blade position if not in the middle of each shelf will at least not be too far off it.

The bookcase side slots can be done by cramping a T-square along each reference line in turn and pressing the jointer against it for accurate fencing. The T-joint allows all kinds of parts to be assembled well away from the jointer's own fencing limit which is close to the board's edge.

Face to face joint

You can increase the thickness of stock that you're able to work with and also prevent components slipping around when glued up during cramping. With this method always fence off one face only, because if you try working off opposing faces the slots won't all line up. If your machine has a high front plate it may be possible to get

Corner joint, the basis of most carcass work

T-joints are easy to achieve when you know how

two rows of biscuits a reasonable distance apart.

Using this method, you could for instance knock up 100 x 100mm (4 x 4in) square newel posts for a staircase using standard 100 x 50mm (4 x 2in) softwood doubled up. It also allows the use of well-seasoned hardwood doubled in thickness, where hardwood twice the thickness just wouldn't be well-seasoned or stable enough to use.

Arising from the need to double material thickness is the problem of how to stop the two pieces slipping around when glued up and the cramps applied. Glue is slippery, viscous stuff and it is difficult to get the component edges flush. If you were going to biscuit them anyway, the problem of slip solves itself. If however you didn't feel biscuits were necessary, the answer is still to use a few biscuits just to positively locate both pieces.

Boxed-up joints

The boxed-up joint is nothing more than four corner joints all close together to form a rigid hollow square shape. This is ideal for table legs, for example, and is immensely strong. As always the components need to be cut carefully to start with, but providing the edges are a true 90° to the faces, once glued and the cramps are put on, the box shape will pull together straight and square and once dry is almost indestructible.

If this joint is done in solid wood the resulting joints aren't very noticeable; however plain MDF or veneered board, which needs its edges taped with veneer, may be a bit more obvious. One way round this is to use the jointer in shallow 'saw mode' and run a groove down each joint and on the unjointed faces as well to give a deliberate decorative effect that disguises the joints.

Mitres

Mouldings such as cornices and plinths need neatly mitred junctions and sometimes a design may call for an angled shape – a corner cupboard that literally fits across the corner of a room, for example.

All jointers can slot 45° mitres either using the fence which can normally be reversed so the 45° face comes into play, or more sophisticated models have been equipped so that the fence can swing right down to give variable mitre angles including acute ones (as in the case of the Ryobi or the Flex Porter Cable). Alternatively, the actual front plate on the blade housing may swing down parallel to the blade (Lamello Top Twenty, Classic, etc.) which, although not as extreme as the former examples, is still useful.

In all cases the work has to be clamped down and the machine brought to the work rather than the other way round. A certain amount of care is needed in order to be successful. Machining into narrow,

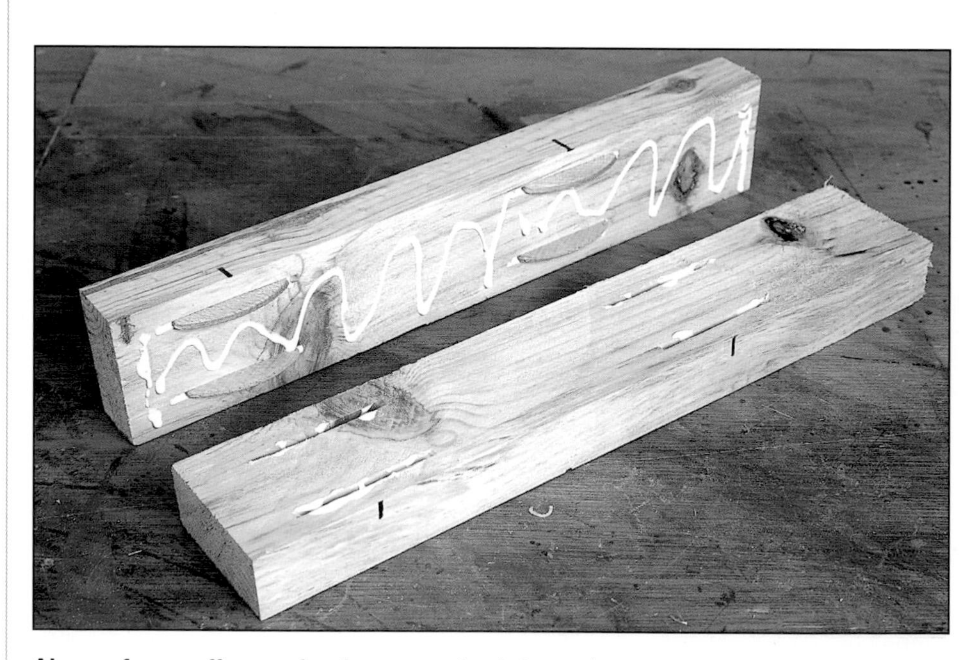
Always fence off one edge for accurate slot spacing

Four closely spaced corner joints make a rigid box section

end-grain mitres must be done with the sprung spikes or other anti-slip devices in place because there is more likelihood of a 'kickback' where the machine will move suddenly to one side thus damaging the slot and perhaps injuring the operator.

Unfortunately, these anti-slip devices tend to prevent the jointer from seating onto the mitre face properly. This is particularly true with the standard mitre fence which only allows an obtuse angle between the fence and the front face of the jointer. Those machines which have full swing-down fences can 'trap' the mitre because the angle between the fence and front face is an acute one, usually at 45°. Here the need for anti-slip devices is less and is worth avoiding, so the machine can sit tightly in the correct location.

No matter how you machine a mitre slot, it is vital that you plunge slowly to avoid any kickback and to get accurate positioning of the slot, although the wood may burn especially as end grain is tougher, with a consequent blackening of the blade. These burnt deposits should be cleaned off or this will only get worse with all subsequent biscuit slotting.

A 'trapped' mitre held in place by the fence and faceplate

Mitres must be cut accurately to work well. A radial arm saw or chopsaw with a fine blade is needed to get good results and plenty of test pieces need to be cut to check that all the mitres are true and will meet nicely. It is not a good idea to try mitring on long edges, such as when making a boxed-up shape. This is because it is difficult to get four (or more) mitres that meet well without some really accurate means of machining them.

Flat mitres used for picture or mirror frames for example, are natural for the jointer. If the frame width is narrow however, the biscuit slots and the biscuits may show at either side. It is possible to offset the biscuit slightly to the inside edge, and where there is a rebate for a picture or mirror, the biscuit can just be trimmed off. All flat mitre joints tend to be a bit weak so if the wood is thick enough, you may be able to use two biscuits, one above the other.

Since some jointers have a gap in the middle of the fence and because you will be cutting into narrow end grain which may cause a kickback, the rule is to use a static set-up for safety and accuracy. This is easy to do and uses the flat underside of the frame as the reference surface.

In the following part we will look at board sawing and advanced jointer techniques.

Double biscuits make a much stronger mitre

Introduction to the biscuit jointer

PART III: MAKING FUNCTIONAL ITEMS

Discover how to make multi-functional items with the biscuit jointer

Most manufacturers of biscuit jointers put a safety warning in their instructions not to use the jointer as a saw. I've used various jointers like this for years without incident. The older Bosch and DeWalt swing-down types are intended for sawing as well as 'biscuiting', while the normal plunge jointer is a less suitable candidate, but can be made to work in this mode.

First of all, make sure you have good extraction (this should be the case for most jointing work in any case) as the amount of dust produced is excessive. A spare blade is sensible as a lot of sawing will wear the tungsten carbide teeth. The DeWalt machine takes a slightly larger, thinner fine-tooth blade, designed for ply cutting. My own experience is that the thicker, standard jointer blade doesn't flex while cutting, unlike the thin one, giving an almost 'planer' finish.

The board needs to be laid across sawhorses or a couple of work benches. If you don't want the top surfaces scarred by the projecting blade, place some scrap board on them. To use a swing-down type jointer, unlock the motor body and swing down to the lowest setting and re-lock. This means you are pushing it from behind. A straightedge is needed such as a lightweight aluminium 'plasterer's feather-edge' which has one tapered edge and one vertical – this is the one to use.

After marking out the size you need to cut, measure the offset distance between the blade and the edge of the jointer base that will run against the fence. Transfer this distance onto the board and place the straightedge on these new marks and cramp in position. Both the Bosch and DeWalt allow the blade to be moved from side to side giving fine adjustment when sawing or biscuiting. Wear personal dust protection and goggles and lean over the board, switch on the jointer, swing down to plunge and proceed to push it along the straightedge until the cut is done. So long as the blade projects through the board slightly, you will get two neat, well sawn edges.

The swing-down DeWalt is perfect for sawing

Plunging effect

The straight ahead plunge type machine is slightly more awkward to use. Retract any anti-slip devices; on some jointers this may not be possible, or you may be able to stick a piece of Formica on with double-sided tape through which the blade can be plunged for sawing. As with all jointers, you have the safety feature of

A careful grip is needed for safe working

Swing-down jointers have an anti-spelch plate to prevent grain breakout

turning the machine on without it being plunged.

Place it against the fence, switch on and plunge carefully – your choice of grip will make a difference – and never hold the tail end of the motor housing on its own, hold the jointer handgrip instead.

Push it along the fence in the direction in which the blade is cutting at full depth until the cut is done, and do not let the jointer move in the reverse direction, as the machine will kick back causing a hazard. Although more care and effort is needed in keeping this type of jointer plunged and on course, it does work and I have used plunge jointers in saw mode when panel sawing, for years.

The blade can cause a certain amount of spelch (breakout or tearing of wood fibres) so the best face should be underneath with the tips of the teeth projecting through the board by just a couple of millimetres. This will reduce spelching to a minimum. This is really only a problem on cross-grain cutting.

> **Safety Warning**
>
> **NEVER** unhook the return springs for sawing or grooving. This would allow the blade to slip in and out of the blade housing freely, and is incredibly dangerous.

Making functional items

This section covers some of the more interesting things you can do with a jointer.

First up is the drawer pull, although you are limited to the maximum blade projection, it is easy to do. Take your drawer front, cramp it down and put a centre strike mark.

Set the blade right up close to the fence (most fences have a hole for the blade to push into safely, or you may be able to stick an MDF sub-fence on: this won't matter if it gets grazed by the blade).

Line up the jointer's own centre mark exactly with the pencil mark and plunge. Move the fence up by a blade's width, line the jointer up again, plunge and continue this until you have removed material to the full thickness of the board leaving a neat lemon wedge shaped cut-out.

All that remains is to sand the shape to remove the blade marks. This makes a small, neat drawer pull. You can try plunging and moving between two strike marks to elongate the slot. However, a lot of control is needed and the result probably won't be as neat as the first version.

Sliding doors

Small sliding doors are quite easy to make, using biscuits as the runners. Let's assume you have a frame for the doors to fit in. Set the jointer to groove (as in saw mode) so that you end up with two grooves in the top and bottom of the frame. Each groove will take one door (a two-door set or if you have an extra long cupboard, three doors in total). Check that both doors will slide past each other with a gap between. Plunge and cut each groove in turn, making sure the jointer is held level as you move along so the grooves remain straight.

Note that the grooves do not need to go right from one end of the frame to the other, so long as the biscuits in the doors are set in from each end of the door. Fold some abrasive and lightly sand the sides of the grooves to remove any roughness that will hamper free-running. Cut the doors to fit loosely from top to bottom and overlapping each other when closed. Put strike marks a short way in from each side of the doors, top and bottom. Set the jointer fence so the slots will be in a suitable position to allow the doors to clear each other when they slide past. Set plunge depth for No. 10 biscuits and make the bottom slots, reset for No. 20s and do the top slots. Glue and fit the right size biscuits in their respective slots cleaning off any excess. When dry, sand each

When sawing, remove or retract anti-slip devices

Drawer pull created using the jointer; accurate alignment on the strike mark is essential

projecting biscuit so it tapers in profile slightly, towards the top. Wax the biscuits, lower door edges and frame grooves to help the doors slide. Then push each door in turn upwards into the top slot and clip the lower biscuits into the bottom grooves. As the doors drop, the smaller lower biscuits fit fully in the grooves, while the larger upper biscuits still project enough into the upper grooves to stay in place.

Slide-on shelves

These are useful where some shelves may need to be added or removed as storage requirements change. Whereas fixed shelves are 'biscuited' on with glue, in this case the biscuits remain in the carcass and don't even have to be glued while the shelves have their ends grooved so they can slide onto the fixed biscuits. When grooving the shelf ends keep the jointer level or use a reference board so the groove stays straight and stops just short of the front edge – no unsightly slot shows. To assist in removal or fitment, the exposed part of the carcass biscuits can be sanded to taper them or the slot sanded to ease the fit. If the biscuits are not glued, they can always be pulled out with pincers leaving a neat slot behind.

Drawer boxes

The biscuit jointer can make a drawer (or drawer box as it is correctly known in woodworking) from start to finish, apart from the sanding.

Start by working out the drawer sizes to fit the carcass in question. You can buy modern 'easy runners' made from cream-white coated pressed steel and fitted with nylon rollers from DIY stores. Allow for the width of these, about 12.5mm (½in) per side and make each drawer shallower than the height of the space available by about 20mm (¾in) so the drawers can be hooked into the runners. Finally, allow for the thickness of the drawer front to be screwed on afterwards and also slightly less deep than the carcass.

Now sketch out your drawers so the sides run right from front to back while the front and back sit inside the sides. The material thickness can vary, but 12–18mm (approx ½–$\frac{23}{32}$in) will allow for biscuits to be slotted in without penetrating through the drawer sides. Make up a jig as shown in the last section of this series, specifically for making drawers. Note that for different drawer widths you will need to alter the jig to suit.

Fitting biscuits to a sliding glass door to act as runners in slots. Note how they have been sanded to a taper compared to standard biscuits

The shelf end is completely slotted apart from the front edge

Strike marks need to go across both components. One component is slotted in the vertical position. Note the groove for the hardboard drawer bottom

You are basically making up a mini-carcass so the same care in organising and marking up parts is needed. Proceed to slot all the same parts in one go before altering the set-up for the other joint halves. Remember to allow for the bottom panels which will be grooved in later. Obviously, the biscuits which hold the drawer box together mustn't project into the space where the drawer bottom groove will be.

The easiest way to do these grooves is probably to fix each drawer component in the vice in turn along with a longer flat board behind it and both flush on the top edge (or make an 'L' jig). This gives the jointer fence a longer surface to run on when grooving. Set the blade depth for about a 6mm (¼in) projection (if the setting dial doesn't allow this you can alter the fine adjuster: don't forget to reset this when you go back to regular 'biscuiting').

Set the fence so the slot will be cut about 8–10mm (5⁄16–3⁄8in) down from the edge, then proceed to the groove holding the jointer level and running from left to right in the direction of cut. Two passes at different fence settings are required to get a 6mm-wide groove so do all components at one setting, then machine them all again at the second setting. Dry assemble a drawer in order to work out the size of the drawer bottoms. Saw these out with the jointer and then assemble each drawer in turn using a reasonable though not excessive amount of glue. Cramp carefully and check for square and leave to dry. The drawer front is an entirely separate item to be considered afterwards.

Rebates

Small rebates for holding panels on the back of furniture are easy to do with the biscuit jointer. Work out the profile measurement of the rebate and set the depth for cutting into the edge (you may need to turn the fine adjuster to get an exact setting) and move the fence so the distance from it to the bottom edge of the blade is the rebate width. Machine from the edge because the jointer fence will need as much support as possible. If it is done from the face first, this might not be the case on the edge cut afterwards. Cramp the board down on the bench for this operation. Plunge and cut a groove along the board edge.

Now put the board upright in the vice and reset the jointer to make the other groove; keep the jointer steady and true because this second cut removes a narrow strip of wood which the jointer was using for support. If necessary cramp a board flush with the top to extend the running surface.

A small rebate will just make sawdust and could be done from the face side only in one or two passes, thus avoiding a lot of resetting.

The waste strip is broken off to show rebate. The first cut is made with the board placed vertically in the vice

Introduction to the **biscuit jointer**

PART IV: MOULDING EFFECTS

Inspiration for using the jointer to add detail to modern furniture

No one is pretending that the biscuit jointer is anything other than just that - a jointer. Nevertheless, I have shown on a number of occasions in the past how the jointer can be extended beyond its accepted limits to add detail to a piece of furniture. Here are a few ideas that suit modern, more simply styled furniture. You might try adding them to a more traditional piece, but they won't be 'correct' in appearance.

Fluted column

The fluted or reeded column goes back to classical architecture. It consists of a number of half-round profile slots in wood or stone, which finish with a rounded, dished shape at each slot end.

The jointer variant is created by running the jointer along at different fence settings to groove the board repeatedly, each groove next to the last giving the wide slot effect. Starting and stopping the jointer at accurately marked pencil lines is important so that you get a neat dished 'sweep' at the end of the slot. Even so, the use of a sharp chisel and some abrasive will be needed to clean it up a little.

Generally speaking, a fluted column would be between two and five slots wide. Therefore, if you have two or more columns to a piece of furniture you can do all the outer slots first by turning each workpiece over, then the inner slots in succession likewise. As with any tricky piece of work, use a test piece to get all the settings right before attacking the actual job. You can hold the jointer to the test piece with the motor off and adjust the fence to just fit in each side of the slots so it acts as reference for transferring the settings to the actual job. As always with sawing and grooving, the anti-slip devices need to be retracted or removed.

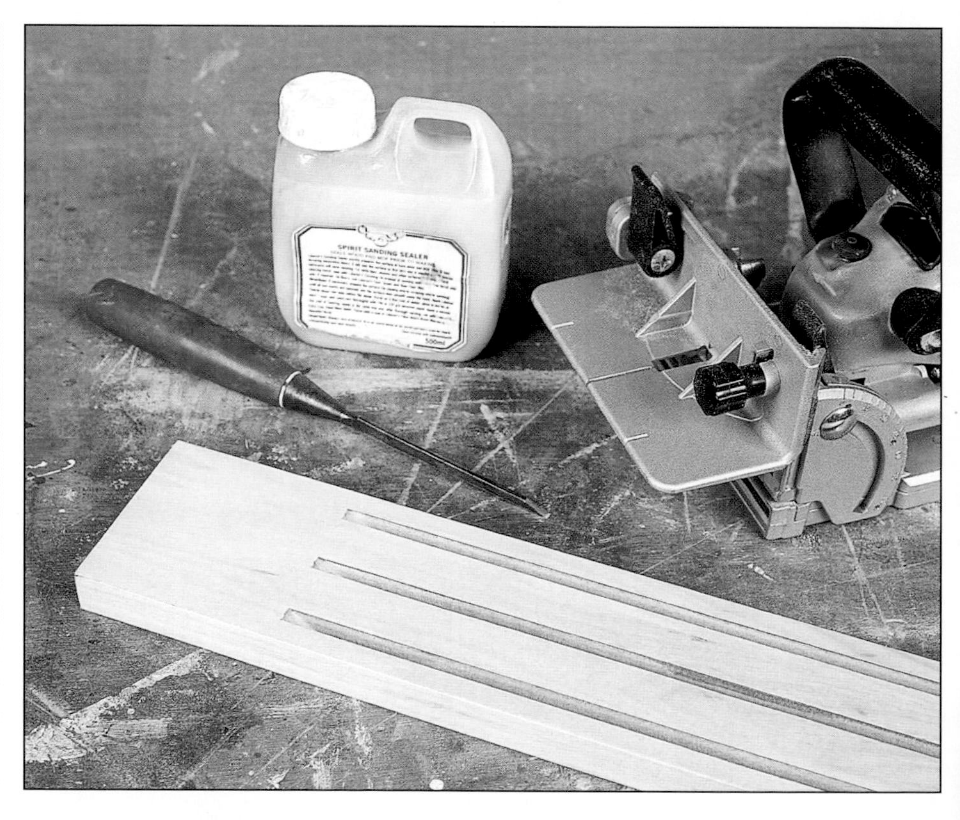

The completed three-flute column. Test cuts are vital in order to get the centre flute the right width

Once this is completed to your satisfaction, the columns can be biscuited to the carcass taking care that the biscuits on the back won't penetrate through the slots on the front.

Alternatively, you can run the slots right through and finish the columns

Precision slot placement

If your jointer lacks kerf centre line marks, you can add them by placing a strip of masking tape along the base (with the machine unplugged). Line the strip of tape up carefully with the centre of the blade from end to end, then press the tape in place. Use a Stanley Knife and a safety straight edge - one with a high edge so the blade cannot ride up over, thus preventing injury - to cut into the alloy casing at each end. Use the tape line underneath to determine the cut line.

The result is a thin, but definite line at each end, which, if the casing is silver or plain aluminium, can have black paint rubbed into the cuts to highlight them against the bright finish. Remove the tape, and your jointer now has another means of precise slot placement.

Creating classic decorative details

off with a plain, larger block at the bottom and a moulding at the top.

Multiple groove effect

This is useful for table edges and the like. It adds detail and interest quickly and easily, and looks impressive too.

Cramp the table top down, adjust the jointer for a suitable but not excessive cut depth and a fence to blade distance of about 4–5mm ($\frac{5}{32}$–$\frac{3}{16}$in), and retract the anti-slip devices. Then, holding the machine level with plenty of downward pressure on the fence, plunge and proceed to groove – in the direction of cut. If two sides of your work support overhang the table top, you can groove both of these sides before having to uncramp it and turn it round to do the other sides.

Reset the fence for the next groove allowing a 3mm ($\frac{1}{8}$in) minimum space between grooves so the remaining wood is strong enough. Repeat as many times as the thickness of the wood allows. With 18–20mm ($\frac{23}{32}$–$\frac{25}{32}$in) material, this means just two grooves, but it still looks good. The top 4-5mm ($\frac{5}{32}$–$\frac{3}{16}$in) of material allows the top edge to be rounded over slightly with a bit of hand applied abrasive paper.

A table top with rounded or 'chopped' (angled) corners looks

The multiple groove looks very stylish – note the top section has to be thick enough to avoid damage in use

A highlight groove improves the look of this desk side and avoids an ugly join

The finished star detail on a block ready to glue to the end of a frieze rail

Producing dentil moulding is a lot quicker than pulling teeth! Note how the jointer is fixed down with blocks. A registration biscuit pushed into a slot ensures the spacing is even

even better with this effect if you are after a 'designer' piece of furniture.

Groove highlight detail

I have already discussed this in part II, under 'Boxed-up joints'. It needs no further explanation, save to say that it can be used to disguise a joint or highlight the difference between two flush surfaces, say a table top that is flush to the underframe, or similarly, the top of a cabinet. In other words, add a little bit of detail where none exists or where cross-grain wood meets the long grain and might otherwise look a bit odd.

Star detail

I still have an MDF coffee table I made some years ago that features this effect. It is best used as an applied block to a larger surface because a bit of trial and error is involved; it's better not to experiment on your nicely made furniture. Instead, work this idea into the overall design if you think there is a suitable place for it. Typically, this might be corner detail, perhaps on the underframe of a table or at the ends of a frieze rail just below a cornice at the top of a bookcase.

Solid wood is not so suitable as it may start to fall apart the more slots you do. MDF seems to fare the best as it has no short grain to worry about; it's formed from a series of compressed sheets of wood-based material.

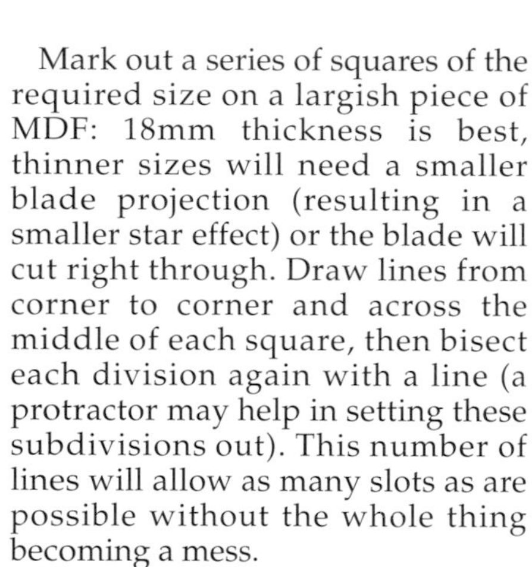

Mark out a series of squares of the required size on a largish piece of MDF: 18mm thickness is best, thinner sizes will need a smaller blade projection (resulting in a smaller star effect) or the blade will cut right through. Draw lines from corner to corner and across the middle of each square, then bisect each division again with a line (a protractor may help in setting these subdivisions out). This number of lines will allow as many slots as are possible without the whole thing becoming a mess.

You need a mark at each side of the blade housing that shows the centre of the blade kerf (slot). Some jointers actually have this marked, though it may not be very clear.

Centre the jointer on one drawn line on the board as well as across the line perpendicular to it. This must be done with care for a neat result. Plunge slowly and let the blade retract, then swap around to the perpendicular line and repeat the operation. Next, start on the major subdivisions and lastly the minor ones. The more cuts you do the harder it gets to line the jointer up in both directions as the guide lines get machined away.

However, you can sight along the outer part of each line for guidance. There is a bit of luck involved which is why you need to do more than you need, then select the best ones and cut them out afterwards. Lastly, sand the edges of the blocks and glue and 'rub' them into position. This creates a suction effect and should be enough to hold each block in place until dry, providing the blocks are lying down so they can't slip off.

Dentil moulding

This is a traditional effect that adds status and grandeur to a piece when added to other mouldings. Fire surrounds and cabinets, for example, will benefit from this moulding.

The jig needed is covered in the last section on the following page, but basically the jointer sits fixed over two boards, between which the strip to be moulded slides under the jointer. A succession of slots at predetermined intervals produces

A slotted frieze rail is easy to make, this time sighting down this jointer's baseplate was enough to get the correct spacing, there are siting marks on the jig as well

The blind scallop is a neat but very effective visual treatment

the required dentil or toothed effect quickly and easily. Afterwards, it simply needs to be cut, pinned and glued in place on the furniture.

Slotted frieze

This is more interesting than a plain rail on a table underframe or frieze rail on a cabinet. The set-up which is detailed in the next section is similar to the dentil moulding jig, only this time it must accommodate a piece of wood up to about 50mm (2in). If you are happy with plain strip along the top edge, 80mm (3⅛in) wide is possible and the groove spacing is closer. A maximum depth of cut is needed to slot the full width of the workpiece properly; the slight curve to the bottom of each groove isn't very noticeable.

Scallop effect

This could not be easier! Taking the example in Part III of a drawer pull fashioned with the jointer by making a series of overlapping plunges through the full thickness of the wood, here is the same thing done in series. Simply take a thin piece of board suitable in dimension for edging a shelf. Make a series of discreet, easy to sand out strike marks at a set distance apart. The photo (right) shows a typical spacing.

Now plunge starting at the top and do all the slots before resetting the fence for the next cut and repeat all along the workpiece and so on, until you have machined right through. The result is a neat set of scallops that need only light sanding. Glue and pin them to a shelf edge to give a new look. This is extremely effective on a dresser for example.

Another variant is to do a series of shallow scallops on thicker material. On a painted piece of furniture the scallops can be painted a different colour to the main surface of the wood or an interesting effect. If you intend doing a lot of scalloping an index stick for marking out is a good idea.

In the following part, find out how simple jigs can be made, to allow repetitious jointing operations with the static or fixed biscuit jointer.

An index stick allows fast, accurate laying out of strike marks

Introduction to the biscuit jointer

PART V: JOINTER JIGS

The series on the biscuit jointer continues, looking at jigs and set-ups

Reference board

The most basic form of static jointing is the reference board. We have already seen its advantages in a previous article, but here we have a more in-depth look. By placing the jointer and workpiece on a truly flat and reliable board, you can use the jointer's underside as the datum. Likewise, the best face of the workpiece is placed face down. The fence is effectively ignored as a means of setting the slot position. However, it can have a residual role in holding the workpiece down onto the reference board. It is also possible to centre the jointer blade in the edge of the workpiece by using packers under either the jointer or board.

These can be veneer, Formica or thin ply, but downward pressure is needed to prevent any tendency of them springing up and introducing an inaccuracy. Some jointers, usually the swing-down saw type, can have the blade adjusted within the body which eliminates the need for packers. If the reference board is large enough it will be able to accommodate carcass panels as well as smaller components.

As always, the workpiece must be clamped both for safety and accuracy. Strips of moulding or narrow pieces can, however, be placed against a clamped-on fence instead. This

The jointer sitting on the reference board, with the fence holding the work down

The framing cam jig

Using a packer on the reference board to position the biscuit slots higher up

obviates the need for repetitious clamping and any resultant damage to the work. On a safety note, it is important to clamp any pieces of softwood with knots, and wear goggles as the jointer blade can dislodge and throw the knot centre towards the operator. Believe me – I speak from experience!

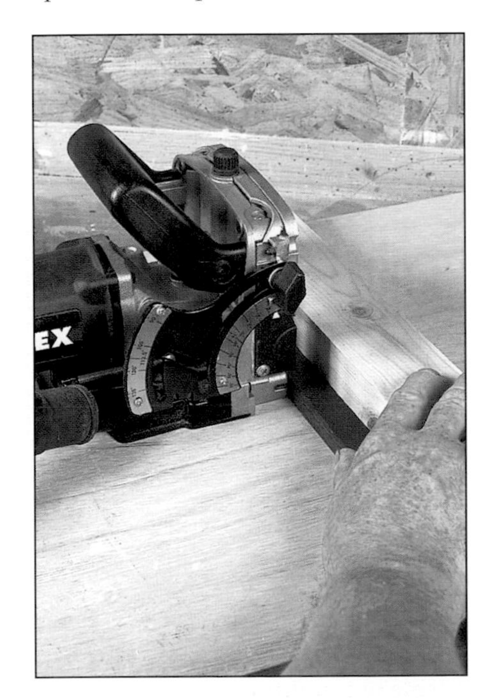

Small sections can be placed against a fence for slotting

Bed Slat jig

Using a reference board, there are a couple of jigs made by fixing either the jointer to it or positively locating the workpiece on the board. Once made, these jigs can be stored for future use. Narrow components are too dangerous to slot at the ends without fixing both jointer and workpiece. The end grain is harder and the contact area too small for safety when plunging. The slots can also be off-centre or show too much at one side and not line up properly on assembly. A typical use is for fixing bed slats, where on average about 52 slats (104 joints) need to be cut per bed. No doubt there are other uses you can think of for this type of jig.

Choose a long board that will accommodate both jointer and workpiece. Fix your jointer down – this isn't as difficult as it sounds. Some jointers come with a couple of fixing holes although these are not adequate on their own. Use short strips of wood to frame the jointer body without obstructing either the extraction port or its ability to plunge. Next, add more pieces on top to hold the body down. Alternatively, plastic fixing blocks for joining furniture can be used. Once you are satisfied the jointer can't move at all, screw two long strips at 90° to the fence, just far apart enough for the slats to fit in the middle, centred on the blade. If all the components are identical in width they should fit snugly between these two strips.

Stack the components near to hand, push one workpiece up to the faceplate with the jointer switched on, and plunge the jointer with the other hand. Turn it around and repeat at the other end of the workpiece keeping it the same way up so the slots are level with each other. Do this as many times as necessary – after the first few the rate of production becomes pleasingly fast!

L-jig

The L-jig is a basic step away from using the jointer on its own. It allows all manner of face moulding work to be done. Make up a biscuited MDF L-shape at exactly 90°, large enough for the jointing you are embarking on. Fix it down to your reference board so there is space in front for the jointer and workpiece to sit on. Providing the components are not too long, they can be stood up against the jig and the jointer can sit directly on the reference board or on packers if the slots are going to be too low down.

The bed slat jig is very quick to use

An L-jig makes face biscuiting precise and easy

If the components are large it is better to lie them down and place the jointer vertically against the upright piece; the effect is the same so it's just a matter of choice. Always cramp the workpiece before biscuiting. You can fit side stops against which the jointer can press, thus determining the outer biscuit slot positions without having to mark them out, although this is only really worthwhile if there are a lot of identical components. The L-jig is also very useful for the safe, quick jointing of mouldings.

Drawer jig

This is essentially like the previous jig with slight additions, in that each drawer size will need the jig to be altered accordingly.

Fit a stop at one side so the jointer is automatically positioned for the first slot. The other side needs a stop block that extends in front of the drawer component so the second biscuit is offset away from the edge, thus leaving a space for the bottom panel groove. A second jig, or removing the L-piece and adapting the first jig, will allow the other half of the joint (the end of the component) to be machined.

Note that this cuts either the left-hand or right-hand joint only (because of the bottom panel). You will need to reverse the stop blocks to do the 'other hand' of the joint . This set-up is easier to knock together than it sounds and providing you mark and stack your components correctly, it works a treat.

Framing cam jig

Framing for pictures and mirrors needs to be held firmly but also released quickly between cuts. It also needs to accommodate different width stock. This jig does both left- and right-hand mitres by swapping the position of the biscuit jointer.

Check the angles of the strips and blocks carefully before using in earnest. The angle at which you cut your mitres is most important of all. The cams allow sufficient quick pressure to be applied and released making fast working possible.

Dentil mould and slotted frieze jig

This jig has been covered in the previous article but I have repeated it as it qualifies as a static set-up. The jigs for these two operations are similar although you will need one for each if you choose to do both. Another simple set-up, it needs two strips of wood either side of the workpiece and should be a fraction higher (pieces of veneer edging tape are useful for this).

Fix the jointer between strips of wood which are exactly 90° to the other pieces and add more to hold the jointer down. Make a test cut with the blade set to the chosen depth. Mark where the next slot should be. In the case of dentil moulding this should be sufficiently clear of the jointer to mark in biro on the guide pieces at the side. Each time you do a slot, pull the wood along until that slot lines up with your marks, then plunge again and repeat ad infinitum.

Dentil moulding is rather repetitious to do but gives a satisfying result

For the slotted frieze, the jig has to accommodate wider strips and the slots are very close together. On the DeWalt swing-down model this isn't a problem because the blade can be moved close to the edge of the housing, which enables you to sight down the housing for each successive slot position. You may be able to do this with your jointer anyway. If you can't, it may be a case of marking the first few slot positions on the workpiece accurately and lining up against an arbitrary mark on one of the guide pieces near the blade housing on the feed side. Once the slotted strip starts to emerge on the other side, make new marks on the guide strip of the outfeed side and use those to ensure accurate repetition slotting.

A last tip is to drop a biscuit into each emerging slot to get precise spacing, or alternatively, fit a thin alloy strip to the jig to do the same job either with dentil moulding or frieze rail.

The drawer jig in use – note the jointer in all these photos is screwed down via two holes provided for the purpose

Introduction to the **biscuit jointer**

PART VI: IN-SITU WORKING

A look at joint work and some other tasks for which the biscuit jointer can be used

Old & antique furniture

If old and much loved pieces of furniture or valuable antiques are not to be ruined, then careful, considered use of hand tools and the proper restoration materials are essential. I wouldn't like to suggest that power tools and antiques mix, because quite clearly they don't.

During the time I ran an antique restoration business I came up against the recurring problem of how to rejoin separated boards on table tops. These could be solid oak, ash or mahogany drop leaf or Pembroke tables. The conventional answer usually meant cleaning the animal glue from the edges, hand planing until true and remaking the butt-joints. In some cases, planing the edges is not desirable as it can spoil the look of a long since opened-up top, although some means of jointing is still required. Inserting a loose, glued tongue wasn't an option since it would mean running the boards over a saw-table with consequent damage to the boards and possibly the operator too. The old pocketed screw fixings or glue blocks underneath were reused, thus holding the top in a fixed position that wouldn't allow for further shrinkage, which could therefore precipitate joint failure again.

The biscuit jointer is an ideal site tool – the handle needs to be removable for internal carcass operations

The jointer's apparent lack of intrusive machining, coupled with the ability to work on an uneven edge and still give good alignment, has the potential for making a better joint – along the lines of a loose tongue, which even if it parted a little, would still hold good, just exposing a bit of each biscuit. It seems I wasn't alone in thinking this and I have since met several cabinetmakers and restorers who use a biscuit jointer in such a way.

Don't sweat the technique

Where safe, practical, or necessary, true the edges with a hand plane (good judgement is needed here) although they may need to be cleaned off first. Next lay each board

A taped and marked-up burr walnut veneered top, neatly rejoined

in the original order and apply masking tape along the top, close to each edge. The tape should not be pressed down too firmly, to avoid pulling any finish off when the tape is lifted. The tape is needed to rest the jointer fence on and mark out the biscuit positions without causing damage. Even so, only soft pencil pressure is needed, otherwise dents will occur which are visible when the table surface is viewed against the light. Proceed to slot the edges, taking care that the jointer is presented level with the boards, since any misalignment may be obvious and cannot be removed by sanding the top!

Use either glued or dry biscuits depending on the particular requirement (dry will allow for shrinkage). Lift the tape very carefully afterwards and if the finish is disturbed be very circumspect about how you treat it. Generally nothing more than an application of a hardening wax polish is acceptable.

It is sometimes possible to carry out this machining with half the table top still fixed to its underframe. This is useful because it results in less disturbance that could otherwise damage rusted-in screws or firmly fixed glue blocks. In this case the jointer can sit in the open space in the middle of the frame.

If you are not confident about using this repair technique, don't do it, as any resultant damage will spoil and devalue the furniture.

Removing carcass back panels

I worked for a bespoke kitchen company for a while and installed a number of kitchens and 'snagged' many others. Snagging refers to any corrections, finishing or improvements that are needed after installation, often at the request of clients.

One such kitchen in London needed a hi-fi unit installed in a large 'island' unit in its centre. This entailed cutting out a back panel in one side of the unit, which is difficult at the best of times as a jigsaw can't get close to the carcass sides and leaves a ragged cut. Handsawing with a keyhole saw is even more impractical. Worse still, I was told to expect ring main wiring hanging just behind the panel, posing a high risk if the cutting out went wrong!

The solution was to use a normal straight ahead type plunge biscuit jointer equipped with efficient dust

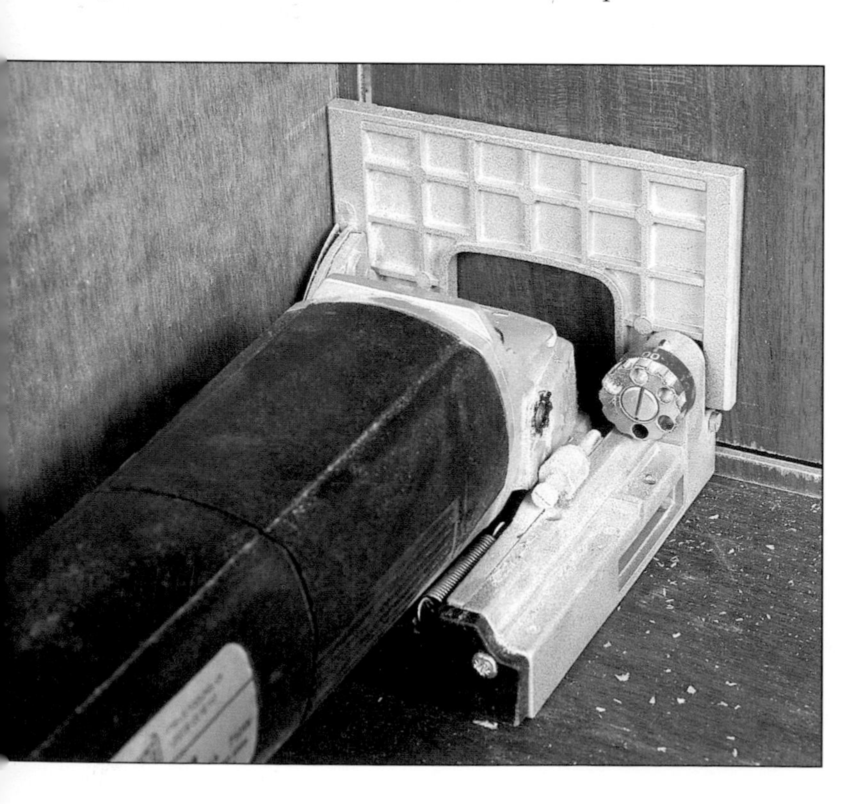

Left **Cutting the corner out of the back panel – note the jointer handle has been removed**

Above **Finishing the panel cutting with a keyhole saw**

Solid wood skirtings like these, and dado rails, can be biscuited in place with the finish already applied

extraction set to a very shallow cut depth without its fence or handle on (this allows the jointer close to the corner when a body grip is adopted). I didn't know the thickness of the back panel, though I could have hazarded a guess based on the standard board thicknesses that we had used.

Firstly, I set the cut depth for just over 7mm (9/32in) as this was the minimum carcass back thickness, including the veneer applied to both faces. I then pressed the underside of the jointer against one carcass side in the corner, plunged and ran along sawing through the board until the other end was reached. This wasn't enough to penetrate so I set it for just over 10mm, this being the next likely board thickness. This time the blade just went through the board. I repeated this around all four sides, until the panel was just fixed at the corners where the blade couldn't reach. This last job was done with a keyhole saw, taking care not to let the blade go in very far. Finally the panel dropped away revealing - nothing! In fact the wiring was off to one side and didn't pose a risk, although using the jointer with its precise depth setting meant that I could work 'blind' in relative safety.

Safety note

As always, it is not my intention to suggest practices that are at all dangerous. On most occasions, the removal of in-situ back panels etc., doesn't include the extra problems such as wiring but is simply to facilitate altering a piece of furniture to suit a new use. Always consider properly any intended machining operation you carry out, that way you should stay safe!

Fitting skirting to room panelling

Once I fitted out a study with maple panelling and then added a matching skirting and dado rail to it. In the end I opted to use maple-veneered MDF for all the flat areas and solid maple for the mouldings. All the panelling had to be made to length and pre-finished to a dark honey colour using spray lacquer. Since the high moulded skirting and dado rail had to be invisibly fixed, biscuit jointing was the natural answer. The biscuit slots around the top of the panelling were done before installation and once the panelling was fixed to the walls the dado could be mitred to fit between the walls and then slotted to match the slots on each respective piece of panelling. It was then glued and biscuited in place and because the room wasn't too large it was possible to 'spring' some softwood battens with protective pads at each end, in between opposing panelled walls in order to hold the dado mouldings tight to the panels until the glue dried. The panelling was

Skirting flat section already fixed to the wall. Biscuits and mastic will hold the top moulding in place

Above **Twinfast screws placed between biscuits will hold any carcass firmly together**

Above **It is normal for kitchen cabinets to have decor panels neatly fitted at the ends**

not pre-slotted for the skirting because I knew the floor was uneven and varied in height. I felt it was better to see what the best installation height was once the panelling had been levelled up and fitted in place.

Overall, the skirting was 150mm (6in) high, with the moulded top section being about 45mm (1¾in) and a lower flat section made of veneered MDF which was 105mm (4⅘in) high.

Method & means

The best way is to fix the flat section only, using a level marked line for the top edge, with biscuit marks along it. The jointer is inverted and held against the panelling making the slots, although care is needed. As this is working freehand to a line on a vertical surface, upside down, anti-slip devices need to be used. Cut the flat section square at the ends, since the lack of mitres won't show and slot to match the slots on the panelling. Add glue to the slots only, biscuit the flat strip on and leave it to dry.

Now biscuit downwards into the top edge of the flat strip. Mitre the top moulding to fit between the panelling and slot the bottom edge to match that on the flat strip (No.10 rather than No.20 biscuits may be needed to avoid penetrating through the profile of the moulding). Now glue and push the moulding down onto the flat strip.

The technique of making skirting in two sections and then biscuiting them together will work in rooms with normal, rather than panelled, walls. You should machine both parts out off-site before the skirting is installed because, unlike panelling, walls are usually quite uneven and could prevent the two rows of slots from lining up with each other.

A selection of mouldings that can be fitted as worktop upstand or lighting pelmet

Kitchen cabinet & worktop installation

The biscuit is ideal for kitchens, wardrobes, etc. Carcasses can be biscuited together although they are usually made from melamine faced chipboard, or MDF which doesn't stick together well. Don't rely on biscuits alone. I use modern twinfast screws in between the slots for extra strength, while the biscuits act as a good locational aid.

Often 'decor panels' which are solid wood or veneered facings for cabinet ends, are fitted to cover up the melamine on the outside. This is a natural job for the biscuit and should be done once the cabinets are fitted to the wall, and after the decor panels have been trimmed to fit.

Modern kitchens often have lighting fitted under the top, wall-hung cabinets. This needs to be hidden with a lighting pelmet. This is made from solid wood with a

Very neat worktop joints are achievable with a combination of the router and the jointer

moulding in the lower edge and is mitred at the front corners. Here the jointer can be applied from underneath the cabinet using the fence, then into the top edge of the pelmet and the two are biscuited together. Some lightweight cramps can be used to hold the pelmet on firmly until the glue has dried.

Kitchen worktops need to finish neatly against the wall or with the tiles fixed to them. A line of mastic is a messy answer and it tends to become mouldy as the silicone denatures. A preferable answer is to have an upstand piece of wood along the back edge of the worktop. This can be moulded slightly (not much as it may attract dust and dirt) and biscuited down into the worktop – provided it is made of wood or standard postform chipboard and laminate, not granite.

Generally it is possible to place the jointer straight against the wall and slot near the back edge of the worktop. If there is a bit of a gap at the back edge the slots may be only half formed and the upstand may have nothing to fit into. In this case it may be possible to press the jointer against a thin packing piece of ply, thus offsetting the slots away from the wall.

In any case the upstand should have its own slots slightly offset so it will be just away from the wall. The reason for this is that walls are rarely flat and the upstand won't fit the biscuit slots because of the wall undulations. I always find an offcut of upstand is ideal for checking the fit.

Worktop joints

Standard postform worktop joints can be machined using a large router and a home-made jig. I won't go into the whole procedure of jointing the worktop as it involves the router more than the jointer. However it is worth pointing out that whereas special worktop bolts are used to pull the joint tightly together, there is nothing stopping it from sliding up or down so the surfaces can become out of alignment. The biscuit is a simple but effective way of solving this problem and three or four placed in between the bolt positions should do the trick. If you have a router biscuit cutter set, you can even slot the last, dogleg section at the front, which a biscuit jointer cannot do.

These are just a few examples of how to put the biscuit jointer to work in awkward or unusual situations rather than just straightforward carcass building. The jointer is extremely versatile and makes a very handy site tool!

The final, almost invisible result

Introduction to the biscuit jointer

PART VII: MAKING A JOINTER TABLE

Using the biscuit jointer in conjunction with a table

On previous occasions I have said that the jointer is ideal as a freehand tool, which is true. This does not, however, render it useless when it comes to static work. Just as a router can be fitted in a table, so can a biscuit jointer. There are a few pre-conditions however.

The first essential is a strong, reliable, flat surface. Secondly, it needs to be large enough to take panels or long pieces of moulding, and thirdly, it needs some kind of vertical fence for holding components and as a means of clamping them. It is also useful to be able to fix the jointer down when jointing work such as narrow components. Unfortunately, this function doesn't fit in so well with the others as it involves damaging the table with screws and the like, so some care is needed if the jointer is fixed down. You can, however, fix the jointer to a small piece of board and use just a couple of screws or cramps to fix it to the table. In such a case a similar packing board is needed under the workpiece to bring it to the same level.

The box section is very rigid. With the fence removed it can be used with clamps, and end stops can be fitted for drawer side slotting and other such tasks. It isn't sensible to use it as a general workbench as it will inevitably suffer damage that will render it inaccurate as a reference surface. This will make it useless.

The completed table

Differing designs

The dimensions can be varied to suit your circumstances and it isn't necessary to stick to the sizes I have used here. The table size is rather wide – longer would be better but it becomes very heavy and unwieldy and the width is more useful if you are edge jointing up to half of normal board width, which is about 600mm (24in). Although pretty heavy, it can be stored leaning against a wall without taking up too much room.

The table is just 100mm (4in) thick with divisions to support and stabilise the top and bottom boards, making them flat and true. This makes it an ideal reference table. The overall thickness of 100mm (4in) also allows the fence or workpiece to be

Cutting out the component parts

The two index sticks used for making the strike marks

cramped down. The end divisions, however, are set in from the edge, allowing the use of smaller cramps if necessary. This table needs some kind of sturdy base for which you can use a couple of trestles or a large Workmate so long as it is securely fixed together.

Fence

The fence stands 150mm (6in) high reflecting the fact that vertical work support must be adequate, especially with longer workpieces that would otherwise be difficult to hold. Extraction isn't an issue, since the jointer is connected directly to a vacuum extractor nearby. Start by cutting out the top and bottom boards from an 18mm (¾in) sheet of MDF (or decent ply). Use either a jointer in saw mode or a circular saw with a good quality fine-tooth TCT blade. Manufactured board is machined properly square so you will get reliably sized boards, although the edges may be a bit rough or chewed up because of transport damage.

If this is so, make your sizes a bit bigger with the intention of sawing several millimetres off these bad edges with the jointer to clean them up. Remember to obtain the correct sizes by carefully marking out, allowing for the jointer's blade to baseplate offset distance. Now saw several narrow strips which can be cross-cut to length for the back and front of the table and the four divisions. While you are at it, cut the

Freehand slotting is possible if the anti-slip devices are in place

Slotting the fence brackets

Dividers give strength part way through the gluing up process

fence parts too. This procedure of accurately pre-cutting all the major parts is standard practice in the trade and it is wise to learn this for yourself as the discipline involved is essential for good woodworking.

Cross-cutting these narrow pieces can be done with the jointer and T-square. Make up an index stick with strike marks based on the length of the table. Work out all the biscuiting positions by dividing the distance between the two outer strike marks so you end up with roughly 200mm (8in) spacing. Use a calculator for accuracy and a steel tape rule to mark it out. Place all the strike marks along the long edges including the fence pieces. Mark up another index stick for the divisions and mark up the top and bottom boards after marking on the boards where the divisions will fit. Always indicate which side of the pencil line your division is to be placed to avoid any problems later.

Do a dry assembly of the table to see how everything fits in place. Take it apart and glue and tap the biscuited joints together with a hammer and a block to avoid damaging the board and cramp at alternate biscuit positions. After a while move the cramps along to ensure all the biscuits have a chance to close up tightly.

The fence needs four right angle brackets. These can be sawn from offcuts and their position should be accurately marked on the long fence boards and strike marks placed accordingly. Glue, assemble and cramp the fence, check it is a true 90° and leave it to dry. For some operations it can be useful to have a low fence such as a straight square piece of prepared 75 x 50mm (3 x 2in) softwood as well as the high MDF one. If you need to construct drawer boxes or require similar operations, cramp two vertical strips of MDF or ply to the fence to hold the workpiece tightly in between and push the jointer against the fence in actual use.

Jointer table and fence in MDF or ply scale 1:10

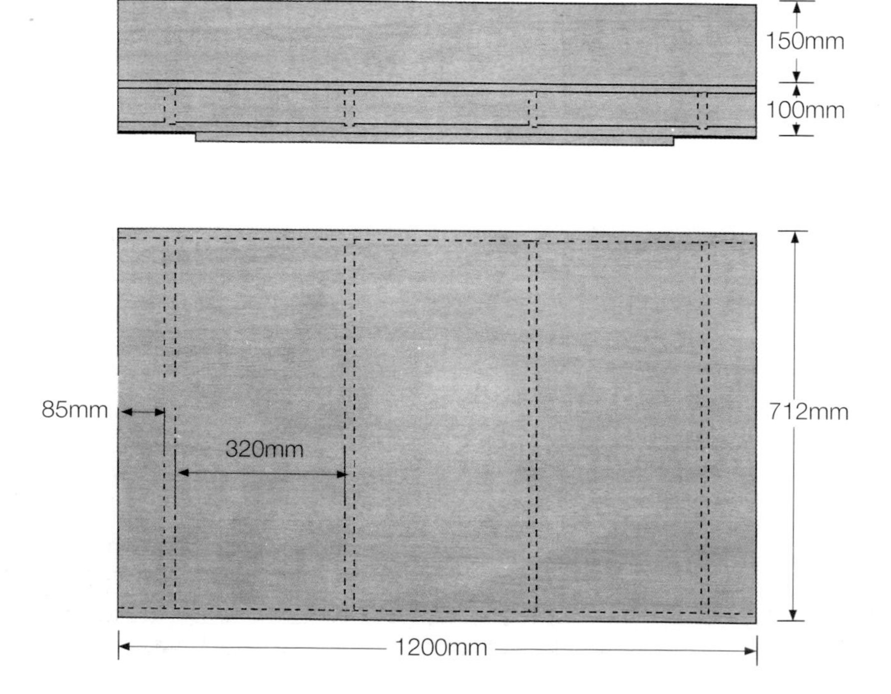

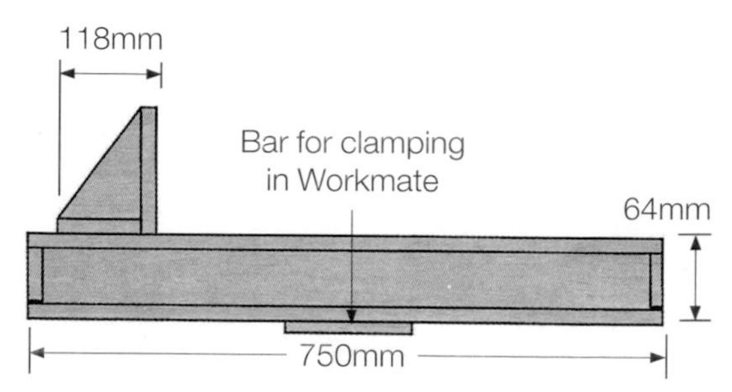

Working the jointer reference table

First of all, make sure your new reference table is flat and true. Do the same with the fence. The fence face and bottom, in particular, need to be at 90°. If there is a problem with any of these things it is now very difficult to correct but at least you will know how accurately you have made the table! At the time I made the table my Workmate was out on loan, so I have

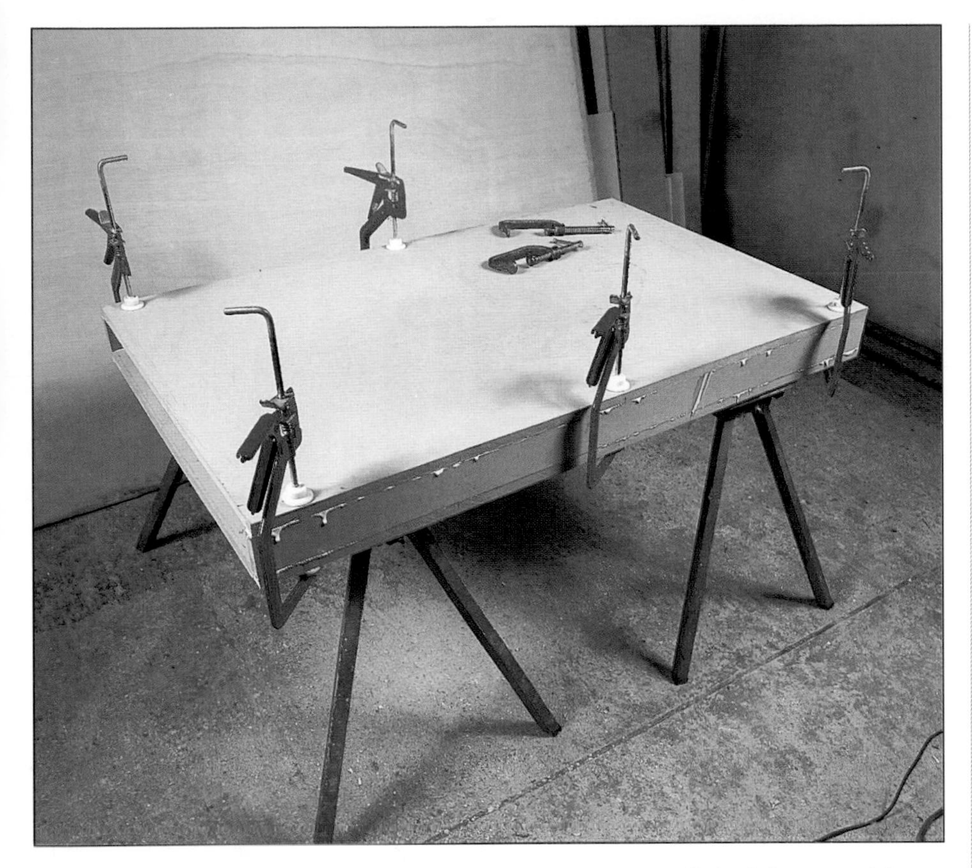

The clamps are moved along after 10 minutes to ensure all the joints are tight

sat it across two trestles for the time being. The standard Workmate will bring the table up to a more acceptable working height. By fitting a strip of MDF underneath the table you can then clamp it between the jaws. The fence isn't subject to the kind of forces that often occur with a router table. The workpiece sits in place and isn't being pushed during machining, nor is any great shock caused by the wood being attacked by the cutter, as a saw type blade is used. Therefore, standard mastic cramps are fine as a means of holding the fence and for work-holding as well. Most jointer users tend to work with the machine's own fence and not with a flat surface for reference. Once you get used to this idea it becomes remarkably easy. You need to put the side regarded as the face side with the strike marks facing downwards as opposed to upwards. This means you either run the marks across the component ends and onto the reverse face so you can still see the marks or use an index stick as I frequently do. Provided you accurately mark the stick, it can be used repeatedly for all similar components and avoids the need to run marks over from one face to the other, by simply marking the uppermost face. Always clamp the workpiece to the fence for safety. Where you are using the fence as a jig, as with drawer box jointing, clamp some stops either side so the component can be slid across to do each slot. As previously discussed, the jointer is fixed down to the table surface. The workpiece is not itself clamped, but everything else is. The work is trapped between the jointer faceplate and the fence. Working in this manner is very quick when you have a whole set of components to make.

Finally, don't use the reference table for any other work as it may get damaged, rendering it ineffective for its true use.

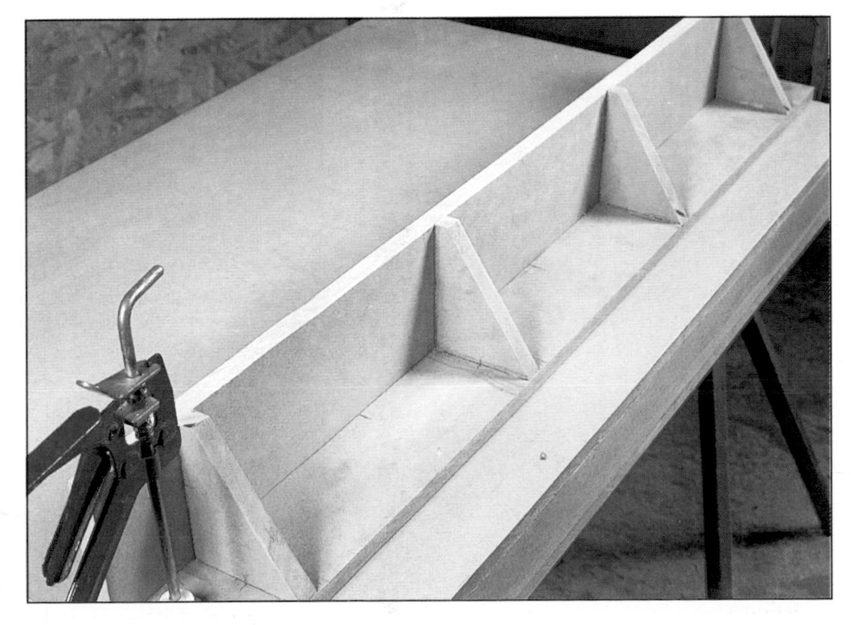

Fence construction details

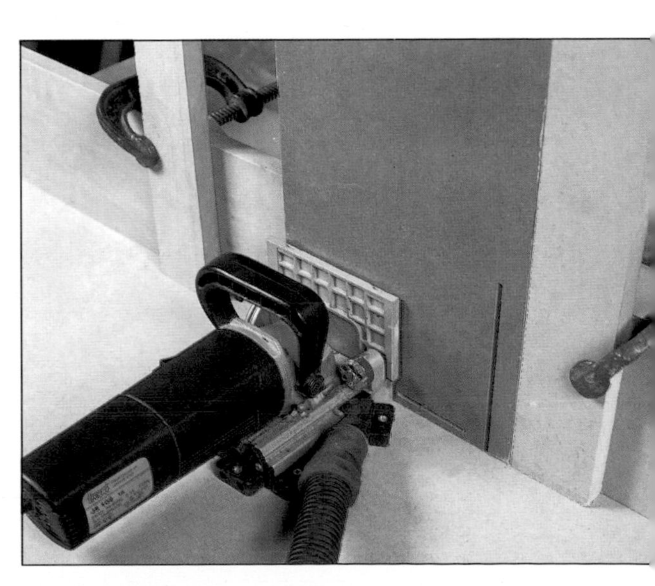

A typical reference operation - a trial cut for drawer boxing. Note that the jointer is with fixed blocks

PART VIII: BISCUIT JOINTER MAINTENANCE

Maintenance is essential to keep your biscuit jointer in tip-top condition

The biscuit jointer is pretty much like any other power tool. It contains parts that move very fast, has a cutting tool (in this case a blade) and over time, all the moving components are likely to wear and may need lubrication and general maintenance.

The plunge mechanism consists of either machined slideways and return springs or slide rods and return springs. Expensive jointers may use nickel plating on one half of the slideway to make for smooth plunging. Medium to low price jointers have both halves of the slideway made from aluminium. This will tend to 'wipe', which means that the metal grains become raised and elongated and rub together. This is peculiar to this metal. It is therefore a necessity to oil the slideways or rods regularly using a standard machine oil. It is possible to use a good quality wax on the rods so long as it is hardening and water-free. There are machine waxes, but my preference is for Liberon Black Bison Wax which works well for this.

A biscuit jointer is not a particularly complex piece of equipment

The plunge rods or slideways on a jointer need lubrication

The next issue is precision. Can you rely on your jointer to work accurately straight out of the box, or after several years of use? Most jointers have minimal adjustments as the majority of the setting up work is done at a factory. Whatever machine you own, an engineers' square is a precise way to check all the relevant settings such as if the fall front is at 90° to the baseplate or not. Using the correct tool you can then reset the offending pointer or component.

During actual machining, there may be some degree of play in the slideway which could result in inaccurate joints. If this is quite apparent it may be that the machine has not been made to fine enough tolerances. Obviously, this sort of wear can creep in on an older machine and may have to be accepted unless you intend upgrading to a better jointer. Generally, the scales on biscuit jointers are not very reliable – check any settings by doing test pieces and measuring the slot position, etc.

Although the blades only cut small slots, the diameter and limited number of teeth can mean they wear more quickly than, for example, a circular saw blade. After a lot of use the biscuits may need a thump to get them in to the slots. This could be the result of the biscuits getting damp and swelling or the blade teeth may have got slightly thinner. Measure the slots, not the teeth, with a vernier calliper, which should indicate if a proper 4mm (5⁄32in) slot is being cut.

It can be difficult to sharpen such small teeth using a diamond hone, but it is possible. Only attempt it on the front and top face but not the sides as it will actually make them thinner. Unfortunately, the only proper answer for a worn blade is to buy a new one at a typically exorbitant price.

Blades need to be cleaned like any tooling. Lighter fuel or wax cleaner plus a knife blade, old tooth brush and medium wire wool can be used to clean each tooth and the blade. This will extend the blade life by reducing friction and subsequent scorching of the wood. Do not re-slot old biscuit joints that may have glue in them without cleaning up the blade afterwards.

Turning to the electrical and mechanical components, there are several wear items. First of all is the switch, which does not have to do a lot but can pack with dust. In this case the switch blades may burn and shorten, thus preventing proper contact. If you are confident with electrical jobs, changing a switch isn't particularly difficult, but if not, leave it to the professionals. The actual running time of a jointer motor is fairly low compared to other power tools such as drills and circular saws. However, the motor brushes which conduct electricity to the core of the spinning motor can wear out over time. Again, these are fairly easy to fit and should be standard replaceable items.

Waxing the author's ELU 177E router legs. This wax works well on a jointer too

The DeWalt plunge machine benefits from accurate setting up every now and then

Jointer blades vary in design but they all wear and get mucky

A useful blade cleaning kit

This jointer switch is discreetly hidden

These motor brushes are held in by coiled springs and are easy to remove

The heart of the machine is the motor core, rotating between the bearings

The mechanics aren't such an easy proposition. The bearings which the jointer relies on for smooth, friction-free running require expert attention if they need changing. Rough squealing sounds can indicate bearing breakdown. The right-angle gears, a sign of the biscuit jointer's close relationship to the angle grinder, are never quiet at the best of times. Somehow, with an angle grinder you don't really mind the rattling grating noise – it is part and parcel of the rough nature of the work. The biscuit jointer is a little more refined, so it seems a bit out of place. The cheaper machines are prone to being noisy and a well-worked machine will, of course, have worn gears, which creates noise. The gears are effectively sealed-for-life with a large dollop of grease pumped inside to keep them running.

Don't try this at home kids: the gear head exposed

If you feel your gear-head needs attention, you will definitely have to contact a service centre. However, with gears or bearings you should get a quote for replacement, as the cost may be a fair part of a brand new machine.

Built-up mouldings on furniture, such as cornices, have been a traditional method of decoration for hundreds of years

Moulding magic

Compound and built-up mouldings can transform a piece of furniture

Historically, both architecture and furniture have been adorned with mouldings of every conceivable kind. Only in this century has there been any serious attempt to ignore ornate built-out decoration.

Even so, contemporary pieces still tend to show a restrained 'signature' in this mode. From an aesthetic and practical point of view, mouldings contribute something positive and quite vital to the work we create.

Figure 1 (page 33) shows a section, not of a furniture moulding, but of a wooden capital and entablature intended to surmount a glued-up wooden column. It illustrates how craftsmen of previous generations have dealt with the problem of large and ornate mouldings: they simply created built-up mouldings, in this case with many pieces.

When to mould

What are mouldings intended for? One obvious answer would be the use of a cornice to 'top off' a piece of furniture, be it a large and imposing breakfront bookcase or a

Spindle moulding is one option, but can prove expensive when it comes to tooling

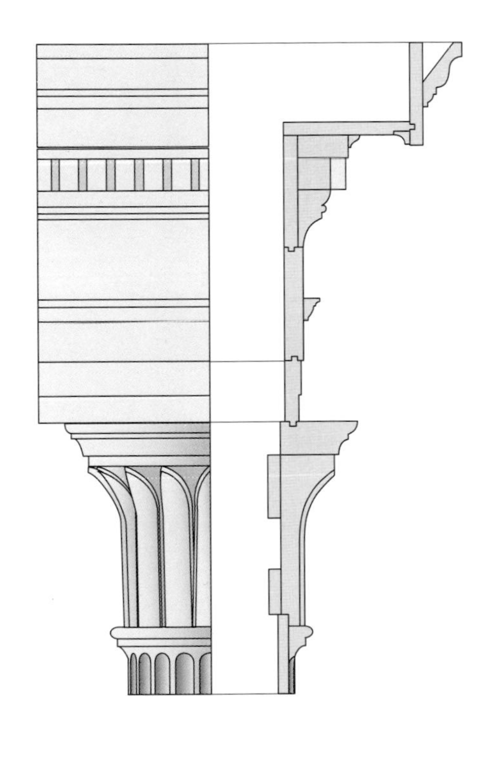

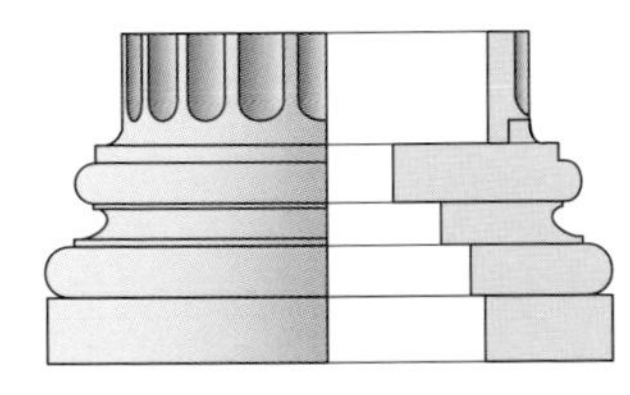

Fig. 1
An example of built-up mouldings at the turn of the century

Cutter choice

If you look at typical reproduction mouldings they all derive from classical Greek and Roman forms and in your router cutter box you probably have a number of these already. The cove, corebox, ogee or Roman ogee, ovolo and even straight cutters are essential for this work. There are now variants such as 'classical' – a cove joined to an ovolo by a 'quirk' or tiny step – and various face-moulding cutters which incorporate a variety of detail to enhance flat surfaces. An all-in-one multi-profile cutter such as the Jesada 656-802 includes both classical and bead profiles and allows rapid re-setting for multiple passes or working narrower stock when making up a compound moulding.

Don't ignore your straight cutters, they may look boring, but a moulding formed only of flat or square sections with one bevelled section can prove the point that size and proportion matter more than how fancy the shapes are. On more elaborate mouldings it is common to have a dentil (toothed) moulding at the base which is achieved with a simple jig and a small router. A flip-down or drop-in stop is needed to ensure perfect slotting and registration each time. By doing this operation on a much wider strip you end up with a slotted frieze rail which could adorn the edge of a table with other mouldings to finish it off.

Built-up mouldings allow greater flexibility through the use of standard cutters

For cornices, a couple of cutters will give you a profile suitable for small cabinets. Add various square stages and you have something suitable for a more imposing piece. Now apply dentil moulding underneath and bingo, it gets bigger still!

A plinth has a wide flat bottom section which not only looks right but simplifies moulding. Unless the plinth is fairly narrow it is much easier to do the top moulding on its own and then join it to the flat section afterwards.

Generally, room skirting mouldings such as torus are not used on furniture, with one exception; the Grecian ogee looks good anywhere, distinguished by an asymmetrical wave form unlike the regular curves of the Roman ogee.

A multiple profile cutter with the finished moulding

A convincing result can be produced through the artful use of several cutters

An alternative to using entirely built-up mouldings is to use one piece of wood, but several different cutters. The result, with a bit of artfulness, can be quite intricate mouldings as shown. However, for it to work properly, you need to plan the cuts first. By drawing out each section of the cut and removing bearings from the equation if they are likely to get in the way, you can get a fairly exact impression of the intended result. You need to think a little laterally, draw and cut out the intended timber section on a piece of paper. Try laying it down or standing it up to show which way is best for each cut.

You can of course machine one moulding from one end of the wood and another moulding from the other end if this helps get the final shape you want.

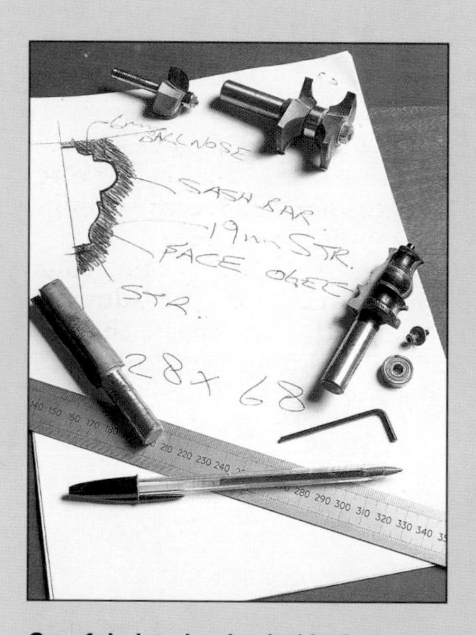

Careful planning is vital before you start

The second to last cut. Note the support strips on the outfeed side

Fig. 2 The result of building-up a moulding from three different sections

Fig. 3 An attractive cornice moulding can be achieved with just simple flat sections

run of kitchen cabinets. Both are visually improved by having a large projecting moulding on top. Another example would be the bolection, a moulding used around the inside edges of framed-up doors, which is generally achieved with one cutter but can be made by applying two mouldings back to back to give the same result.

Another good example would be the mid-height moulding around a cabinet or bookcase, dividing the upper and lower sections with a visual effect similar to a wall-mounted dado-rail. Finally, there is the ubiquitous plinth, often up to 150mm (6in) high depending on the piece of furniture.

There are certain conventions about the general appearance of mouldings and their proportions and size in relation to the furniture they are attached to, but it is hard to cover such a huge subject in one article – there are books on moulding styles, but studying existing buildings and furniture is probably the best way to learn.

Technique

The small workshop has two basic options for making larger furniture mouldings in sections, by using a

A moulding and the usual means of fixing

A jig for routing a frieze moulding

small spindle moulder such as the Elektra Beckum TF 100M, or a large router such as the DeWalt 625K or the Trend T9. Since the final profile is made from several smaller sections there isn't too much between these machining options.

Spindle moulder

If you are lucky enough to own a spindle moulder, a modern safety block with interchangeable profiles is a doddle to use, although you may want to acquire more profiles for greater choice. Since many of these blocks are not overly high, the profiles need to be built up just as with the router, the difference being that less passes are needed to reach the final shape.

Small mouldings should be machined on a wide board and cut off on the saw. The results are cleaner with less burns, tearing and chatter-marking than you tend to get with the router.

Router

With the router, careful setting of hold-downs or pressure fingers and more passes, including a light final pass to remove machining defects, is essential as these mouldings are often needed in longish lengths and any flaws will be highly visible.

One-piece cornices are face-moulded and then angled before fixing in place. However, built-up cornices are more solid and can have the back edges all lining up, except perhaps for the bottom strip which can extend, thus allowing a means of screwing to the cabinet top. A neat means of aligning all these pieces is to use biscuits which prevent the slip of the glue from pushing them out of line when cramping-up. This technique can be used for invisible fixing of mid-height and plinth mouldings too.

Built-up moulding

One advantage of a built-up moulding is that if it doesn't look right you can always reduce it by a moulding, by running it through the thicknesser, or make a different section and add that to the other ones instead.

Although the grain direction is the same, you should pre-sand all components before assembly and glue-up as neatly as possible, wiping off any excess carefully and lightly, and sanding again when dry.

Applying

When applying the mouldings to the furniture, mitred junctions are needed: a decent compound mitre saw with a fine-tooth blade should give good meeting-joint faces.

No matter how good your craftsmanship, an un-adorned cabinet looks no more than a glorified packing case. Fitted with well-proportioned mouldings, it suddenly becomes a visual feast of detail!

Fig. 4
A frieze and mouldings give detail to a table edge

SANDERS
OFFICIAL JOURNAL OF THE
the

The linenfold effect on the finished chest

Blanket coverage

Cheating is fine when the result is a beautiful copy of an early oak chest

English oak selected and machined ready for use

I JUMPED at the chance when I was asked to make a blanket chest based on one featured in Ralph Fastnedge's book *English Furniture Styles*. Although I have made many pieces in English oak, the disciplines of hand carving involved in achieving linenfold panelling always put me off.

But thanks to Wealden Cutters' new linenfold cutter set my excuses have run out. Their cutter profiles produce a convincingly effective substitute for the real thing.

My own substantial collection of cutters has been almost exclusively Wealden from the year dot, so I have no hesitation in recommending them. Equivalent cutters

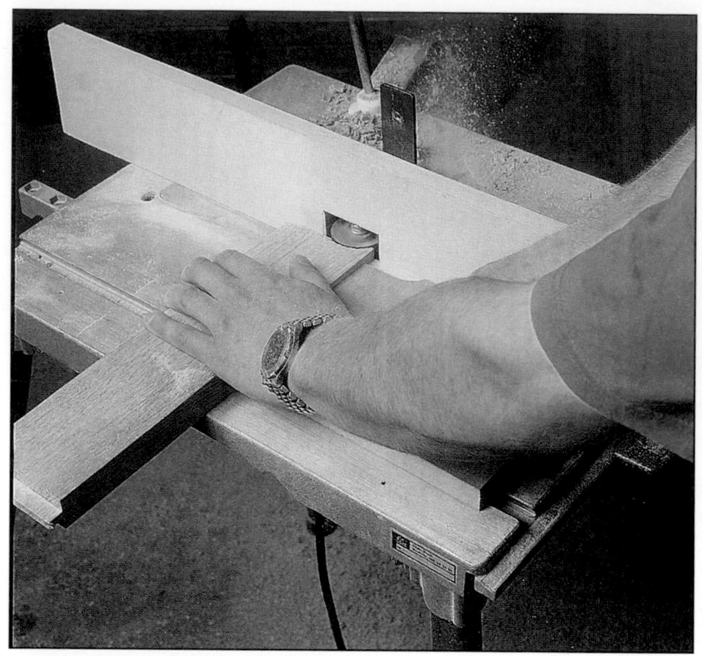

▲ *Cutting tongues on stiles*

▲ *Bottom piece showing tongues, leg cut-out and groove*

▲ *Stopped chamfers and cutter*

made by other companies can be used for all the operations in this project except, of course, the linenfold work.

Flighty oak

Because oak is a wasteful timber with a flighty nature, purchase double the amount of timber required for the chest, to allow for wastage.

For the dimensions of the chest I scaled off the drawing in the book, but it could be made to any size, remembering to keep it in proportion.

I used some thick air-dried, hurricane-felled oak and cut all the components oversize, planed them over-thickness and left the timber for some weeks to acclimatise before re-machining the pieces to the finished size.

Because this is meant to emulate an early piece of furniture with linenfold detail, the stock thickness needs to be 25mm (1in) for the stiles and rails and about 16 to 18mm (5/8 to 3/4in) for the panels. The legs are of two pieces of 25mm (1in) oak to give the required thickness. I reserved the ray-figured boards for the linenfold panels. To make construction easier treat each face of the chest as one complete item. The front and back and the lid comprise complete 'units', and the ends and bottom are fitted afterwards.

T & G cutters

Wealden's Shaker-style large tongue-and-groove (T & G) cutter set allows neat jointing and panelling without having to resort to mortice and tenons. A router table and a large router will be needed for this operation.

Calculation of component sizes is all important. Mark the square face sides and edges of the components when planing to size and work to these marks as a datum throughout the project to ensure flush joint faces.

Cut the stock for the legs and stiles somewhat over-length, ready to be cut to size later on, but cut the rails and muntins exactly 24mm (15/16in) longer than the distance between the stiles or legs. This is to allow for a 12mm (15/32in) tongue each end to fit the depth of groove created by the T & G set.

The panels need to be about 2mm (5/64in) shorter than the rail, including tongue, so that when slid into the groove there is enough free play to allow for assembly.

The T & G set comes with shims to get the right fit, so it is sensible to make several trial joints first and mark the correct shim with a felt-tip pen so that the right one is used.

Rout the scribing cuts first (the tongue) and then the profile (groove). I did some of the grooves at full cut depth but found the 'ragging' of the edges unacceptable and swapped to 'pre-scoring' – this means a first cut at about 2mm (5/64in) deep to give nice clean edges followed by a full 12mm (15/32in) pass which should remove the bulk of the material without disturbing those edges.

Because the panels need a slightly looser tongue, a different shim is needed.

All the components for the end and base can be cut at the same time as the main ones, but on final assembly they might need slight re-machining.

Chamfers, grooves

The stopped chamfers on the lid frame are applied with a 45° cutter, either using a fence on a router table or

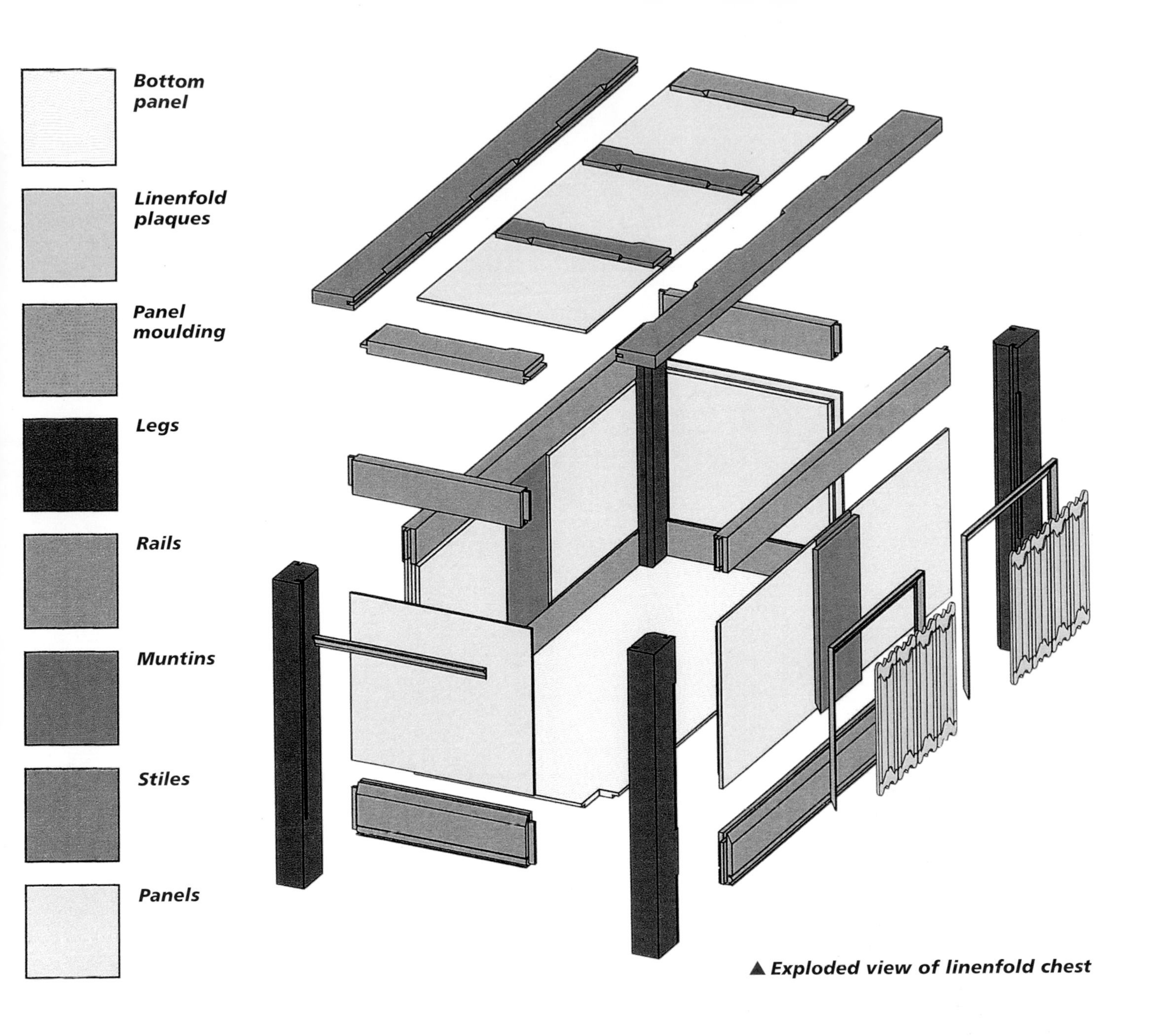

▲ *Exploded view of linenfold chest*

"Don't bother to glue the base strips in place, as they must be allowed to shrink"

with the router hand-held working off the side fence. Ensure you have made pencil marks for the start and stop points and don't hold the wood in one place on the spinning cutter too long as doing so would result in a burn mark.

The panels are butt-glued together, then machined and sanded to a finish before assembly takes place. They are flat on the outside but project slightly on the inside of the chest due to their thickness. Use the same 45° chamfer cutter to put a bevel on after tonguing their inside face.

Also before assembly rout large edge beads on the front of the lower rails and a groove on the reverse to take the chest bottom panel. To avoid breaking through the wood, the groove should be higher than the bead.

The large chamfer running down the inside corner of the legs can either be done now or after the first glue up.

To make the routed small stopped edge bead look as if it has been achieved with scratchstock, whittle each end of the cut with a chisel, and sand lightly.

Fitting frame

All of the frame parts should be sanded before assembly.

After a 'dry-fit' trial run, glue up the front, back and lid items separately with PVA or Cascamite and cramp up using sash cramps. Place paper between the cramps and the timber to avoid staining from the metal.

Leave to dry then trim the legs to finished length.

Lay the back of the chest down and dry-fit the end parts and the front on top of it.

The base, consisting of a series of planks, tongue-and-grooved all round and with the grain running from back to front, can then be cut to size.

Make cut-outs on the two end planks to fit around the legs; place them in their groove each end of the chest. Then fill in between them with the rest of the planks, using a square and a scribe to mark the size.

Mark and cut each one individually until there is a small gap. Trim the last plank to a snug fit when the last tongue is machined.

Gluing, sanding

Now glue the whole chest together. Don't bother to glue the base strips in place, as they must be allowed to shrink. Use protective pads and sit the cramped up chest on a flat surface to make sure it is square – sight across the top to check if it is 'in wind' (twisted). If both ends are exactly in line there is no wind. If they are not, adjust by placing a small packer under one leg, then leave the glue to set overnight.

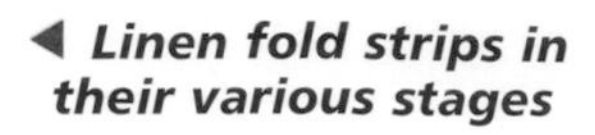

◀ ***Linen fold strips in their various stages***

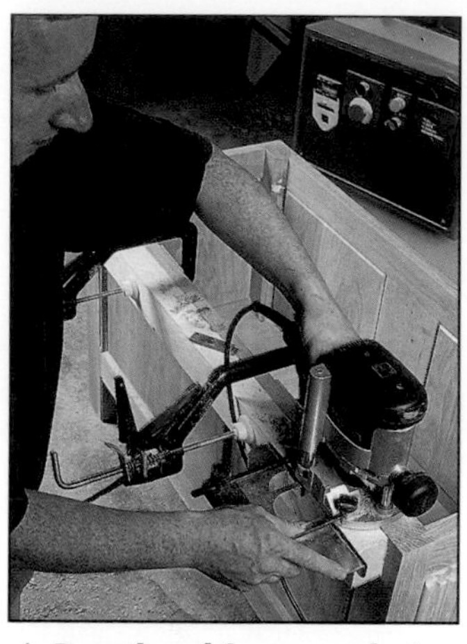

▲ ***Routing hinge sockets – note bar clamped to chest to provide router with a running surface***

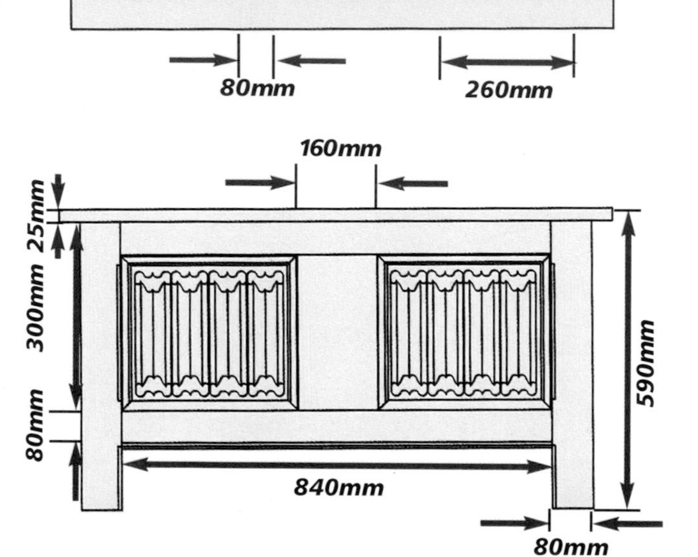

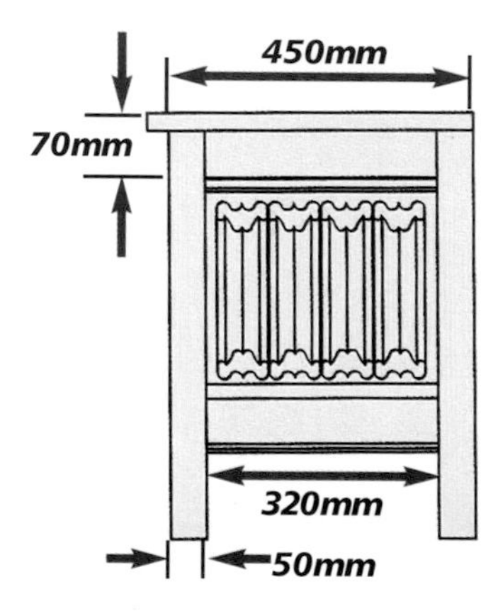

Bailey's tips

Leaving glue to become congealed – but not set – makes cleaning up neater as it can be done with the second best chisel rather than by wiping and washing off the surplus, which raises the grain and can push glue into the pores of the wood. To get the amount of glue right, I favour using a slim wedge cut on the bandsaw as an applicator, or a dis-penser with a spout.

When preparing the small mouldings use a wide board of the right thickness and machine one edge, cut it off on the saw and repeat as necessary – then sand carefully.

To avoid kickback when doing stopped cuts on the fence, apply the far end of the work against the fence, slowly swing the front end against it and feed the wood over the cutter.

The 'horns' on the lid stiles can be trimmed to length then sanded all round. Then, with the box open in front of you, check that the lid fits and overhangs the front and sides correctly.

There may be a slight step where the frames are joined. This will need sanding flush, taking care to avoid the projecting bevelled panels. I worked over all outside frame surfaces and top edges with my 4in belt sander and sharp 120 grit.

Moulding frames

The front and back feature a plain bevel along and a classic profile panel moulding around the other three sides. The ends of the chest also have the bevel on the top of the bottom rail, but the moulding is applied only across the top. A narrow border will separate the linenfold plaques and panel mouldings.

Cut the mouldings with a mitre saw, then glue them into place, holding with masking tape until dry. Note that the vertical pieces on the front and back are next to the edge bead so need to be rounded over with abrasive paper until they look right.

Lastly, remove sander scratches by running an orbital sander and 180 grit over the whole chest.

All arises (sharp edges) need to be taken off by hand with a quick flick of fine abrasive and the ends of the legs chamfered to reduce any carpet damage.

Linenfold process

Unlike the woodworkers who made early oak chests and panelling, thanks to Wealden we need only give passing concern to the linenfolding as it is machined as plaques and applied afterwards.

The plaques are made from stock 75mm (3in) wide and 10mm ($^{3}/_{8}$in) thick. When calculating the size of the chest, make sure the panel sizes measure in multiples of 75mm (3in) plus the size of the border you need.

The prepared stock must be profiled in two passes as the cutter does one half of the width. Adjust the fence so that the second cut cleans up and the 'folding' needs only limited sanding.

Next, carefully cut the pieces to length using a table or radial arm saw; make sure more lengths than you need are cut in case some are imperfect. Unusually, the scribing cuts are done after the profiling.

Then make a jig which clamps the plaques and has a special profile at the end. In combination with the relevant cutters, this produces the full effect of the scribing cut. Wealden provide a full-size template for the jig which is transferred to the MDF or Tufnol jig material.

First, set the inverted plaque to one line and, using a straight profiling cutter with a bottom bearing, run along the shaped edge of the jig to scribe one half the width of the plaque.

Invert the plaque to shape the other half, then pull it back to the second marked line on the jig. With the small

▲ ***Routing internal chamfer on leg***

▲ ***Fitting bottom pieces***

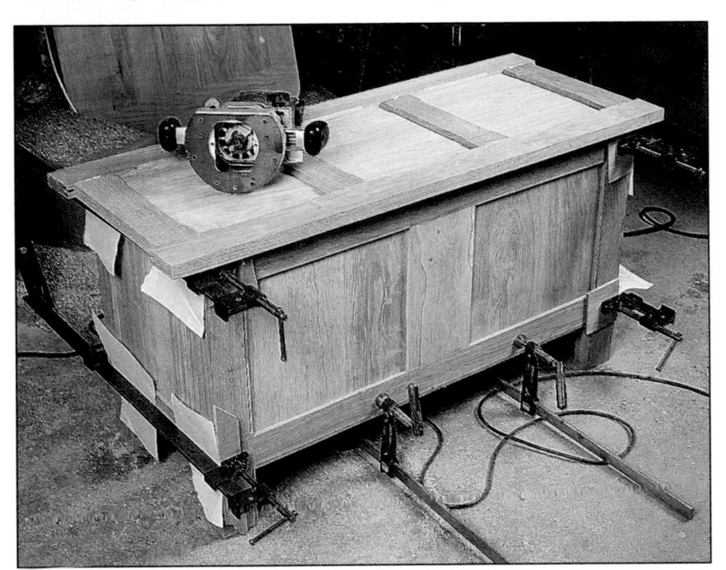

▲ ***Main carcass glued up***

Tooling up

The following were used in this project:

▲ ***Wealden linenfold cutters and others used in the project***

Wealden Tool Co: Linenfold set, Large tongue and groove set, Chamfer T916B ¼ shank, V Groove T128 ¼ shank, Hinge morticing T310 ¼ shank, Panel trim T8018B ½ shank, beaded edge T2503B ¼ shank, T2504B ½ shank, Classic panel guided T1622B ¼ shank.

bearing-guided cutter provided, move the router across the jig and clean off the top of the exposed area of the plaque, so producing a 'carved' effect at the end of each strip.

After a light sanding the plaques can be applied to the panels on the chest. I put an even layer of glue on the backs of four linenfold plaques, placed them on a blank panel and rubbed them gently into place – though a bit of gentle weighting down would be a good idea.

If you don't put glue near the edges, it shouldn't ooze out when the plaques are in place.

Sinking hinges

Mark positions on the back top rail for three 2½in brass butts. They will be sunk into the rail but not into the lid using the router with a 12 or 16mm diameter hinge mortice bit.

With the router stationary, plunge it so the hinge mortice bit just touches a flat surface. Then place the thinnest part of the folded hinge between the depth stop and turret and lock the stop at that depth, lowering the stop a little more if the cut appears to be too deep.

Clamp a board against the top rail to give a larger surface and set the side fence on the router so the hinges will have half the 'knuckle' projecting from the rail. Now machine out the hinge slot, starting along the edge to avoid tear-out.

Cut carefully up to the end marks, then square out the corners with a sharp chisel.

Inside detail ▶

Screw on the lid then take it off again to apply the finish before replacing it.

Finishing

Apply by brush two coats of Liberon finishing oil to reach all the in-between bits, wait a short while and rub off to produce a gentle sheen.

Then apply a coat of Liberon Black Bison clear wax for a soft feel and a pleasant smell. Lastly, rub down the hinges and screws with fine abrasive to get rid of the factory 'drawn' finish.

Some hot tips for making radiator covers

Radiating style

RADIATOR covers – once the province of posh clubs for the rich and famous – are now playing a stylish part in many home decoration schemes. They are relatively simple to make with router and cutters – and can represent a profitable little sideline for professionals.

Design factors

They must be wide enough to allow for the radiator valves to be operated, and not so shallow that, should a hot radiator move away from the wall, the grille panel would be pushed off.

The proportions of the cover can be changed to suit, perhaps by increasing its height or length or by upping the number of grille panels from two to three. Where possible, all radiator covers in one room should be set at the same height.

I build mine from 18mm (¼in) thick MDF because it is cheap and stable enough to cope with heat variations. Making from solid wood isn't a realistic option as it tends to move a lot with extreme changes of heat, although the same effect can be obtained by using veneered MDF with thin solid wood mouldings around the edges.

On a sheet of paper, and to a convenient scale, sketch out the board size 2440 by 1220mm (8 by 4ft). Draw on this the width and number of strips of all the components required in order to devise the most economical cutting plan.

Carcass construction

A portable circular saw and a straight-edge does for ripping everything slightly oversize. Then plane all the edges smooth with a router (photo 1).

Cross-cut components to length with the exception of the plinth and grille frame parts, which are dealt with later (photo 2).

▲ *Photo 1* ***The sheet of MDF is trimmed to size and edges cleaned up with a router***

▲ *Photo 2* ***Small components need a jig to aid with dimensioning***

"I machined the top's edge moulding with the router inverted in a table, but freehand routing it is also possible"

A short strip jointed onto the base of the carcass ends creates a step to accommodate the grille frame (photo 3).This is achieved with a biscuit-slotting cutter used in the router. For safety's sake, leave these strips long for the slotting process, cutting them to length afterwards (photo 4).

Note that each slot is marked in the centre and on either side. This enables the router to be moved along so that a slot long enough to accept a '20' biscuit can be created.

Glue these pieces in place and leave to dry.

I machined the top's edge moulding with the router inverted in a table, but freehand routing it is also possible.

First, produce the major curve by routing a largish roundover, then use a 6mm diameter roundover cutter to rout the top again, but on the other side (photo 5). Applying two curved mouldings on opposite sides of a board will inevitably leave a slight point where the workpiece runs against the fence, but this can be sanded out.

The long edge is easy to machine, but take care to give maximum support to the work-piece when routing the ends with the fence gap set small (photo 6). A steady hand while pushing the board past the cutter will help, with any slight deviation in cut being sanded smooth afterwards.

Next, use a square to mark the underside of the top, so providing lines for the outside of the end panels (photo 7). Joint these with biscuits and mark them accordingly.

Cramping on an 'L' jig (photo 8), allows the router to slot the underside of the top while the more conventional approach is used for the slots in the panel ends. Dry-fit the

"Cramping on an 'L' jig allows the router to slot the underside of the top while the more conventional approach is used for the slots in the panel ends"

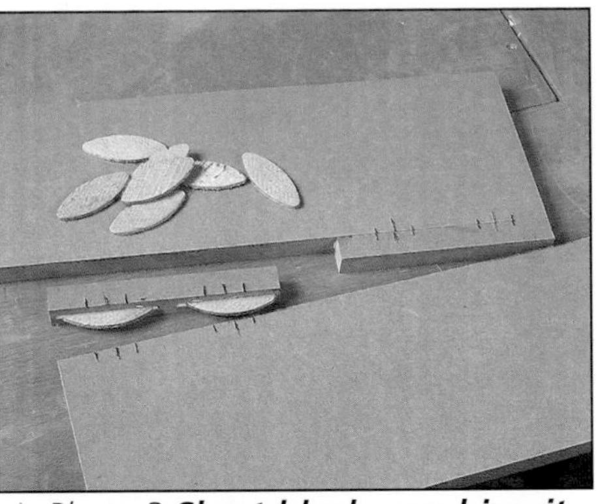

▲ Photo 3 **Short blocks are biscuit-jointed to the base of the carcass ends to accommodate the grille panel**

▲ Photo 4 **For safety, rout the biscuit slots before cutting the blocks short, feeding in at the far end first to avoid kick-back**

▲ Photo 5 **The moulding on the top is formed using a large roundover cutter followed by a smaller one on the other side**

▲ Photo 6 **Use a false fence with a small gap to support the work-piece when routing the ends**

▲ Photo 7 **Mark the positions for the biscuit-jointing slots**

▲ Photo 8 **A right-angle jig aids biscuit slotting inside the ends of the top**

Grille choices

Grille possibilities vary from expensive brass in diamond, rosette and mesh patterns, to cheap punched hardboard obtainable in a number of patterns ready for painting. Any of these can be fitted in place, using panel pins or a tiny wooden fillet, after finishing the cover.

If using a paint finish, ensure the cover and any hardboard grilling is primed. Denib between coats before applying a top coat of gloss, satin or decorative paint effect.

▲ *Various grilles types can be used according to budget: brass from the most expensive brass diamond; rosette; and mesh pattern, punched through polished brass to punched hardboard*

▶ *The grille fitted into the panel*

Tooling up

- *Biscuit-slotting cutter*
- *Straight-fluted cutter*
- *Large roundover cutter*
- *6mm diameter roundover cutter*
- *Moulding cutter – any classical profile, for example Grecian ogee or Victorian torus*
- *45° V-cutter*
- *Profile and scribe cutter set*
- *Bearing-guided rebating cutter*
- *Titan 3mm roundover bit*

ends and measure across at the top to arrive at the correct width for mitring the plinth.

Plinth

The plinth moulding can be a Grecian ogee (photo 9), a Victorian torus or any suitable classical profile. Run the moulding on enough stock to go round the cover, allowing extra for mitres and mistakes.

The mitres can be cut either with a mitre saw or, preferably, with a router fitted with a large 45° V-cutter, the work being run against a T-square fence.

Trim the ends of the long piece of plinth so that the distance between the internal mitre corners is the same as the previously taken measurement (photo 10).

Now butt-glue this plinth piece in place, cramp and check the cover for square by measuring the diagonals from corner to corner (photo 11).

Cut two small blocks of MDF, apply glue to two of their faces and rub them into the internal corners between the plinth and the end panels. The blocks will back up and strengthen the plinth's butt-glue joints (photo 12, page 45).

▲ *Photo 9* ***A Grecian ogee moulding is just right for the plinth***

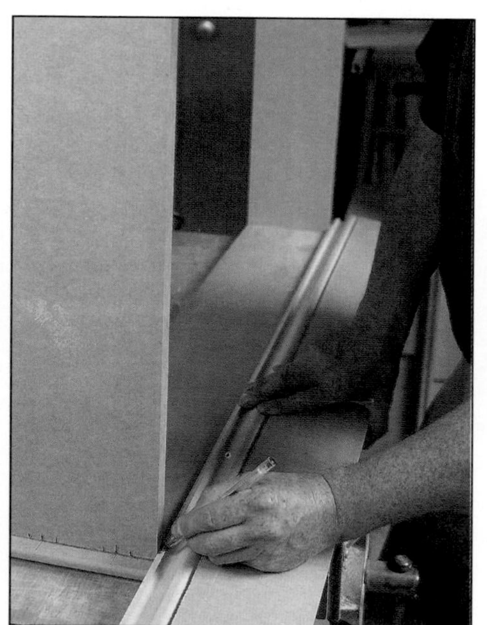

▲ *Photo 10* ***Carefully mark the inside edges of the mitres***

▲ *Photo 11* ***Firmly clamp the plinth in place until the glue is dry***

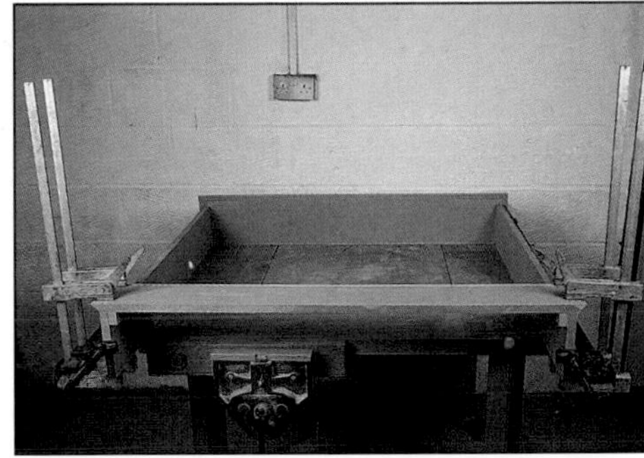

▲ *Photo 12* ***Glue blocks inside the cover to help hold plinth in place***

▲ ***Front and side elevations***

▲ *Photo 13* ***The grille panel frame is easily made using a profile and scribe cutter set***

▲ *Photo 15* ***Mark out the ventilation slots top and bottom of the panel***

▲ *Photo 16* ***Using a straight-edge, rout the ventilation slots***

▲ *Photo 14* ***Make sure the grille panel is square when cramping-up***

▲ *Photo 17* ***Add a decorative moulding with a 3mm roundover cutter***

"Fit it tightly before planing top and bottom to enable the panel to be removed for access to the radiator taps"

Cut and mitre two short lengths of plinth, one for the right-hand end and one for the left. Glue them in place, butting them up tight to the existing mitres, and cramp up.

The top edge of the long plinth must be backed up with a 30mm (1⅛in) strip of MDF, glued in place to strengthen the narrow edge of the moulding. Ensure no gap shows below the grille panel.

Glue the top in place. When dry, fill and sand any gaps or blemishes.

Grille panels

The grille panel is the same width as the cover, and the height is the distance between the top of the plinth and the underside of the top. Fit it tightly before planing top and bottom to enable the panel to be removed for access to the radiator taps.

The side rails, top rail and intermediate uprights – muntins – are 75mm (3in) wide. Perspective effect means the bottom rail looks better if it is about 15mm (⅝in) wider than the other components.

Use a profile and scribe cutter set to make the frame, adding 19mm (¾in) to the length of the top rails, bottom rails and muntins to allow for their scribe cut (photo 13).

Leave the stiles overlength for trimming after assembly.

Set up the router table with the cutter in scribe mode, and rout the ends of the rails, and the muntins supporting them, with a push-block or protractor fence. Leave a minimal gap in the fence to prevent workpieces pulling into the cutter as they come off the bearing.

Reset the router with the cutter in profile mode, then, by taking test cuts on offcuts, check that the profile lines up correctly – without a step – with the scribe-cuts on the rail ends when the joint is assembled.

As components must be turned over for this operation, play safe by marking the face to be profiled.

Mark the centre positions of the muntins on the rails and place a matching mark in the centre of the ends of each muntin.

Pre-sand all the moulded edges, glue and cramp all the frame parts together, measuring from corner to corner to ensure squareness, (photo 14).

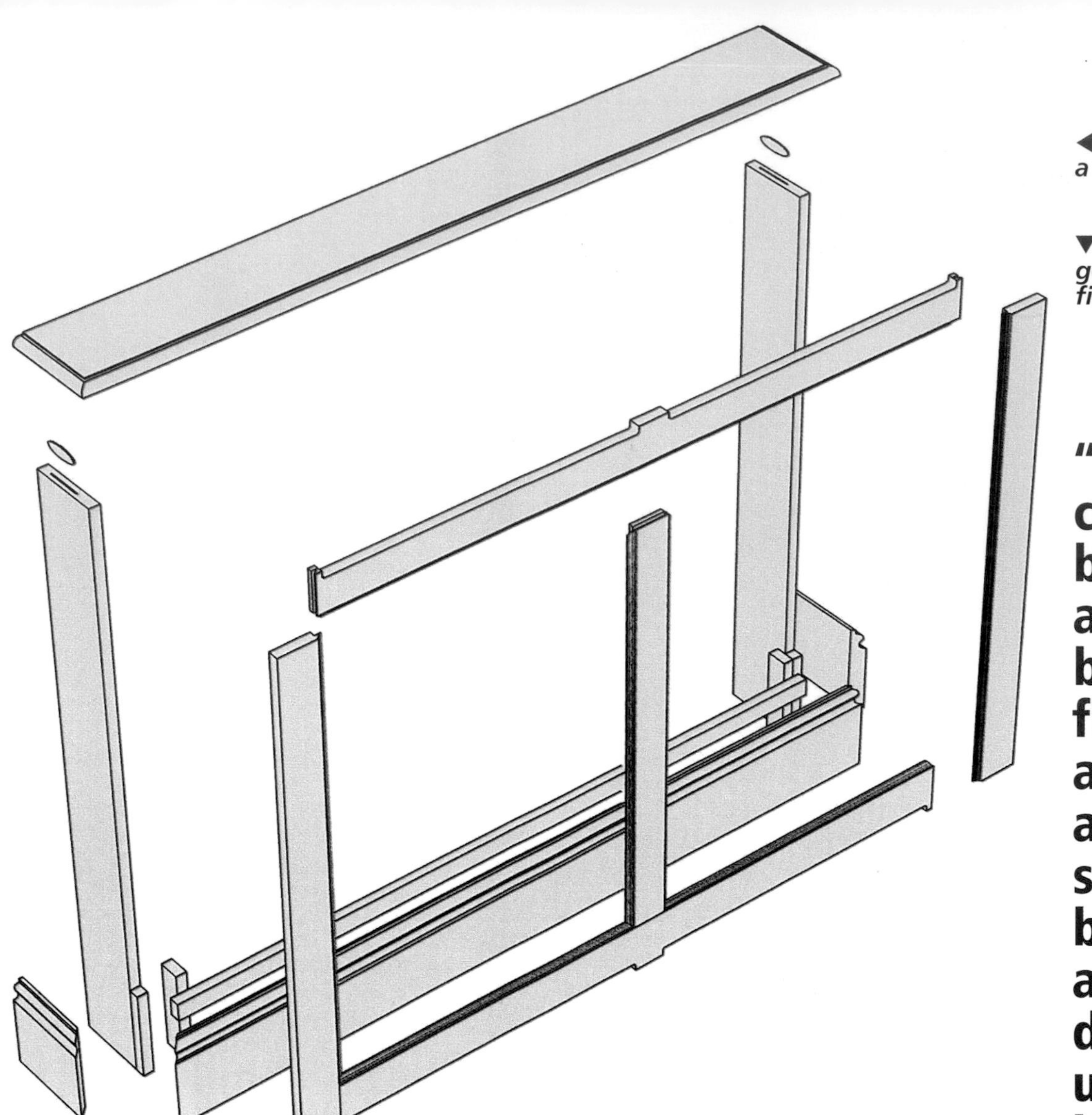

◀ *Exploded drawing of a radiator cover*

▼ *Radiator covers look good with a painted finish*

"The radiator cover must be scribed along its back edge to fit as closely as possible around the skirting board and accommodate any unevenness in the walls"

Once dry, trim the panel frame to a loose fit in the carcass, using a straight cutter in the router and running it along a straight-edge, starting with the two long edges. When sized correctly, sand all round.

Use a bearing-guided rebating cutter to achieve a 10mm rebate for the grille.

For the ventilation slots at the top and bottom of the panel (photo 15, page 45), mark them out, then make successive stopped cuts so they line up with the muntins (photo 16, page 45). A 3mm Titan roundover bit, set to make a slight step, achieves a nice moulded finish to the slots (photo 17, page 45).

Finishing, fitting

The radiator cover must be scribed along its back edge to fit as closely as possible around the skirting board and accommodate any unevenness in the walls. Place a level on its front and tilt the cover accordingly.

Open a pair of compasses up to the widest gap between the wall and the cover and mark a line all round the cover, keeping the point of the compasses in contact with the wall and skirting.

Jigsaw along this line to achieve a tight fit, that may still need a bit of tweaking.

Fix the cover with screws and masonry plugs, first checking for pipes and wiring. ◪

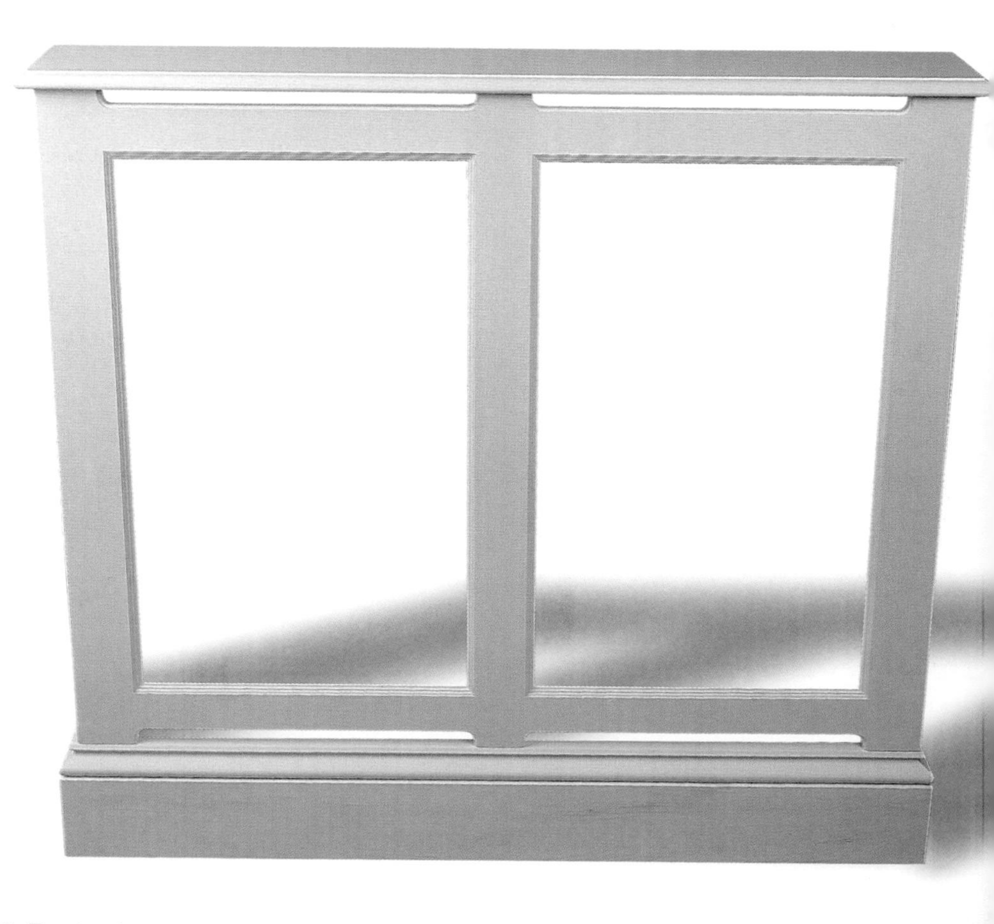

Stoke the fire

Warm up your router and make a pine fireplace surround

A FIREPLACE is a perfect focus for a room, however existing fireplaces often lack something i.e. an impressive surround to show it off to best effect. Here is a design that will transform your living room and put the heart back into it!

I have used softwood, because it is cheap and can be purchased ready-prepared. The sizes shown on the drawings are only for guidance because each household's requirements are different.

"Getting an even result takes a bit of care and will start with accurate marking out"

Fluting the uprights

Cut the uprights to length and mark out the fluted sections allowing for the plinth blocks beneath. Likewise, mark where the reeded strips will go (see figure 2, page 49) – the space remaining should be sufficient to take the roundel design. Mark this out on each stile ensuring it is centred.

Using a corebox bit of 16mm diameter, rout the flutes in the uprights on the router table, having first put pencil marks on its reverse side and on a subfence attached to the table's fence. This means you can 'drop on' and start and stop the cuts accurately. Move the fence between cuts to get the right spacing – use a trial piece each time to check that it looks OK. Remember that the workpiece can be reversed to rout the flutes at the other side of the column, rather than resetting the fence for every fluting operation. Getting an even result takes a bit of care and will start with accurate marking out.

▲ *The flutes are routed by lining up pencil marks and lowering the workpiece onto the cutter*

Roundels

The roundels need to be machined at the top of each column. This is done freehand using a thin sub-base of MDF screwed onto the router's baseplate using whatever threaded holes are provided. Fit a panel bead cutter which gives a suitable roundover effect for the centre 'boss'. The outer rings are cut with a 6mm straight bit – measure the distances needed to give the correct radius for each operation (several are needed to get the final effect).

"Here is a design that will transform your living room and put the heart back into it!"

▲ *The pine fire surround ready to fit*

▲ *A sub-baseplate is made to machine the roundels*

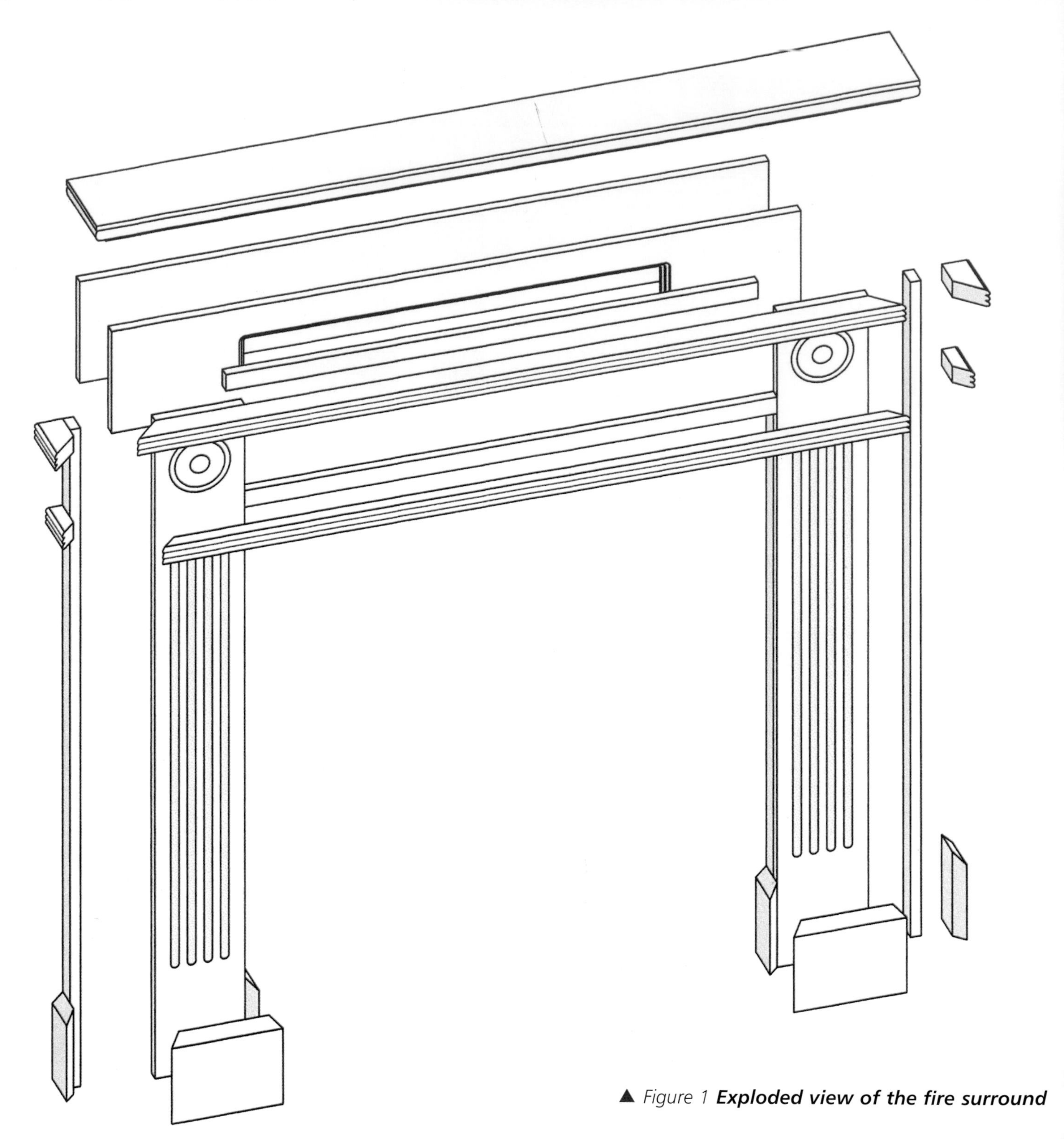

▲ *Figure 1* ***Exploded view of the fire surround***

Mark these positions on the sub-base and drill at each position ready to take a small piece of studding. Make the drill hole slightly smaller than the studding – say 4.5mm for a 5mm diameter stud. Thread the studding into the first hole, then drill. Use a test piece and make a circular pass to create the roundel effect. Move the studding to the next hole, change to the straight bit and carry on machining until the whole thing is complete. The outer ring is created with the panel bead cutter again, with a new stud hole so it is offset to the outside of the slot. Rout this with the straight bit. The result is that with care only the outer edge of the slot will get rounded over. Check that it looks OK, then do it for real on the columns.

Crosspiece

Cut the crosspiece to length, allowing for it to go most of the way behind the columns which it will be glued and screwed onto. Mark out the recess in the middle that will have a moulded edge. I was originally going to make an MDF template to suit this shape and use it with a bearing guided 'classical' face mould cutter. However I had just finished making my new spindle moulder sized router table so I was keen to try it out, rather than using a template. I cut the recess out by 'dropping on' and running the workpiece against the fence; the ends are routed using the protractor to guide it. Remember that several passes are needed to cut right through to full depth. As I didn't have a template suitable for a classical cutter with a top bearing, I chose the good old 9.5mm ovolo instead, as its bottom bearing will run around the recess. Glue the panel behind the recess and fix with panel pins.

Glue the crosspiece or fascia behind the columns and screw from behind ensuring all is square.

Columns, plinths and mouldings

Next cut some spare 25mm (1in) or 19mm (¾in) thick wood or MDF into strips and glue and pin these behind the columns down the full length of each side to make them look deeper than they really are. Do the same with the underneath edge of the crosspiece, these pieces need to sit against

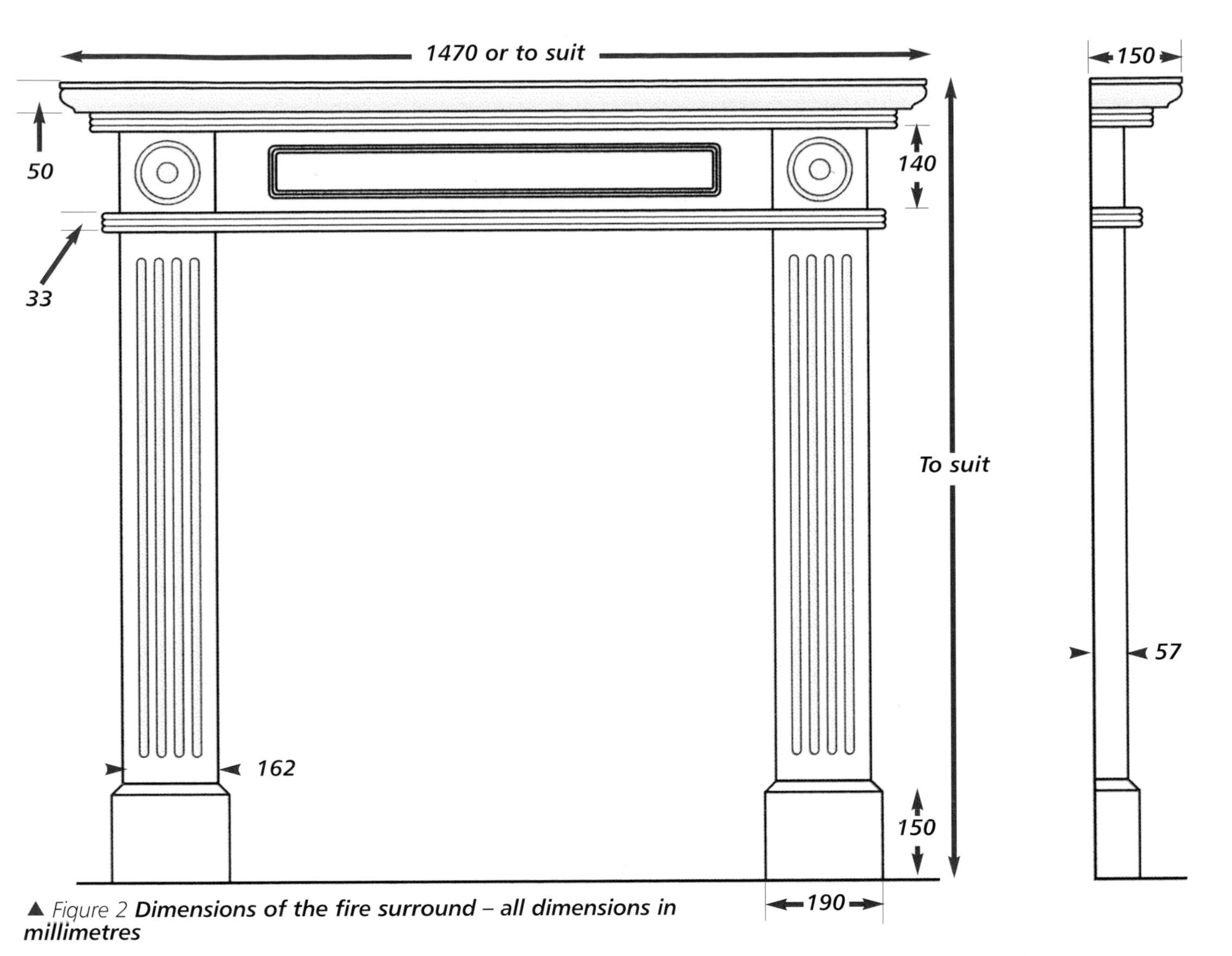

▲ *Figure 2* ***Dimensions of the fire surround – all dimensions in millimetres***

▲ ***A straight cutter is plunged through the workpiece to create the cut-out in the crosspiece***

the wall once the mantle shelf is fitted.

To make the plinths, rout a 45° angle on the front of a wide board using a bevel cutter. Cut pieces to length and mitre the corners around the base of the columns. Glue and pin them in position.

The projecting reeded edges are created next, using 33mm (1⁵⁄₁₆in) wide (finished size) stock and a reeding or ogee panel cutter. If the cutter you have isn't wide enough, reverse the workpiece and rout it twice to give a double width of reeding. Note how the upper section of reeding projects further than the lower one to give better proportion, this is easily achieved by using thicker wood. I found the ogee panel cutter was slightly narrower than the prepared stock so I used the point on a marking gauge to whittle off the slight overhang on the edges before sanding.

Mitre and fit all the reeding, making sure it runs level all the way round. To make up the gap where the crosspiece sits back from the face of the uprights cut strips of stock the same thickness as the columns and the same width as the mouldings. The top moulding is set flush with the top edge of the surround, ready for the mantle shelf to sit on. I used PVA and panel pins for fixing them on, followed by a rub of filler in each hole.

"I was going to use a large ogee cutter belonging to a fellow woodworker, it would have looked nice – but he'd gone on holiday!"

Mantleshelf

The last major job is machining the solid mantleshelf (ex 50mm (2in) stock). I was going to use a large ogee cutter belonging to a fellow woodworker, it would have

▲ ***The cut-out is then moulded on the front making sure fingers are kept well clear***

▲ *On the reeding use the point of a marking gauge to cut off the waste left by the cutter*

▲ *The ends of the mantleshelf are tricky to rout, an extension to the table will help*

looked nice – but he'd gone on holiday! After a bit of head scratching I settled on a trusty Wealden grecian ogee which is normally intended for skirtings.

Routing the cuts across the grain is the most difficult as you need to support a quite substantial piece of wood, without it tilting, while running it carefully over the cutter. A through fence helps, as does some kind of extension fixed to the side of the table.

I screwed a scrap piece on the back at the edge of the mantleshelf to stop the break-out that would normally occur. Rout the left edge, then the front edge, and lastly the right edge. To get the right depth quite a few passes are needed so as not to overload the router or cutter. The overhang may be a little uneven on the underside, this can be cleaned up with a sharp chisel, then sanded. Invert the mantleshelf and glue and screw it to the surround, using strips of softwood if necessary.

Finishing

Whether your fire is ever lit or not, it is wise to seal the reverse of the pine as well as varnishing or applying sanding sealer to the front as it will be more stable. Use mirror plates fixed to both sides of the columns to attach it to the wall, ensure that the wall fixing screws are set close to the columns so that, as the pine shrinks with room heat, the screws will slide in the mirror plate holes. Use a metal primer on the mirror plates and then use emulsion paint the same colour as the walls to disguise them.

The result is a grandiose fireplace that will impress all your friends.

Tooling up

- *Wealden Cutters used*
- *Two-flute, bearing-guided rounding over cutter*
- *Point round cutter – for reeding*
- *Core box cutter*
- *Bearing-guided sunken profile cutter*

▼*The cutters used*

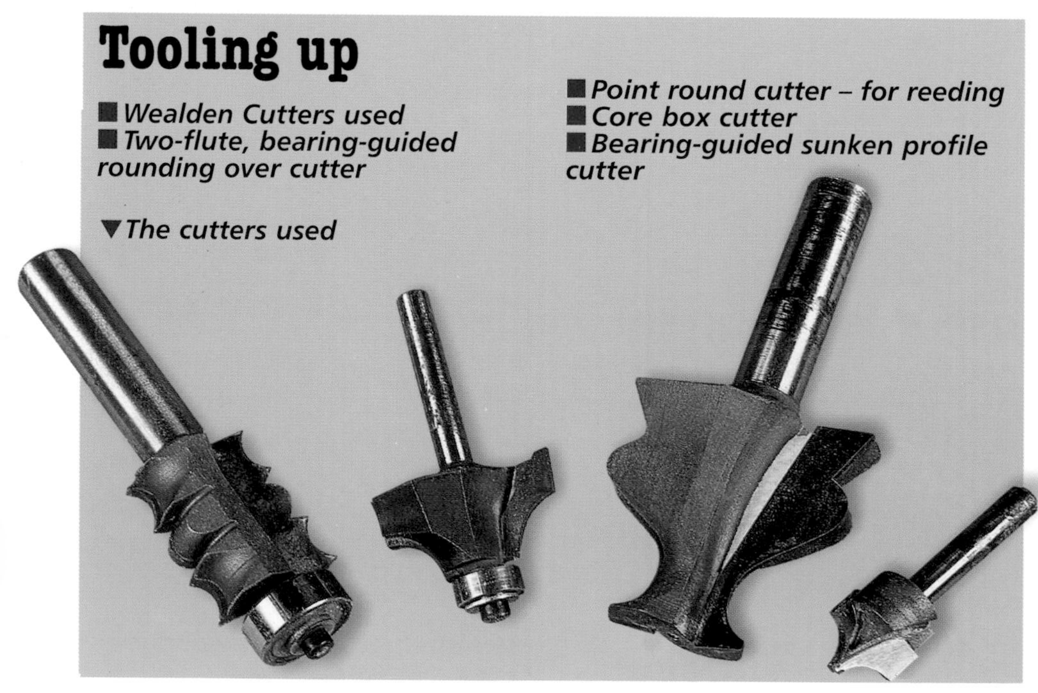

▲ *Screw a piece of scrap wood to the back of the mantleshelf to stop breakout*

On the case

Store your router and cutters safely in this sturdy case

I FIND the standard metal cases made for storing routers rather unsympathetic and prefer to make my own wooden ones which are designed to accommodate both cutters and extras. My router is the standard Elu MOF 177E, but this case can be adapted to suit any large machine. Take the measurements of the router's unplunged height, width and depth. Then adjust the sizes to suit it, leaving space to fit in a fence, fence rods, extraction pipe, guide bush, nuts, spanners, a minimum of 12 cutters on a slide-out board at the top, and collets. If you are working away from your base it is important to carry a selection of cutters to include straight, rebate, ovolo, cove and panel trim, which should cover most types of work.

◄*Set up the dovetail jig for cutting the corners of the case*

▲*A home-made case for your router can be tailor made to fit all accessories as well*

Case

The case is made from 15mm (5/8in) ply with a 6mm (1/4in) back panel and a 9mm (5/16in) door. The cutter board is 15mm (5/8in) thick with stopped holes to prevent the cutters falling through.

In the bottom corner is a slide-out case which contains all the bits and pieces such as guide bush, spanners and small nuts and bolts for fitting accessories. The fence and rods are clipped into the case separately using spring clips and wooden blocks glued to the case interior. The router has a wooden base surround and turn-buttons to hold it securely in place.

The case's jointwork is a good excuse to use the Trend dovetail jig, the resulting joint giving strength on the corners and looking suitably craftsmanlike at the same time.

Construction

Measure and mark out the case sides, top and bottom. The sides are 9mm (5/16in) shorter than the overall height as the dovetails are lapped, not exposed.

For both sawing and trimming, I find the Mini-Mach vacuum table very handy – all you need to do is find a flat non-porous surface, place the Mini-Mach on it, attach a

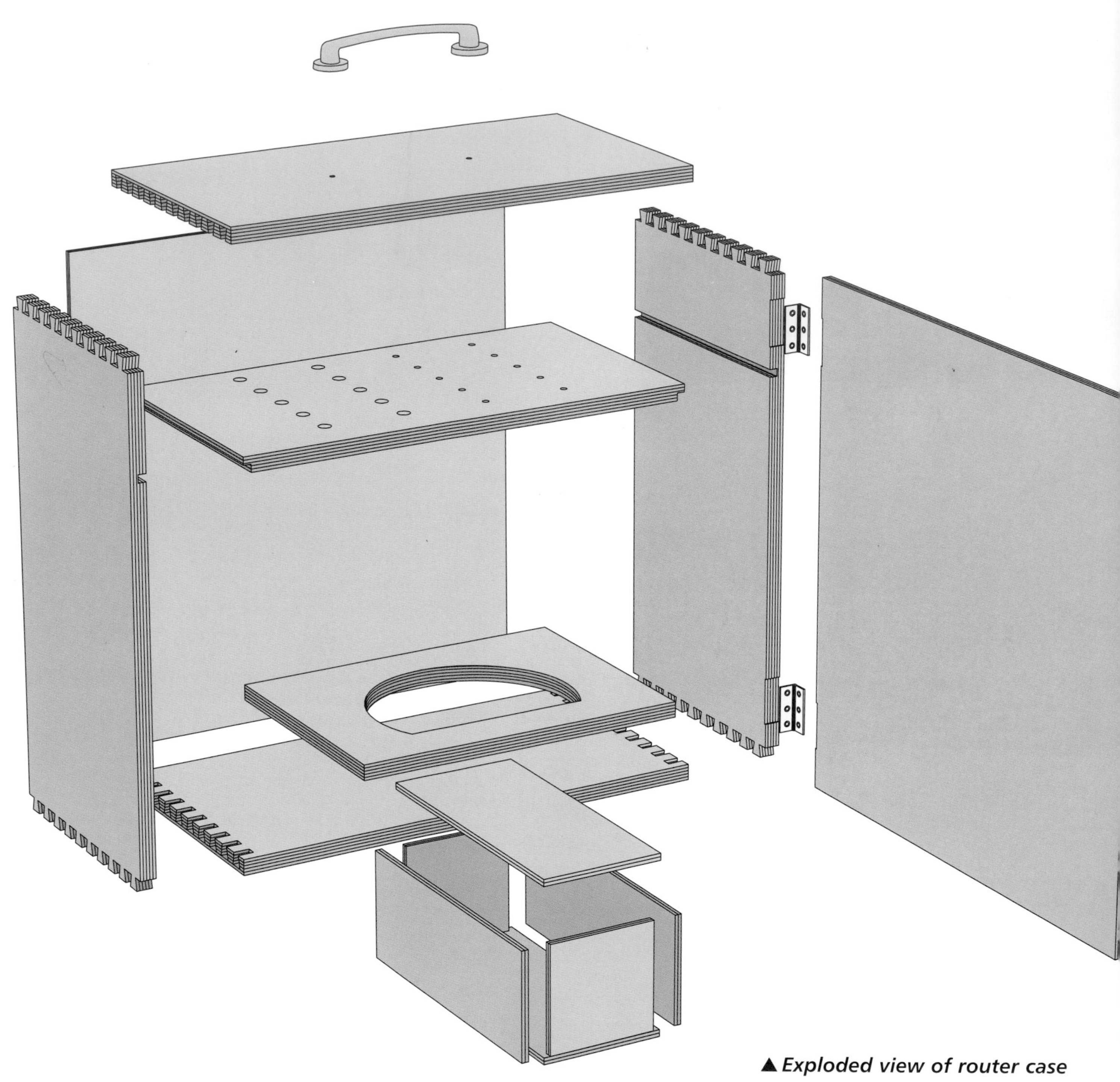

▲ *Exploded view of router case*

domestic size vacuum cleaner to the outlet, and place the board to cut or trim on top, overhanging and ready to machine. Ensure the cutter or blade cannot damage the Mini-Mach and that a reasonable number of 'cells' are covered by the board. If your board isn't quite flat, the foam cell walls will take care of this by squashing down under vacuum pressure – I have sawn ply into strips, lengthwise first, and then cross-cut and trimmed in one go using a router on the MiniMach and a small T-square held in place with spring clamps.

Next, mark the shelf grooves about 95 to 100mm (3¾ to 4in) down from what will be the internal dimension after the dovetails are cut, allowing 10mm (⅜in) for each set of dovetails, and slot about 6 to 7mm (¼in) deep with a 6.4mm straight cutter using the MiniMach and the router's own fence, setting the facings close together for support.

"The case's jointwork is a good excuse to use the Trend dovetail jig, the resulting joint giving strength on the corners and looking suitably craftsmanlike at the same time"

Dovetail jig

Now set up the dovetail jig. This needs to be screwed to a bench edge, or something similar. You could of course use a piece of thick board which can then be vacuum mounted on the Mini-Mach!

▲ *Dovetail joints look neat and make the case extra strong*

▲ *The back is pinned on and then cut to size with a flush trimmer*

If you are familiar with the Elu jig the principle is the same – set the standard left hand end stop so that when the components are in place, the socket positions will be centred under the template. Each set of stops exactly offsets each of the matching components so that they will line up correctly when assembled.

Cramp the piece to form the socket half of the joint wrong-side up, lying flat on the top of the jig. Now fit the template over it and, holding it down firmly, tighten it up using the knurled brass nuts. The jig should be factory set for making the basic dovetail joint but the manual will explain how to adjust it for different joints.

Having found the correct height setting for the template, insert the vertical component which will have the tails, wrong side showing, and push it tightly up under the template and cramp in place. Now uncramp the socket component and push it tightly against the vertical piece and recramp.

It may sound complex but it isn't in practice! What you have done is to set the jig both in width and in height for cutting an entire set of parts – and the jig remains this way until the job is done. Each time you cut a matched joint, you offer the vertical piece up first. Cramp it, and then butt the flat piece against it, and cramp that too – always wrong side outwards.

Routing

Now take your router and screw the Trend guide bush in place. This fits the jig exactly and has a proper square profile that will run in the jig. Don't use pressed guide bushes that have a rounded internal shoulder.

Fit the dovetail bit – there are alternative cutters available for other joints in conjunction with different templates – and ideally you need a fine depth adjuster, as this allows fine height setting and prevents accidental unplunging.

Sit the router on the right hand end of the jig and adjust the plunge height so that the cutter shows 10mm (⅜in) below the jig. If the router can't plunge low enough you may need to loosen the collet and slip the

▼*Before gluing the case together rout the grooves for the sliding cutter shelf*

▲*Rout a rebate on both ends of the shelf so it slides in a groove*

cutter out slightly.

Use scrap pieces for making a test joint – make a habit of sliding the router in from the front of the jig and withdrawing it in the same way which ensures that you need not worry about damaging the work or the jig if the motor is running.

Switch on, push into the first recess and pull out following the shape of the jig, then push into the next recess and so on.

Because a dovetail cutter 'undercuts', it can seem a little aggressive, so keep firm control of the machine at all times. It is worth going back to the beginning and repeating the operation to ensure the tails are properly rounded for a good fit. Remove the router and switch off.

Joints

I found with my test joint that breakout occurred on the wrong face of the tail piece, so to counter this I cramped a piece of scrap 6mm (¼in) ply against the face each time, which dealt with the problem completely. The joint was, if anything, too tight, and since the cutter does both halves of the joint in one hit there seems little you can do to adjust the fit.

When assembling the joints I used a little glue and sash cramps, with wooden pads the full width of each joint, to apply even

▼*A jig and guide bushes will accurately place the holes for the cutter shanks*

▲*With the shelf pulled out, cutters are easy to select*

pressure for neat closure. The result is that the joints are tight, neat looking, and incredibly strong.

It is important to remember that the dovetails must be on the side pieces because the weight of the case demands it – if they were at the top and bottom the case could fall apart when lifted.

Inside

Trim the slide-out cutter shelf so it will fit easily in the already formed grooves. The tongue at each end can be made with a small rebater, as the bearing will run along the edge of what will become the tongue – and again this can be done overhanging the edge of the Mini-Mach.

Check the shelf is a loose sliding fit, and make a strip jig for the small router – which makes drilling of shank holes easy. Mine are quite widely spaced but you can set the rows closer to take more cutters if you wish. The standard 17mm guide bush will allow the use of both ¼in and ½in shank cutters, thus giving a mixture of shank holes if needed.

Pin a slightly oversize piece of 6mm (¼in) ply to the back with one edge flush to one side, and then sit the router on the back panel with a bottom bearing guided trimmer fitted, and run round to clean off the excess ply.

Hinges

The case obviously needs hinges, and if they are not the thin pressed type, they will need to be recessed in. A small router is ideal for this as it will have to sit on the edge, but you should always cramp a thickish piece of wood, say 50mm (2in), along the side to give extra support. Mark the hinge cutouts with a knife. Plunge the cutter to sit on the case edge, then put the thinnest part of a folded hinge between the

▼*Housings for the brass hinges are cut in with a router*

▲ *Other accessories can be secured with stick-on Velcro*

▲ *Turn-buttons hold the router securely and spring clips hold the rods*

depth rod and on the capstan stop, and lock the rod. This will give the depth setting – now machine between the knife marks, backfeed the router using a shallow cut in from the side to pre-score the ply. Then, running in the correct cut direction, move in to full width and remove all the ply in the recess area, and try the hinge for fit.

Screw the door in place with the hinge side flush and, as before, trim the other three sides off with a bearing guided trimmer, and then fit the small case catches.

Inside case

In the bottom left hand corner of the case is a box containing all the minor odds and ends – such as nuts, bolts, and guide bushes. The sides can be tongue-and-grooved if you use solid wood; ply tends to be more fragile when cut open so I glued and pinned my box together. The lid is fixed with stick-on Velcro pieces and this 'cheat' method is also used for holding the dust spout inside thecase.

Fitting

The router sits in a hole cut in a piece of ply which fits between the small case and the other case side. Draw the router base shape on the ply, cut it out and glue in place. Make some pads to glue and screw back and front, on which to fit turn-buttons – each held with a single screw and bevelled on the underside to turn and grip the base easily. The fence and rods are fitted separately using spring clips, and there is plenty of room for other accessories which can be installed with a little ingenuity.

Finish

Tool cases often don't have any kind of finish, but bare wood does get dirty and marked so a couple of coats of varnish are a good idea.

I have fitted a door handle, but if you intend carrying your case around a lot, use a proper case handle which can be obtained from a good ironmongers.

Finally, fit the accessories, cutters, and router into the case!

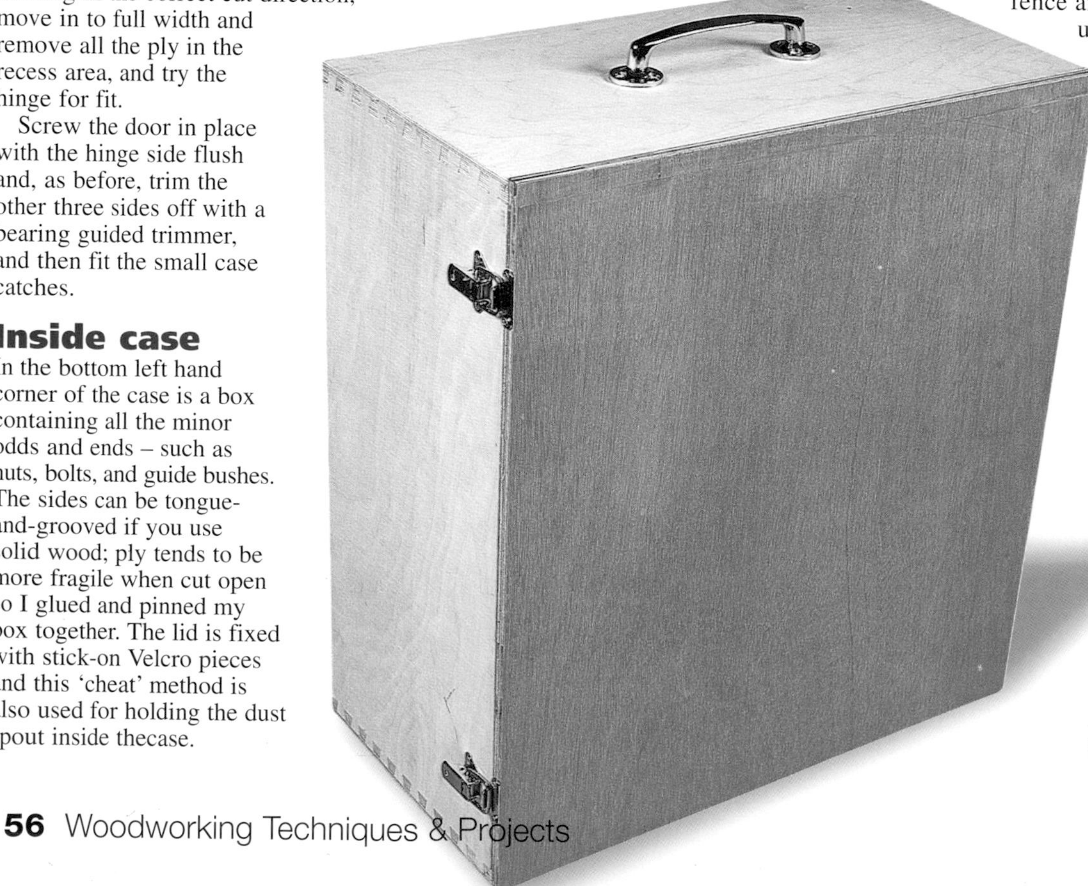

◀ *All latched up and ready to go*

Elu
Made in Italy
MOD: MOF 177E TYPE4 Nr. 4018847
240V~
50-60Hz 8.5A 1850W
8000-20000/min
V/920113-07/06
CE

Bed and boards

The first of a three-part project uses cutters to make a headboard and matching footboard for a bed

IN this and the following two articles I shall be producing a double bed in pine, a great material that can be finished in its natural colour. In this case I may be tempted to try my hand at a hand-decorated paint finish.

This first part of the project involves making the existing headboard and adding a matching footboard, and these can be attached to a standard divan-type bed. In the next two articles I will be making the parts that will join the head and footboard together to make it into a bed in its own right that only requires a mattress, and a drawer to fit underneath the bed. I have made this project to suit a double mattress but an adjustment in the measurements is all that is required to make a bed to suit any size of mattress.

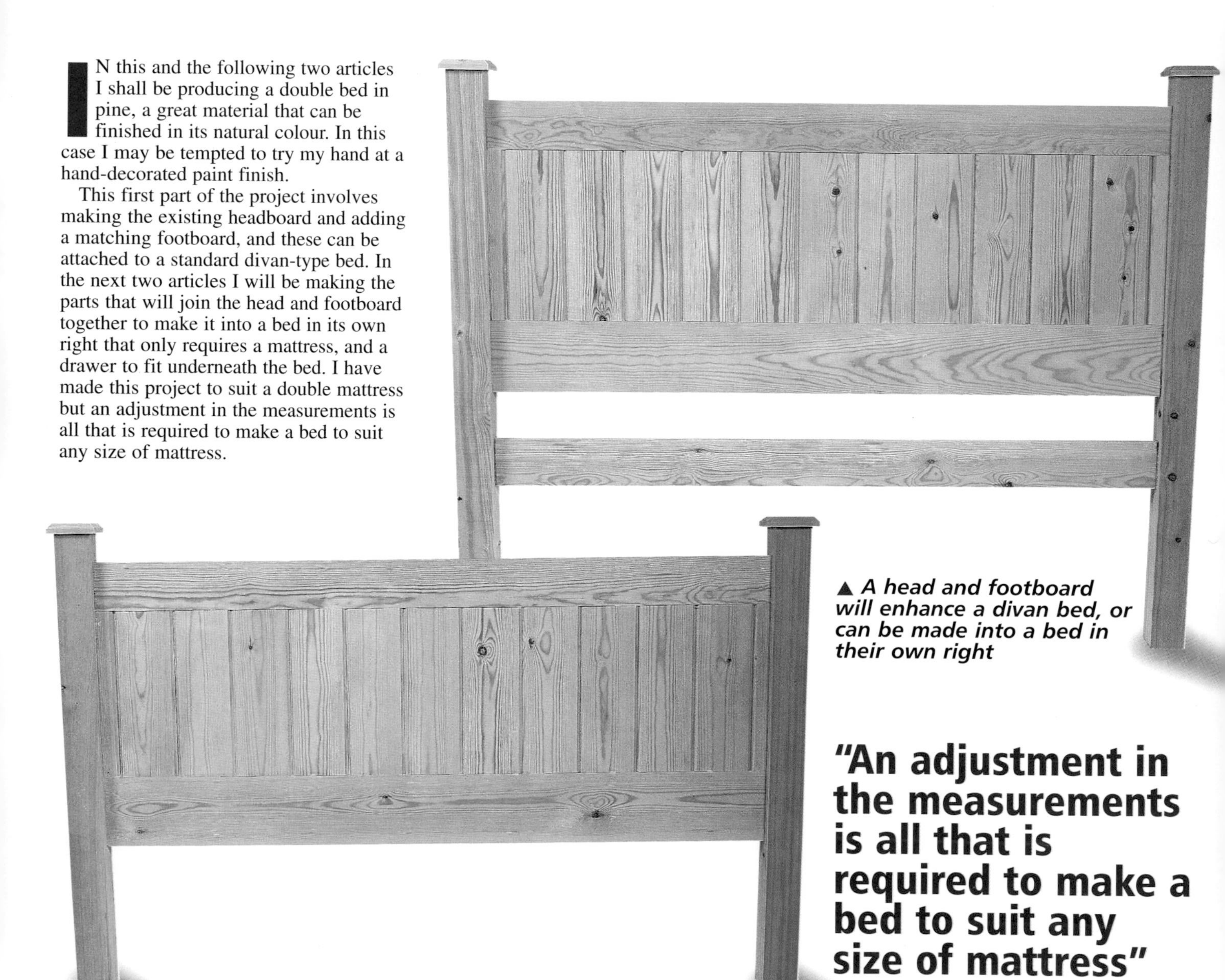

▲ *A head and footboard will enhance a divan bed, or can be made into a bed in their own right*

"An adjustment in the measurements is all that is required to make a bed to suit any size of mattress"

▲ *Mark the positions of all the mortices*

Marking up

Firstly, measure the bed accurately, both the divan base and the mattress on top; determine the position of the solid frame inside the base because you will need to fix the head and footboards by screwing through and into them. Note how the tongue-and-groove 'V' (TGV) infill is the same height for both headboard and footboard, although the footboard itself is lower and the headboard has an additional rail to allow for fixing into the divan base. Using the same amount of TGV unifies the design and simplifies setting out. The tongue-and-groove is 'V'-moulded on both faces to look the same from both sides – not strictly necessary with the headboard.

Each frame has mortice and tenon joints, and the TGV is let into a narrow groove all round. Prepared softwood is used throughout. Start by cutting all four legs, then mark the rail positions on one leg, followed by the mortices.

These are 14mm (9⁄16in) wide, and are 15mm (5⁄8in) less in height at both top and bottom for each rail, except for the narrow rails where they are reduced to 10mm (3⁄8in) at the very top and very bottom; this avoids having to remove too much of the tenon on these narrower pieces. Now transfer these markings directly onto the other legs. A large router with two fences and a 12.7mm straight cutter is needed.

"As heating of the shank takes place I would advise that you use the cutter with the longest cutting edge possible"

▲ *A pair of side-fences are useful to stop the router from wandering*

▼ *Rout a central groove for the TGV tongues*

▶ *The three stages of creating TGV*

Cutting mortices

I based my choice of cutters on the comprehensive Jesada Router Magic Bit Set, but as long as the relevant cutters are to hand the make is irrelevant.

I thought I had all the required cutters, only realising when I came to cut these mortices that I was short of a long and strong, straight bit!

Using instead the set's 12.7mm cutter – which is the same size as the shank – I plunged it until the shank entered the hole and achieved the required 40mm (1½in) depth of cut.

This technique may sound far from ideal, but this happens with some pocket or mortice cutters anyway. As heating of the shank takes place I would advise that you use the cutter with the longest cutting edge possible.

Using a pair of side-fences prevents the router from wandering when cutting the mortices. Set the cutter to line up with one side of the mortice. Machine, then lift the router off, turn it round and cut the other way to create a 14mm (9/16in) wide socket, which I made 40mm (1⅝in) deep.

Once all the processes of TGV have been achieved a Stanley knife can be used to clean up the fluffy end grain

Dry-fit the frames together to check how much TGV is required

"This groove must be deep enough to take the tongue on each outer piece of TGV"

Rails, tenons

Once all mortices are done, machine a 6mm (¼in) groove centrally and 8mm (5⁄16in) deep from one mortice to the other – excluding the bottom-most rail on the headboard.

This groove must be deep enough to take the tongue on each outer piece of TGV.

Cut all rails to length and, on the router table, form tenons which are just shorter than the mortice sockets – say 38mm (1½in).

Use a mitre protractor and a backing piece to prevent tearing on the back face. Machine the flat faces, reset the cutter height and stand the rails on edge, doing the 10mm (⅜in) set backs first, and then resetting to accomplish the 15mm (⅝in) ones – this order avoids mistakes!

Round the mortice corners with a chisel until they fit the sockets; you should aim for a snug fit that will allow for glue. At this point dry fit the full frame assemblies and check what length the TGV will need to be, excluding the tongues.

Tooling up

Router:
- *Jesada router cutters*

- *12.7mm straight cutter*
- *Large-diameter straight cutter*
- *Jesada groover*

Close-up of the boards when fitted into the head and footboard frames

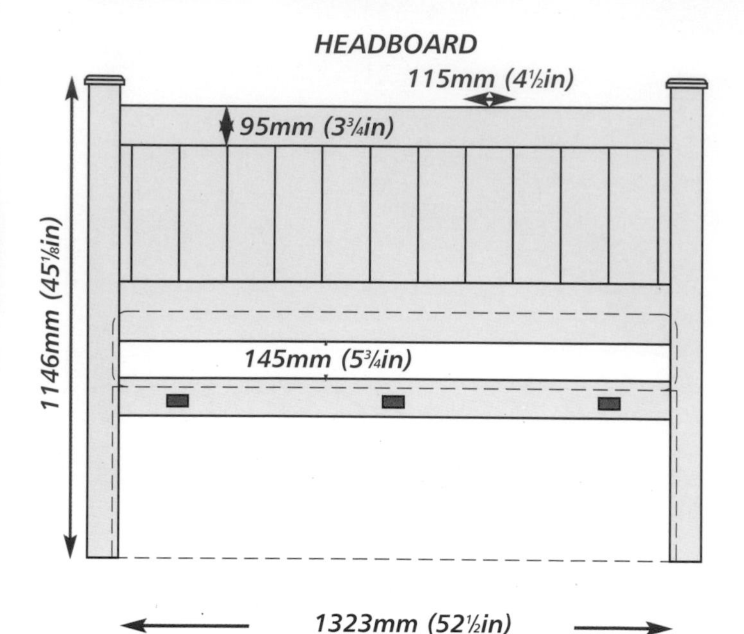

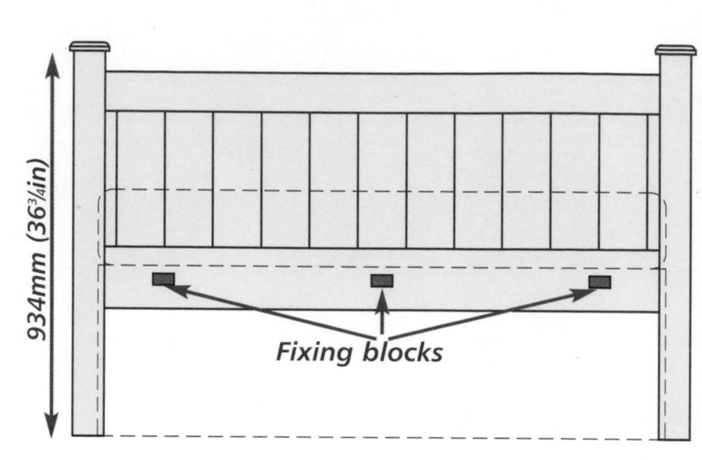

Dotted line = outline of divan bed and mattress

▲ *Dimensions of the head and footboards*

Grooving rails

Now fit a grooving cutter in the table mounted router. Jesada do a neat set of groovers with one arbor, bearing and spacers.

Disassemble the frames and groove one long edge of all the rails to a depth of 15mm – except the base rail on the headboard – ready to receive a tongue when assembled.

The creation of TGV requires three separate cuts to prepare it. Start by forming the grooves on one long edge of each only – if you have already cut the blanks to length they will run flatter against the fence.

After ensuring that the groove is central and about 8mm (5⁄16in) deep, fit a large-diameter straight cutter and form the matching tongues on the opposite edge as if making very thin tenons.

After checking for a neat fit, 'V' groove all four long edges. Tongue the ends of each TGV section, taking care not to make the tongues longer than about 13mm (½in), otherwise a gap will show top and bottom once assembled into the frame.

Assembly

With as many TGV sections fitted as possible, assemble both frames to check the fit. Push these tightly to one end and measure the resulting gap.

"There is room for a mistake here, so have some spare pieces just in case"

Divide this figure in two to find the widths of the two missing pieces needed to fill in the gap at each end of the frame.

On one side a groove and a new tongue are needed; on the other an extra tongue is formed. As one new one is required add on the extra tongue width. There is room for a mistake here, so have some spare pieces just in case.

Take each frame apart again and apply glue to the tenons which go into one leg. Assemble this end of the frame, then put in a narrow piece of TGV followed by all the the rest of the TGV and finishing up with the other narrow piece, so achieving a balanced look.

Glue the other leg on and, after ensuring that the whole frame is square, cramp it up. If necessary apply some cramps from top to bottom of the frame so that the rails close tightly against the TGV.

Finally, make up some caps to go on top of the legs, cut them to size and bevel them around the top edge with the 'V' cutter, then glue and pin them on.

Because the legs would stop the rails sitting tightly against the bed base, make up some strips to screw on the base and into the rails.

Apart from the finishing, the existing bed can be dressed with the new frames, ready to await the completion of the project – and a whole new bed – find out how in the next part. ◪

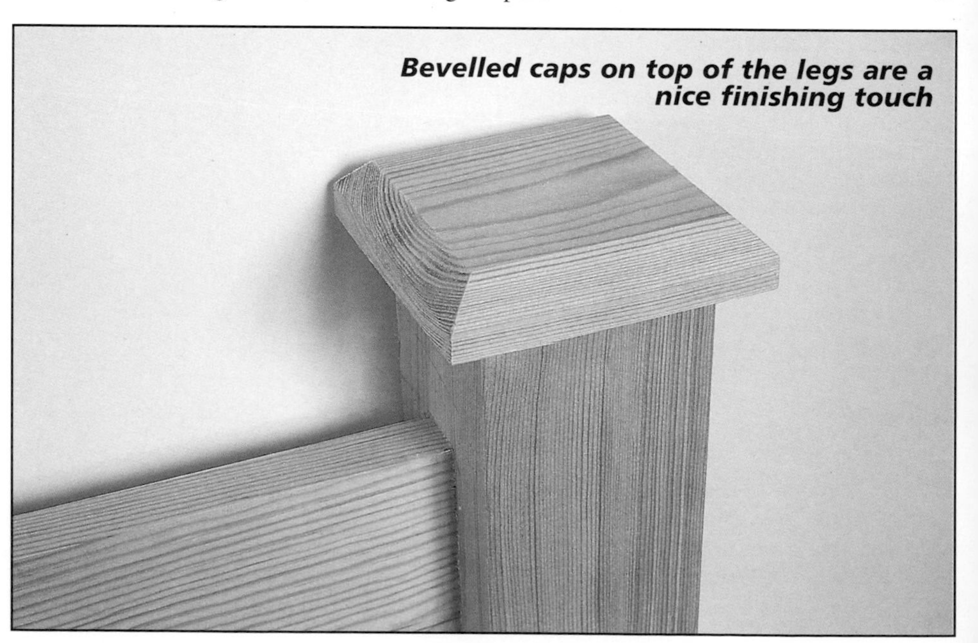

Bevelled caps on top of the legs are a nice finishing touch

Making connections

Continue with your bed project by adding a frame

IN the previous article I showed you how to make a pine tongue-and-groove headboard and footboard for attaching to a divan-type double bed. This part deals with converting the headboard and footboard, by machining the bedposts to allow the attachment of the side rails, making a replacement frame and slats, and thereby creating a complete bed without the need for a divan base.

An essential ingredient is a means of fitting the frames together which is demountable and does not depend on complicated jointwork.

Bed connectors are ideal, obtainable from specialist suppliers like Häfele, Tradecraft Supplies or Isaac Lord.

Start by obtaining some decent softwood, and check it is true along its length as the bed side rails, centre support and the slats must not be bowed.

The two wide side pieces not only couple the head and footboard together but also have a 50 by 25mm (2 by 1in) rail running along the inside for the slats to lie on.

The slats of a double bed must be supported centrally – unnecessary with a single – and this is achieved by notched blocks fitted at each end of the bed.

"Check that the height mark is the same on all four posts by marking the height on a stick – also known as a rod – and using this to avoid mistakes"

▲ *An attractive bed completed*

Tooling up

- *Small router*
- *Fence*
- *Jesada 16mm straight bit*
- *Jesada 6.4mm straight cutter*
- *Jesada 45° cutter*

Connectors and posts

Cut the bed side rails to length, then prepare to machine the recesses for the bed connectors.

The Häfele bed connectors I used couldn't be simpler. Made of plain steel, the more load that is put on them, the better they lock together.

Because they don't come as left- and right-hand fittings, the only critical position is the bottom of the tapered slots in the receiving half. The hook-in part of the connector sits here when coupled.

Assuming the side rails of the bed will be centred on the head and footboard posts, draw the rail section on the post to see exactly where the receiving part of the connector will be situated.

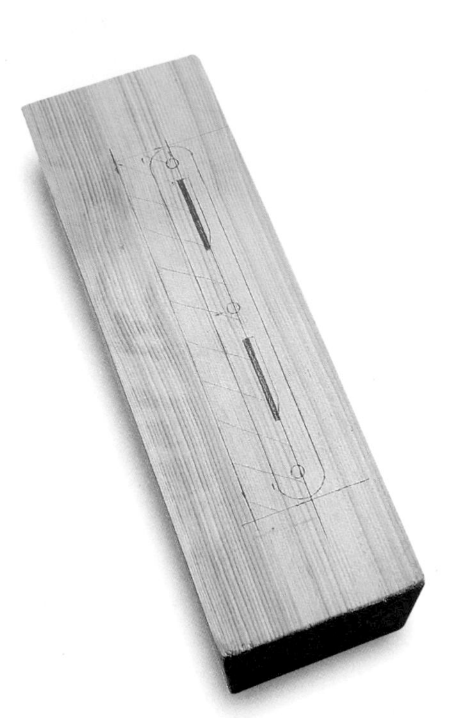

▲ *Mark the position of the receiving plates on the bed's legs; use an offcut for setting up the cutter and to use as a test piece for fitting the two components together*

▼ *Rout the housing for the receiving plate; note the length of the deeper central slot allows for the hooks*

▲ *Make up a template to rout the housings in the side rails*

"Ensure that the slot goes down the post further than the opening in the steel plate as the hooks will slide downward to engage"

Check that the height mark is the same on all four posts by marking the height on a stick – also known as a rod – and using this to avoid measuring mistakes.

The hook part of the connector will be set flush into the inside face of each side rail so you can align the receiving part, centring it for height, with the rail. It is in fact offset to one side although the amount is slightly different between the left- and right-hand bedposts.

Draw around the plate with a sharp pencil, then, using a router fitted with a side-fence and a 16mm straight bit installed, make the slot in one pass. To set the plate in flush make the cut just over 2mm (3/32in) deep, the same thickness as the plate.

The two narrower, deeper slots needed to take the hook part are cut with a 6.4mm straight cutter; ensure that the slot is machined down the post further than the opening in the steel plate as the hooks will

▼ *The plates in place, ready to fit together*

▲ ***The side rails have a batten attached to the inside to support the slats***

slide downward to engage.

The other half of the connector must be set in flush with the inside face of the side rail and is centred for height.

A template is necessary as the ends have a curved shape and must look neat. A 16mm guide bush with 6.4mm cutter works well and produces a good fit.

Make up the two notched blocks for the central support rail, a nominal 300mm long by 10mm wide (12 by 3/8in). Cut their 60mm (2 3/8in) high notches centrally, just wide enough for the 10 by 25mm (3/8 by 1in) centre support to fit snugly. Bevel for a better finish.

Slats and slat rails

Fit the two halves of each connector, assemble the bed then screw on the slat support rails and the notched blocks.

I set the slat rails down just enough for the slats to end up about 6–8mm (1/4–5/16in) below the top edge of the side rails. This allows the notched block on the headboard to be fitted at the same height as the separate lower rail of the headboard.

Screw on the slat rails at each end and check they are level all along; if not, push the rail up or down in the middle before driving a screw home to hold it level, then secure it using more screws in between.

Measure the centre slat support and cut it to length, then, with a handsaw, saw the ends to fit in the notches so it is flush with the top.

▼ ***A central support rail for the slats fits into a slotted plate***

▲ *Slats are held in position by stapling seat webbing to them; they are spaced apart with an offcut*

▲ *Tidy the ends of the webbing by folding over and stapling*

Now measure the gap between the rails at both ends of the bed and the middle. Any slight bow in or out in the centre can be eliminated later (see below) by screwing down the middle slats.

Cut the bed slats to fit neatly between the side rails. The number of slats is determined by the gap between them, which should be about the same as the width of each slat.

Assuming 21 slats each of 45.5mm (1$\frac{25}{32}$in) finished width – I used a calculator to work that out! – I found that I would have a gap between the slats of 45mm (1¾in) – close enough.

With the slats carefully spaced, run two strips of upholstery webbing over them and staple the webbing with an industrial-quality stapler. Tension and staple the webbing to each end of the bed and then gap the slats accurately with the aid of a spare 50 by 25mm (2 by 1in) piece of slat timber.

Shoot two 12mm staples diagonally into each slat before moving on to the next – don't be tempted to put in all the staples on one side first as the results may be uneven.

Release the webbing from the bed ends, trim and staple over the webbing ends, roll up the slats and turn them over so the webbing and the staples are on the underside.

Pull the whole lot out flat and put the mattress on. The slats will stay put without further fixing, but now is the time to screw down one or two middle slats if necessary to hold the two side rails the correct distance apart.

Finally, apply your choice of finish to the whole bed.

The bed is now complete, but could take a roll-out storage drawer, if desired, and I'll be making that in the next part.

"The number of slats is determined by the gap between them, which should be about the same as the width of each slat"

▲ *The addition of side rails and slats finishes the bed which now awaits a coat of varnish or paint – and some bedding of course*

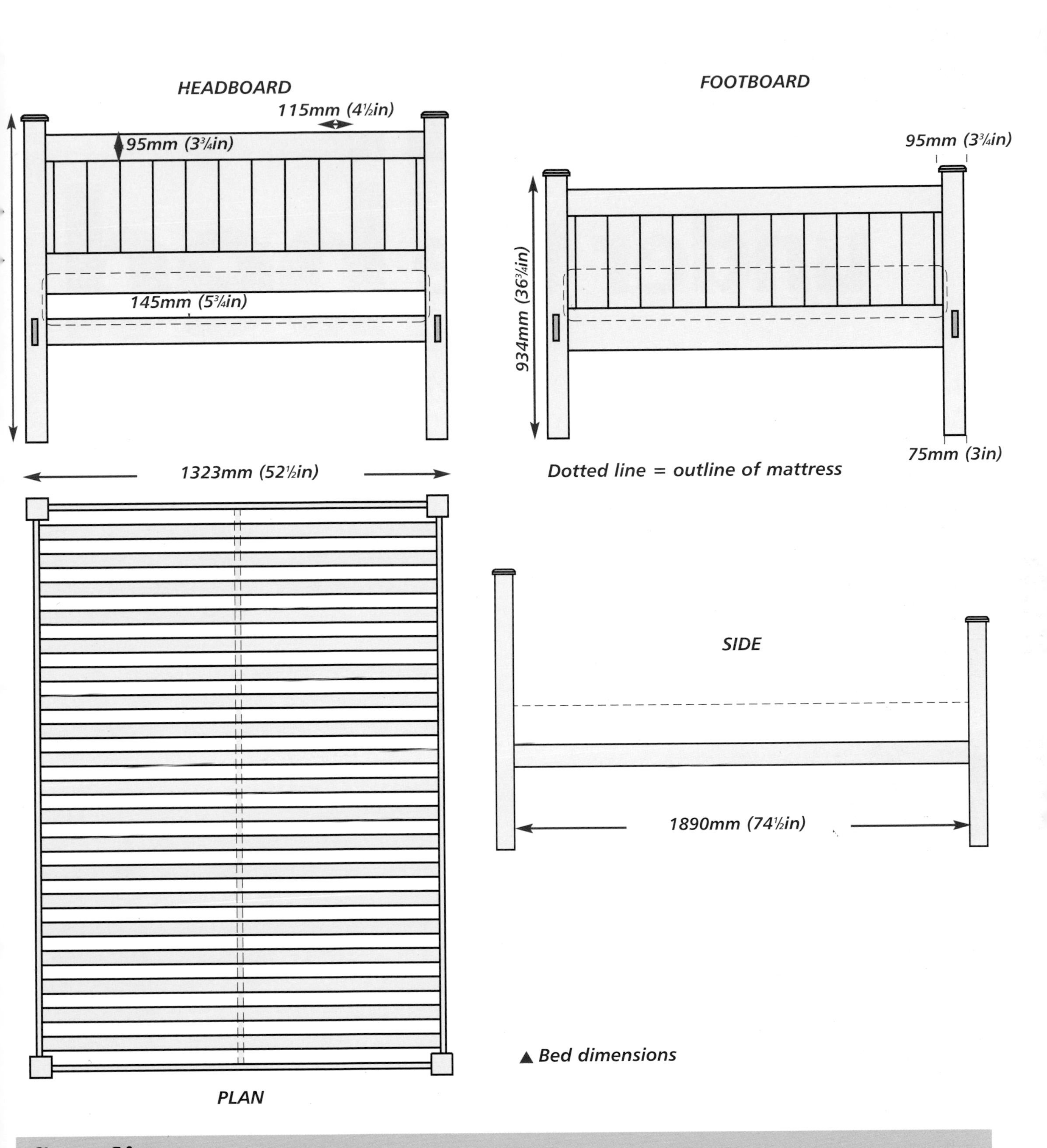

▲ Bed dimensions

Suppliers

Häfele UK Ltd, Swift Valley Industrial Estate, Rugby, Warwickshire CV21 1RD, Tel 01788 542020, Fax 01788 544440.

Tradecraft Supplies, Unit 11, Broadway Green Farm, Broadway Road, Lightwater, Surrey GU18 5SH, Tel 01276 474302, Fax 01276 477200.

Isaac Lord, Unit 5 Desborough Industrial Park, Desborough Park Road, High Wycombe, Bucks HP12 3BX, Tel 01494 459191, Fax 01494 461376.

Russian under the bed

In the final part of the bed project make and fit a useful storage drawer to go underneath

A large drawer is the perfect complement to the bed

TO complete my bed project, covered in the two preceding articles, I am making a drawer to go under the bed.

The bottom of the drawer is light-coloured Russian birch ply and the front, back and sides are in pine to match the bed.

For simplicity, I have chosen to have one drawer at the footboard end of the bed, which will run on heavy-duty industrial-type castors.

Making wide boards

The drawer front comes up higher than the front of the frame, so the gap between them is concealed. There is a close, neat fit between the bed posts, and as the drawer side width is a fraction narrower than the front, the drawer slides smoothly between the legs.

The first job is to make boards wide enough for all the components. Softwood often isn't available in pieces of the correct

Tooling up

Jesada cutters used

- *Glue joint cutter*
- *Slotter set*
- *9.5mm straight cutter*
- *V-groover*
- *45° chamfer cutter*
- *12.7mm cove cutter*

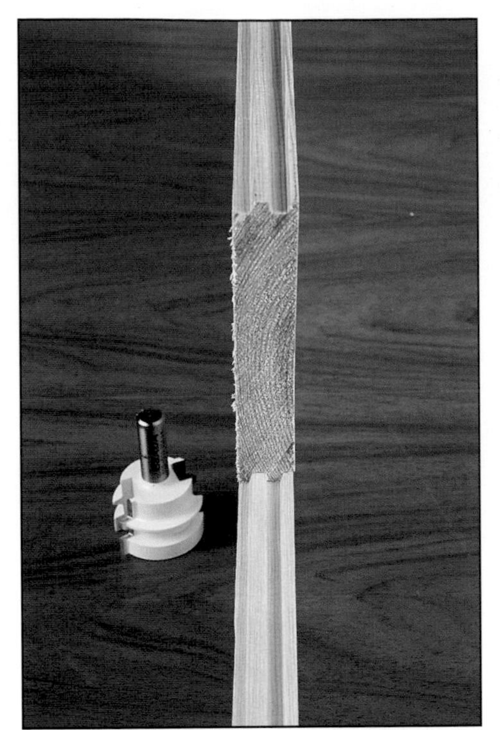

▲ *The glue joint cutter makes another appearance*

▲ *Grooves are formed for both the joint and drawer bottom*

width, so narrower pieces must be joined together. I used 120mm (4¾in) wide prepared boards which, when edge-jointed, can be cut down to width afterwards.

The best way to fit the boards together is to use a gluc-joint cutter like the Jesada 655-501. This is more secure than a tongue-and-groove joint, and gives plenty of strength.

To even out any tendency to bow, make sure each alternate board has its annular rings lying the opposite way.

Set up the router table so the centre of the glue-joint cutter is centred on the board thickness. This ensures good flush faces when joined. If the cutter isn't centred it will cause a step which will need sanding out.

Also, use flat, unbowed boards, otherwise there will be a lot of mismatched edges.

"Brush-glue the edges and assemble the boards, holding them tightly in sash cramps"

There is no bearing on this cutter, but if you set the fence on the router table carefully, and do some test joints, tightly-jointed edges are easily produced.

I was lazy and machined the edges, turning each board over before doing the other edge. This meant I could choose which edges best fitted together, and allowed me to get the annular rings running alternately.

Having assembled each group of three boards, I sawed to width, taking off the surplus glue-joint edges in the process.

Brush-glue the edges and assemble the boards, holding them tightly in sash cramps. Smears of glue would mark the surface and mean extra sanding out, so wash off the excess with a damp cloth and leave to dry.

Also, if the wood is to be stained the colour will not penetrate glue-smeared grain. Any sanding needed to level the boards' joints should be done now.

▼ *The slotting cutter set up to form the tongue*

▼ *The drawer's corner joint is designed to give maximum strength when pulled*

▲ *V-grooves decorate the drawer's face*

▲ *A cove cutter creates the finger pull on the underside of the drawer front*

▲ *Sturdy castors are required to take the load*

Corner jointing

Because this isn't a small cabinet drawer, I decided to use a simple tongue-and-groove joint for the corner jointing. This needs some care in setting up and machining.

Cut all the components to their respective widths and lengths. The drawer sides run from front to back, with a groove routed on their inside faces, both front and back. Machine a tongue on the ends of the front and back boards to lock into the side grooves.

The joint is produced this way so any strain caused by pulling on the drawer front won't pull it right off; also, the highly visible drawer sides then look neat.

Make the front and back boards the measurement between the sides, plus about 9mm (⅜in) for each of the tongues.

Grooving, sanding

Next, set up the table to do the grooving. Cut a 9.5mm (⅜in full) wide groove in the drawer sides, then use the straight cutter to cut grooves on the bottom inside face of all the boards.

These grooves will take the 9mm (⅜in) ply drawer bottom, which needs to start 40mm (1⅝in) from the bottom edge of each board.

The groove is positioned so that the drawer sides and back come down a little over the castors to hide them as much as possible. There should be a 10mm (⅜in) exposure of castor on all sides.

I used the Jesada Slotter set to form the tongue. Since the groove depth needs to be 9mm (⅜in), I used the fence of the router rather than the bearing table for guidance.

The panels are too wide to use a mitre protractor to push them, so press the panel end against the fence and slide it

"Some sandpaper on a block will remove marks from any type of sander"

▼ *Fill the drawer up with blankets, sheets and all sorts of other stuff*

past the cutter, holding a backing piece behind to avoid tear-out or spelching.

Sand all parts before assembly. I use a random orbital sander to reduce the amount of swirly rings that a conventional sander produces. However, a flick over, along the grain with some sandpaper on a block, will remove marks from any type of sander.

Cut the birch ply 2mm (1/16in) smaller than the overall distance between the deepest part of the side grooves.

With the front and back in place, glue and assemble the drawer, taking care to brush the glue onto the tongue before fitting into the slot. Use three 50mm (2in) panel pins per joint to hold them together, and punch them in for filling later.

"Don't wander or you'll take a chunk out of the edge!"

Drawer front

The drawer front is a separate item, and covers the joints on the front of the drawer box. Use a V-groover to create two deep grooves, each centred at 55mm (2⅛in) from each long edge, then use the V-groover or a chamfer 45° cutter with a bearing, to create two smaller bevels along the very edge, top and bottom.

Mark out the cut-out shape along the bottom edge. The bevelled ends to this cut-out are chosen to match the rest of the design.

Use a jigsaw or bandsaw, and clean up with abrasive paper. Invert the drawer front and use a 12.7mm cove cutter with a bearing to make a hand-grip shape along the edge of the cut-out.

Don't wander beyond this area, as the bevel on the front face will not give any support to the bearing, and you will take a chunk out of the edge!

Finally, screw the drawer front to the drawer box with the bottom edges flush, and any side overhang equalised. Fix the castors underneath near the corners using short fat screws.

Because this is an awesomely large drawer, you can fill it with blankets, woollies, crumpled shirts and whatever else you have, then push it under the bed and forget about everything in it!

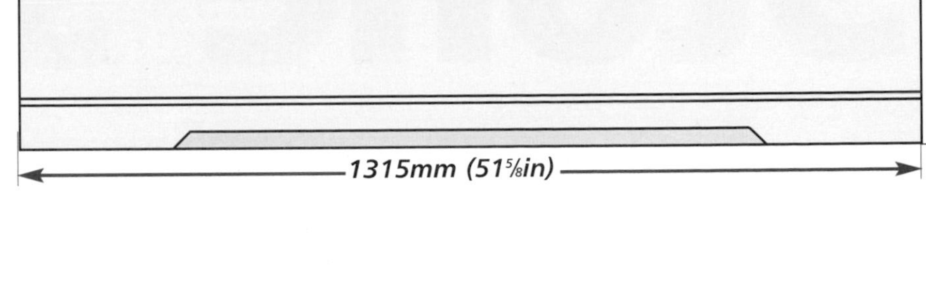

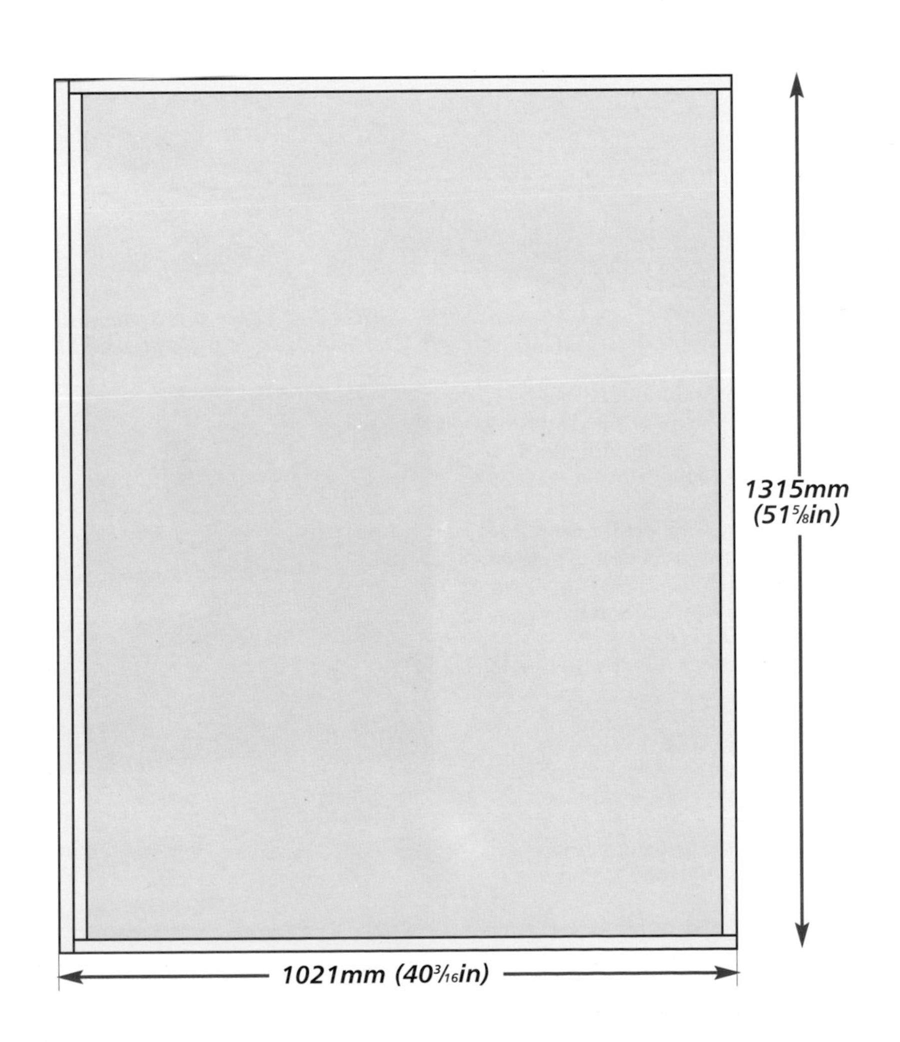

▲ *Dimensions of under-bed drawer*

Stone store

Rout a protective box to keep your oilstone out of trouble

▲ *A box for your oilstone will keep it in good condition*
▼ *Cut the two long parallel slots in the jig*

ONE of the most useful basic workshop items is a good oilstone, because we still need all the basic handtools despite the onslaught of routers and other powertools.

Planes and chisels need regular sharpening and frequently don't get it! I own two stones, one is standard coarse and medium grit, the other a much finer stone which definitely deserves a box, especially as it picks up dust and chippings and leaves oily abrasive particles wherever put down.

Measuring up

Measure your oilstone and make a jig for use with a router and guide bush that will create recesses in the base and lid of the box. Most stones are now standard metric sizes, in my case this was 200 x 50 x 25mm (8 x 2 x 1 in).

Use a piece of thin ply or MDF for the jig and measure the difference between the cutter and the guide bush. Divide the result and you get the amount by which the jig aperture needs to be over and above the size of the stone.

Allow a fraction more so the stone will actually fit, but not enough for it to slip around.

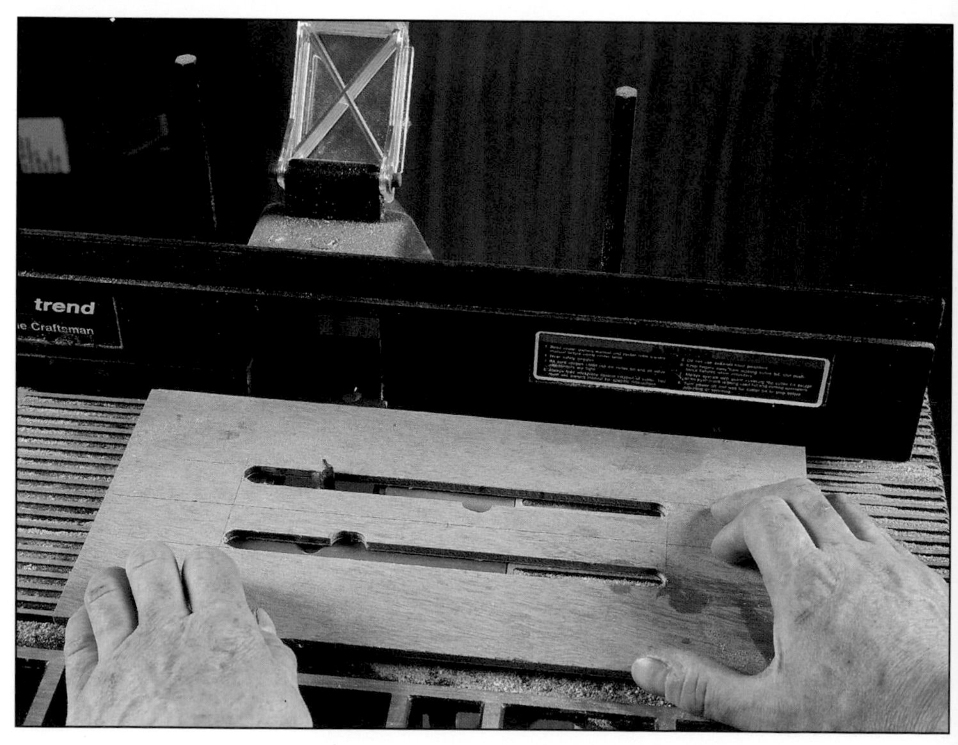

▲ *Set-up for the end cuts that will complete the cut out*

▲ *Fix on the runners that will position the jig*

"Beech is commonly used, but I have a penchant for good quality ply"

Tooling up

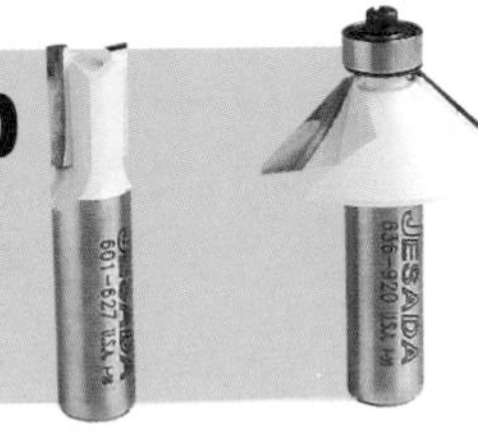

- *Straight cutter*
- *Bearing guided 45° cutter*

Slotting

Set up the router table with the fence loosened at one end so you can drop the ply onto the cutter well within what will be the waste area. Move the fence forward and lock it once the cutter is touching the marked line.

Hold the ply carefully against the fence and move up to the cross lines at each end so you have a neat slot. Switch off, lift the ply and turn it, then repeat the operation, ensuring you end up with parallel slots the correct overall distance apart.

Fit the mitre fence, or use a square piece of board, and machine the end slots. It is important to support the right-hand end, as the cutting action can cause drag, and you will end up with a slightly uneven slot.

Repeat at the other end, taking care as the waste piece comes away. If necessary use a file to tidy the aperture.

Saw and glue two strips of softwood either side of the aperture, leaving a centralised parallel gap between to take the width of the box (mine was 70mm). Cramp, clean off excess glue and leave to dry.

"Allow a fraction more so the stone will actually fit, but not enough for it to slip around"

▼ *Carefully rout the recess in the ply*

▼ *Slide the jig along and rout the second recess, making sure there is enough space between the two recesses*

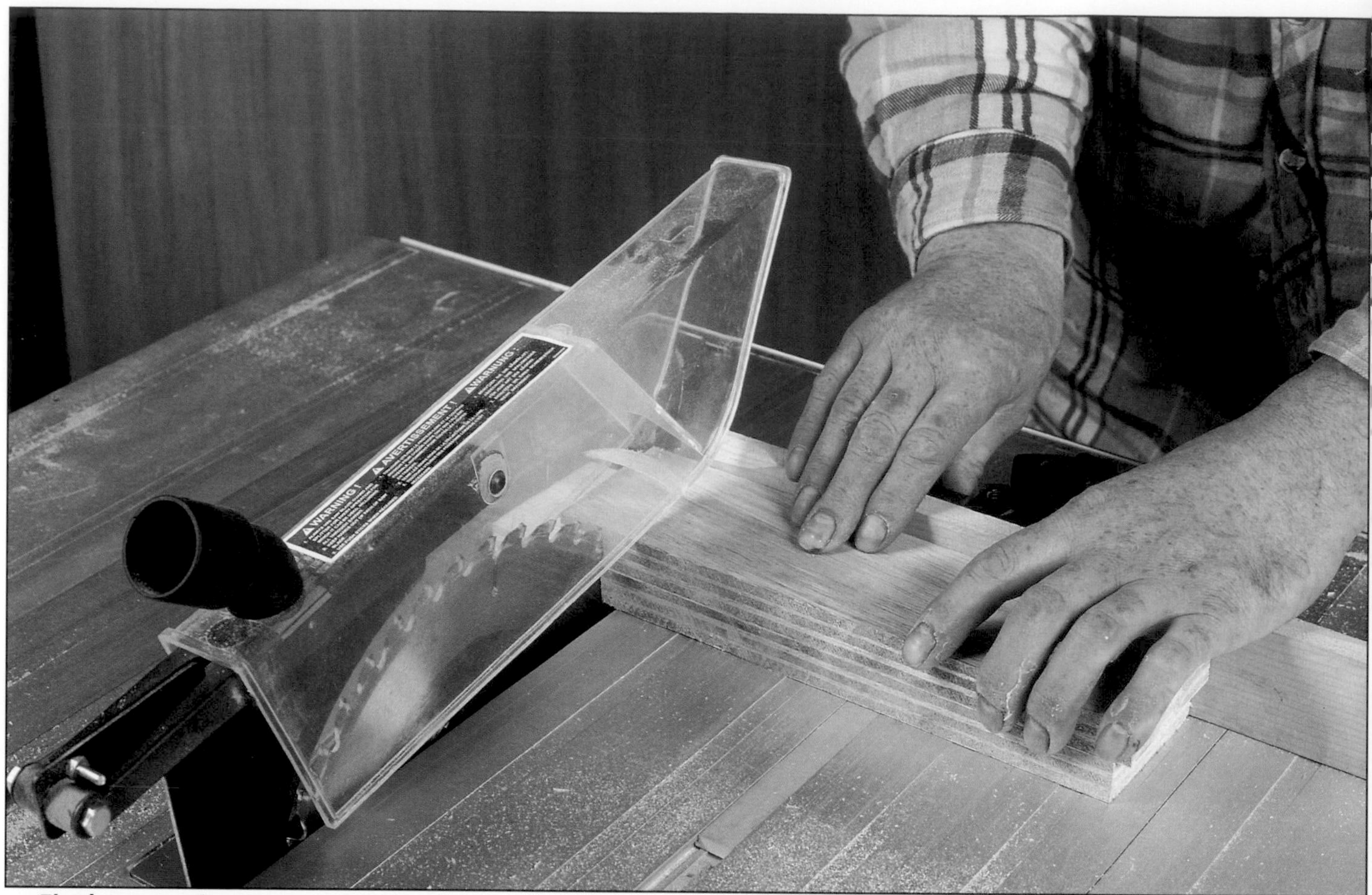

▲ *Fit the two pieces onto the oilstone and while it holds them together cut the box to length*
▼ *Rout the finger grips using lines marked on the box and sub-fence to position the cut*

▲ *Rout a small chamfer all around the top and bottom of the box*

Jigging

Choose your box material. Beech is commonly used, but I have a penchant for good quality ply, especially if it has an interesting colour with a finish applied.

Cut and plane to width a strip long enough to do at least one box, though you may want to make up several more if you own other stones, but bear in mind they may be different sizes.

The wall thickness is slightly greater at the ends because of the 'short grain'. By having a jig that straddles the wood you can slide it along and make as many parts as there is wood for.

Cramp or pin the jig so it can't slip, sit the router on and adjust the depth setting for a 13mm deep cut. Use the depth turret for machining in three passes to depth.

Move the jig along and repeat. The distance between isn't critical, so long as the recesses aren't too close.

Guide bushes are often deeper than the 6mm ply that I favour, so I ground one down so it doesn't protrude below the ply.

Tight fit

Square the recess corners with a chisel; if you don't fully square the corners on the bottom box-half it will hold the stone nice and tight, while the top half will lift off easily. Fit the two pieces around the stone, check it fits and closes, then mark

◀ *Drive panel pins into the underside, leaving the points exposed so they grip the bench and hold the stone secure while in use*

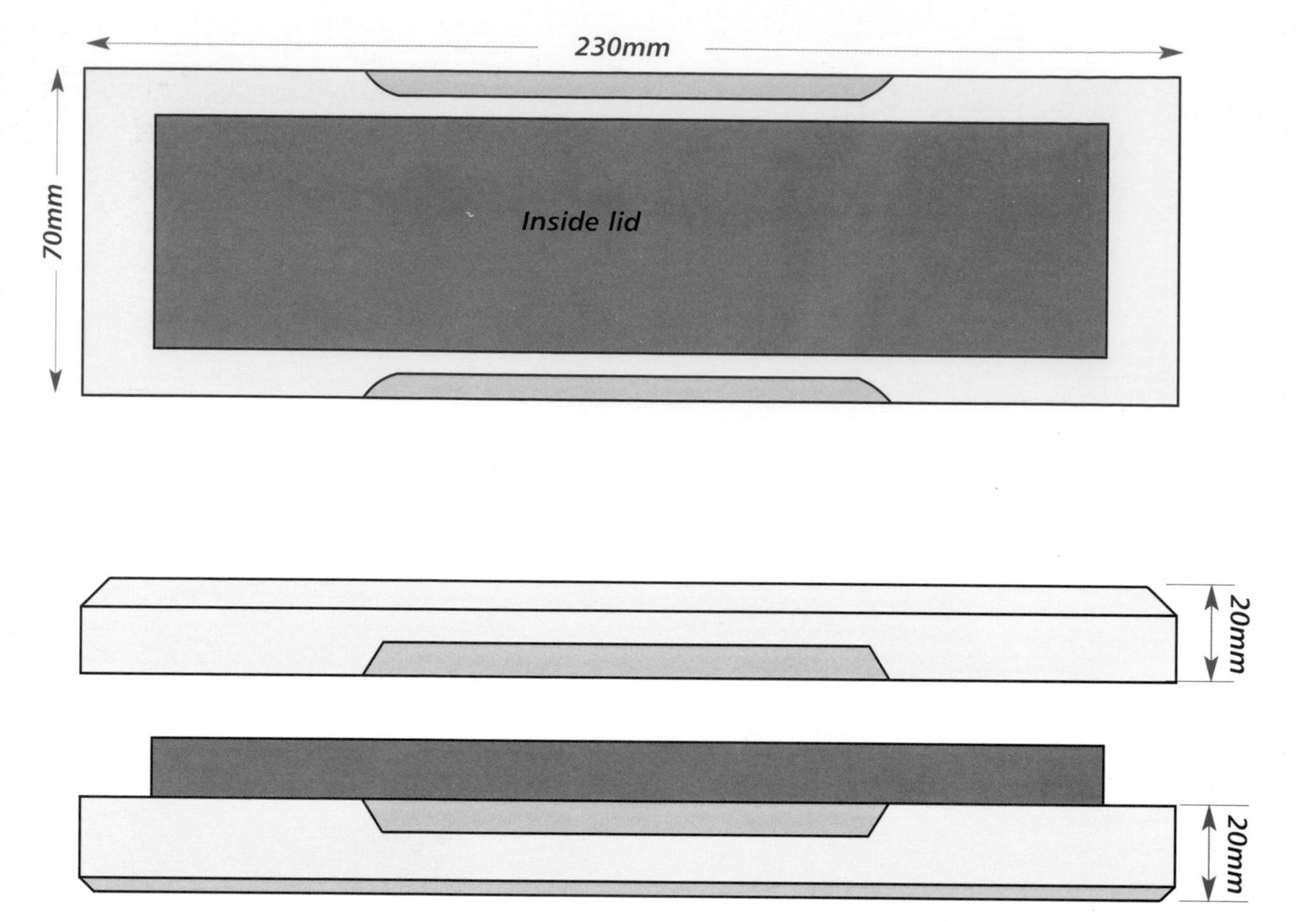

one piece where the box ends should be.

Crosscut the 'sandwich' on your marks to give neat matching ends – don't accidentally cut through where the stone is! Apply all faces to the belt sander, with the stone still locking it together.

Chamfer

Remove the oilstone and set up a chamfer cutter in the table to create the finger grip. Fit a sub-fence and make a test cut on a waste piece of ply. Switch off and mark the ends of the chamfer on your test piece, then turn the cutter till it just rubs against one end of the stopped chamfer.

Transfer the mark onto the sub-fence and repeat at the other end. Mark each side of the box lid where you want the chamfer to start and stop, transfer these marks across both the top and bottom halves, and use the sub-fence marks as guide points for starting and stopping.

Apply the wood on the far end mark first to avoid a kickback. Move it smoothly along, sliding the tail end away when you reach the second mark.

Don't linger during the cut as it will burn. Reset the cutter a fraction higher and pass again to remove any burns.

It is possible to fit start and stop blocks on the sub-fence. These are more positive if you are making several boxes.

Finishing off

The last operation is to machine the lid top edge all round with the same chamfer cutter, though at a lesser depth, then make a small chamfer on the base as well.

▼ *The finished item ready for use*

Fine sand all faces and apply a varnish on the outside. For the final touch, pre-drill and fit panel pins so the points just protrude underneath, holding the box firmly on the bench-top when sharpening.

Rack attack

Tidy up your music collection with this smart CD rack

▲ *Keep those unruly CDs tidy in this neat revolving rack*

MOST people accept that music CDs give perfect sound, but storing them is another matter. As my collection grew into an unruly pile on the floor I finally gave in and made a revolving CD rack in ash which holds 40 CDs. It takes up a limited amount of room, and looks good anywhere in the home.

The slant of the slots holds the CDs in place and makes for a more dynamic design when filled. This gives a bit of complexity to the design, but a challenge is nothing to be scared of!

Setting out

The key to making this rack is the setting out. You have to know exactly what size the components need to be, and have accurate spacings for the slots.

Start by drawing a side panel showing slots for 10 CDs. Mark even spacings between, plus 5mm extra at each end – this will be the length of the tongue which locates each panel into the top and bottom.

I decided on an 11.5mm ($\frac{29}{64}$in) slot width to comfortably slide a CD in, and a 9.5mm ($\frac{3}{8}$in) gap between, with each slot 8mm deep. The slot angle is 35°, resulting in a panel 326mm (12$\frac{51}{64}$in) long by 95mm (3$\frac{47}{64}$in). Accurately prepare some 20mm ($\frac{25}{32}$in) thick ash (finished size). All parts must be identical and square.

Slots

Make a jig from 6 to 9mm ($\frac{1}{4}$ to $\frac{3}{8}$in) thick ply, with an angled slot towards one end to allow a guide bush to run in. I used a 9.5mm straight cutter with a 17mm guide bush. Any suitable combination will do, providing you make a test slot first to check that you can create the 11.5mm ($\frac{29}{64}$in) width CD slot needed.

Machine a short angled slot next to this, the width of a CD slot and the correct distance from the centre of the guide bush slot. This will give an exact reference position for each successive slot you make.

Screw two strips of wood on the underside so the blanks fit tightly between. Make a test piece first. Position the blank so one end is just in line with the edge of the guide bush slot and cramp in position.

This should leave just enough at the end to form the 5mm ($\frac{13}{64}$in) tongue. Once the first slot is made, uncramp and slide the blank further underneath so it appears underneath the reference slot in the jig. Reclamp, machine the next slot, and so on.

Side strips should prevent the wood breaking-out at the end of the slots. Create four blanks in this way, then fit the side strips on the other side to create the other four that are a mirror image of the first four. Stick some abrasive on a board to keep it flat and sand all sides and edges of the components to de-fluff them.

▲ *Make the jig for slotting, note the smaller slot to the rear for visually spacing the slots*

▲ *Mark out the jig for creating the housings in the top and bottom panels. The asterisk indicates the datum 90° corner*

▲*Using the plank technique, see panel, to rout the slots*

Top and bottom

Accurately mitre together each of the four pieces needed for the top, bottom and the base. This is quite an undertaking and will show just how good your work and mitre saw is.

A fine-tooth blade, careful setting up, and a test piece are needed to verify that you can get good accurate meetings of all the joints.

The top and bottom can just be butt-glued together, but the base, which is thicker, needs two rows of biscuits for strength, this is because it carries the whole weight of the rack and the CDs. The slots for this are produced with a jointing cutter used in the table.

Tongues

Draw a full-size master drawing or 'rod' of the plan view on a board. I like using white MFC, melamine faced chipboard, the lines are clearly visible and you can use an eraser if you make any mistakes.

Note how the panels sit in pairs offset to each corner, leaving an unfilled space in the middle. This needs a 58mm (2 9/32in) square piece of ash to complete the equation.

Draw on the 'rod' 6.4mm (¼in) wide strips aligned to the inside of each panel where their housings will be situated. The tongues on each panel will be flush on the inside slotted face as a result.

Now make a ply jig with slots to take a small guide bush in combination with a 6.4mm straight cutter. The jig will need two good meeting edges at 90° to each other as it fits flush at the back right-hand corner when clamped on the bottom panel.

The two slots are at the front left-hand of the jig, and there is extra board to the front and side for the router to sit on. The resulting slots on the top and bottom ash panels must match those on the rod exactly, and stop just short of the panel edge so the housed joint is hidden.

Each slot runs slightly beyond the panel at its back end, so the square end of the tongue fits easily into the slot without having to round the tongue or trimming off.

The plank trick

I have a technique for working on small or awkward to cramp workpieces. Screw a long 25mm (1in) or thicker board to the workbench so it projects right out in front. It is then easy to apply cramps along each side and to machine without hindrance.

The deflection of the board caused by plunging the cutter is small, a heavy router will need a thicker board to support it.

Just as pirates of old liked to make their victims 'walk the plank' this is 'routing the plank'.

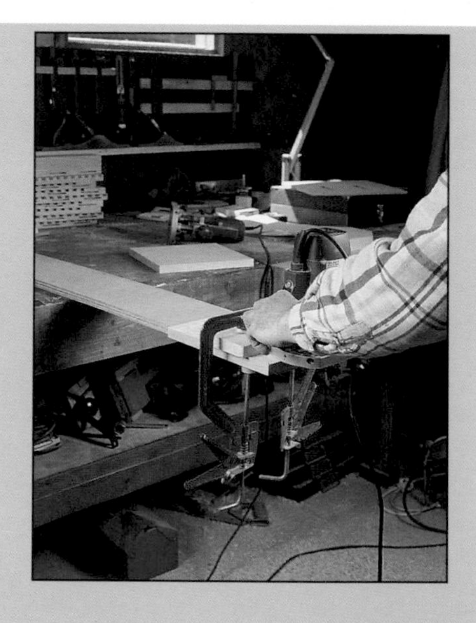

▶ *The plank technique gives good all round access*

▼ *Again using the plank method, rout the housings in the top and bottom panels*

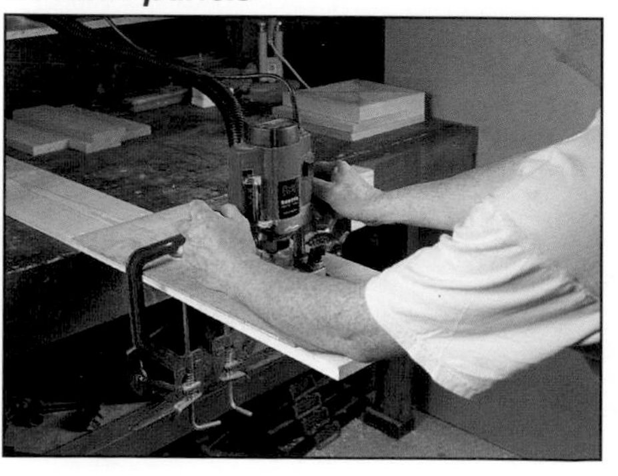

▼ *The jig when flipped over will create the mirror image housings required for top and bottom*

▼ *Rout the tongues on the ends of the slotted panels, machining two together helps to keep them square*

▲ *Nip off the end of the tongues so that the joint doesn't show*

▲ *Use an index stick to position the biscuits slots in the edges …*

▲ *… and faces to ensure they all line up*

Cut the pieces for the top and bottom panels and the base exactly to their respective sizes, ensuring that the finished corners meet exactly at their mitred junctions in each case.

Using the router and a straight-edge, mark the correct offset for the cutter to edge-of-base distance. Place the jig on the bottom panel and cramp in place so the back right-hand corner and edges line up together.

Rout this and the previous operation by 'routing the plank' as mentioned in the sidebar.

Machine the housings 5.5mm ($\frac{7}{32}$in) to 6mm ($\frac{15}{64}$in) deep to leave clearance for the end of the panel's tongues. To cut the housings in the top panel, which is a mirror image of the bottom panel, flip the jig over and mark the critical corner, then rout all four sets of slots as before.

Check that each panel sits in the correct position, flush with the edge of the top and bottom panels and the right width apart to take the CDs cases.

Index stick

All the vertical joints between the panels and the ash 'core' in the middle are made with No.10 biscuits to prevent breakthrough.

Use three per edge and make an index stick with lines 25mm (1in) apart which the cutter must run between to make the slot long enough for the biscuits to fit.

Fit a small block at each end of the index stick so it fits tightly on each blank. Now you can offer each piece up to the cutter in the table and machine the slots exactly, without marking them all individually.

Some joints are on the edges, others are on the unslotted panel faces, so take care in checking which you are doing.

The face slots need each panel to be held vertically as you push it onto the cutter. Always place the furthest end of each panel against the fence first. Don't allow the panel to move backwards over the cutter or it may fly out of your control.

Always swing the panel right away from the cutter once each slot is made so you don't graze the wood between the slots.

The square core piece is 10mm ($\frac{25}{64}$in) shorter, so adjust the blocks accordingly. All like components will be interchangeable as a result of using the index stick.

Dry fit

Dry fit everything to check that it goes together, then sand all internal surfaces to a finish, taking care not to round over any edges. De-fluff the slots with a folded piece of abrasive paper.

Glue the central panels onto the square core first inserting biscuits and ensuring glue doesn't seep out on the slotted face, if it does wipe it off thoroughly with a damp cloth.

Cramp and check all panels are at 90° to the core piece. Sand the resulting flush surfaces flat. Next glue and biscuit the other panels on and check with a square. Any failure to get this right means the whole thing will not go together when the top and bottom are fitted.

Now glue the top and bottom on, cramp well together and leave to dry.

Dry fit the components together on the 'rod' to make sure they will fit

Glue and assemble the main unit together

▶ *Exploded view of CD rack*

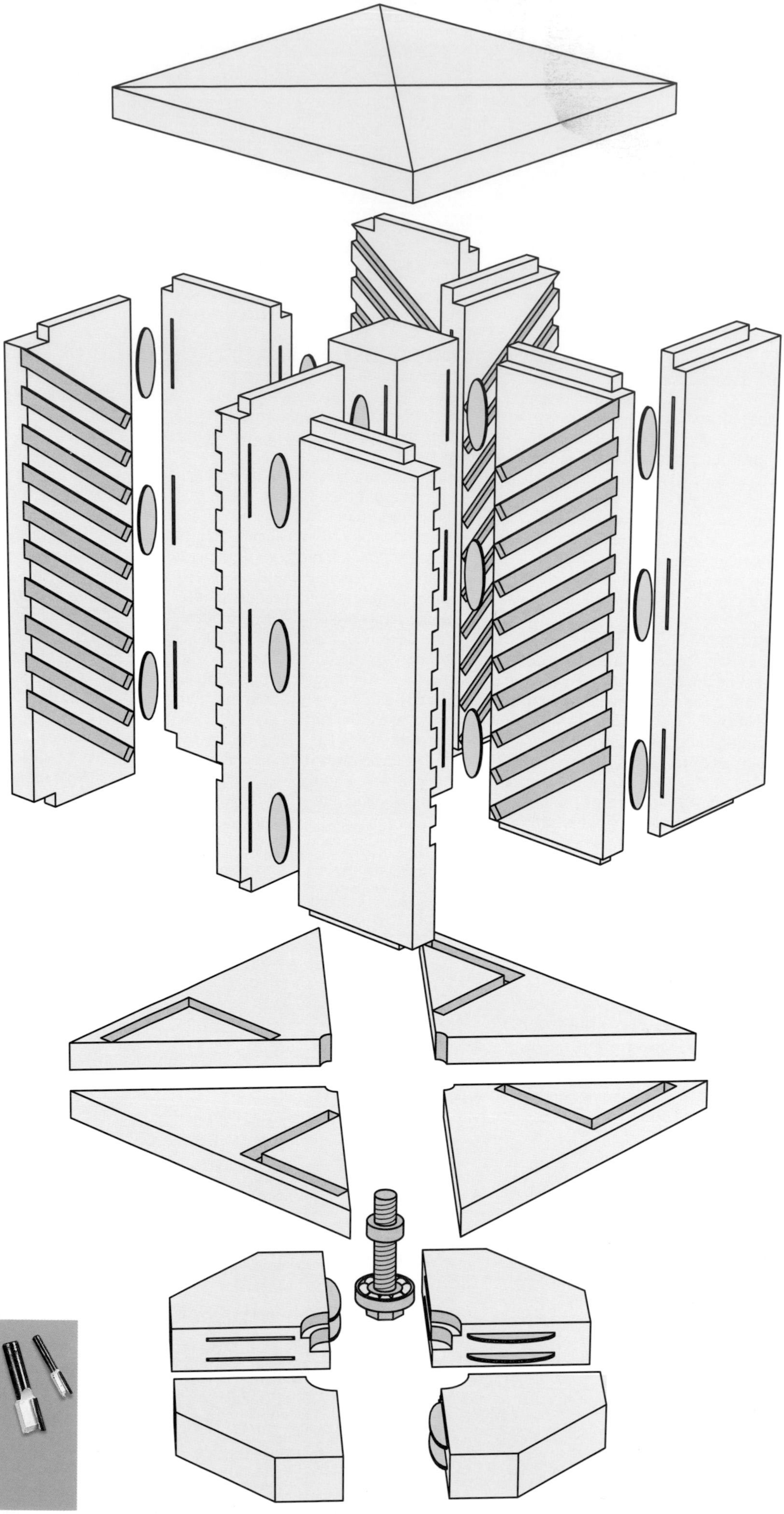

Tooling up

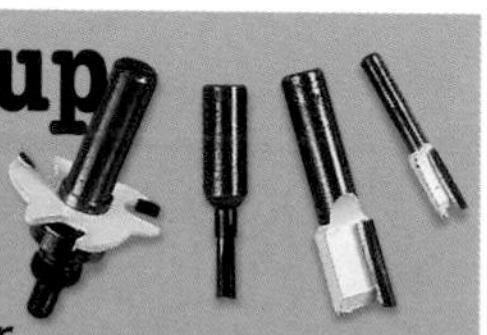

- *Slotting cutter*
- *6.4mm straight cutter*
- *Large straight cutter*
- *9.5mm straight cutter*

▲ *Assemble together the bolt and bearing for the swivel, note the housing in the underside of the base*

▲ *Apply a finish to the rack to protect it and enhance the grain*

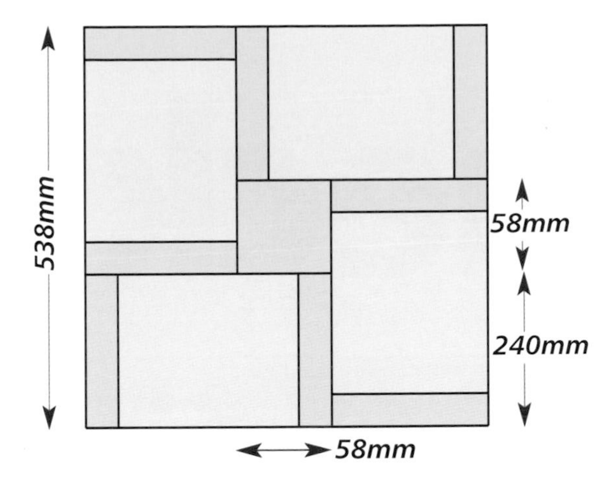

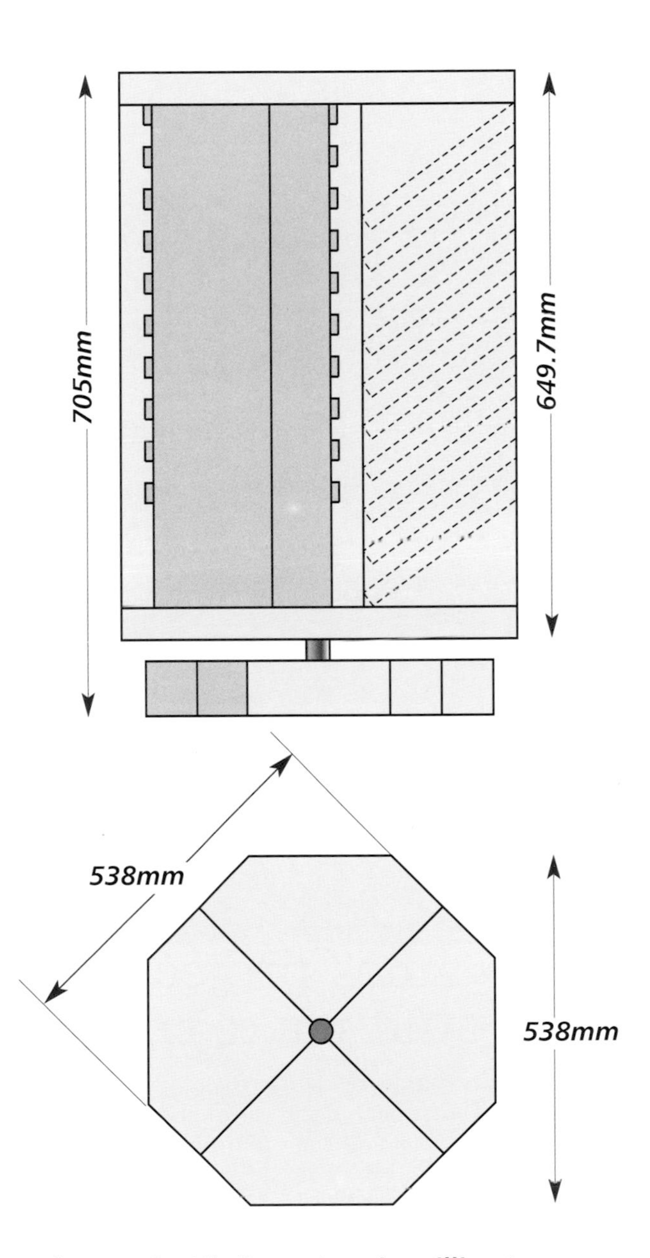

▲ *Dimensions of CD rack. All dimensions in millimetres*

Bolting up

The base must be cut to an octagon, close to the marked lines, then trim with a router and straight-edge. Machine with the grain to avoid tearout.

The CD rack swivels on a large bearing, and a long bolt with nut that fits, in this case a 10mm internal bearing diameter. Draw around the bearing, placed dead centre on the base, take a router and large straight cutter and freehand rout by holding the base.

Work up to the line and check the bearing fit. Adjust by routing until it is a hammer-tight fit. Don't knock it right in or you may not get it out again. If you have a jig passion it would be possible to make one for this process but I decided it would be quicker to rout freehand.

Fit the bolt in the bearing and tighten the nut. Now make a further recess underneath so the bolt head will turn freely.

Sand the CD rack to a finish all over, use filler for any flaws or slight gaps, if needed.

Finishing

Upturn the CD rack and mark dead centre. Take a big router with a long 9.5mm cutter, stick some abrasive on the router base so it won't slip around, and make a neat full-depth plunge to drill the bolt hole.

If necessary, trim the bolt to fit the hole and file a bevel on the end to help it start threading, then wind it in with a spanner.

Apply a suitable finish such as sanding sealer or spray lacquer (nothing oily though), tap the base onto the bearing and apply some protective felt or baize. Stand the rack up the right way – it's done!

The last and most vital bit is to fill up the CD rack, pour yourself a nice cold drink and unwind after the stress of this project, listening to your favourite tunes!

Check make

Sit down, relax and do battle

This neat games project is sure to provide hours of fun and would make the perfect present

I FANCIED a game of chess but found my board had been on the receiving end of one of my dog's chewing fits. This prompted me to make a fun project for games designed to sit on a table, with lift up lids and two compartments for chess or draughts pieces.

Sizing up

It is 380mm (15in) sq. excluding the edge mouldings, with a piece of 9mm (23/64in) birch ply for the top, as it is strong and will resist any tendency to bow when the sawn veneer squares are glued in place.

The base is a piece of 6mm (15/64in) hardboard, rigid and easily covered with baize or felt on the inside surface. The shallow birch ply sides are sandwiched between the top and bottom, needing to be just deep enough to hold the chess pieces with the largest diameter bases, about 38mm (1½in).

▶ ***This scruffy chess set is what mine looked like even before the dog got hold of it!***

▲ *The box corners are housed together, so first cut the rebate...*

▲ *...then the housings*

Box

The sides and centre division are tongue-and-grooved together using a 4mm straight cutter. Offset the tongues to the inside face of the sides, and in the case of the division, do the same, just take care when marking out that the division is centred even though the tongue and groove isn't!

Aim for a tight but not forced fit. Glue all the joints and hold together with veneer pins which can be punched in later. Check the sides and division are square, and leave to dry.

Glue and pin on the base, cleaning off any glue showing on the inside. Once dry, punch in the veneer pins and fill, use a block plane to flush the base if it overhangs anywhere. Belt sand the outside faces using 120-grit to get a clean finish.

▼ *Assemble the components together and make sure they are square*

Top

For the top, take the ply square and use the table saw to bisect it down the middle. The loss of the saw kerf width can be made up with a strip of a suitable wood later.

Choose some dark and light timbers to form the alternate squares. I bought a cheap box of offcuts by post from Craft Supplies of Derbyshire. These are intended more for turnery, but many are large enough for this purpose.

Measure the total area of the two boards and divide by eight to arrive at the square size. Note that the maple inlay does not need to be taken into account at this stage, as we will simply rout a groove along the junction of all the assembled squares.

Set up the table saw for producing approximately 3mm (⅛in) thick sawn veneers. How you do this is important for safety and consistency, so make sure that you use pushsticks and follow a safe procedure.

Prepare plenty of thin flat strips to make the squares, also cut lots of thicker sections of the maple for thicknessing, ready for the inlayed lines.

Cutting squares

A hand mitre saw is a quick, easy way to cut the strips into squares. Put a strip of MDF on the bed to support where the cuts are made, then clamp another piece on the fence as a stop.

Cut lots of each colour wood until you have a bit of an excess, then choose the best looking ones. Lay them alternately on the two boards. Ensure the first playing square at the bottom left-hand corner as you face the board, with the join running across, is a light square and the grain runs crosswise.

Check for grain match, and slide them off in the right order. Use a spreader to apply PVA glue all over the boards. Lay the pieces back on one by one, pressing them tightly together and down onto the boards.

Use some packing tape to hold all the squares together. Make sure they line up flush and parallel with the underlying boards, and cramp both boards firmly face-to-face, sandwiching a piece of paper in between to prevent them gluing together, and leave to set.

Depending on how well-sawn to thickness the veneers are, you can either get away with a thorough belt sanding to level the squares, or if more needs removing, some very fine passes through the thicknesser can be tried. This may cause a bit of tearing if there is short or angled grain.

▼ *Run out some decorative moulding for the box edges*

▼ *Use a small straight cutter and side fence to cut in the hinges*

▲*Machine the thin pieces required for the top*

▲*Accurately cut the squares to size*

Strip jig

Make up a jig board with one long stop to press the two playing boards against. Line them up to each other in their correct playing order so the cross-grain direction of the squares will be grooved first.

Screw strips against the other edges of the boards to hold them tightly together. Make up a T-square for the router which sits right across both boards, with a slot big enough to admit a guide bush.

Screw two squares of board either side, overhanging the chessboard so cramps can be applied to the T-square to hold it in place. Make sure the guide bush slot is exactly 90° to the right-angle piece fixed to the T-square.

Line the T-square up on a joint between two squares, fit a 2mm straight cutter in the router and set the depth to that of the veneer. Rout along the join, working backwards and forwards several times till the chippings clear out of the slot. Repeat this along all joins and the outer edges too, also making sure to centre the cutter on the edge of the squares.

▲ *Glue them to the top and hold them firmly in place with tape*

Maple strips

Take the sawn maple strips and thickness to size, taking repeated fine passes through the thicknesser until you reach a size that will, edgeways, fit fairly easily into any of the routed grooves. Now use your tablesaw set-up to cut these flat strips into nearly square sections, take care, using two pushsticks and no fingers.

Apply glue to the grooves and tap the inlay evenly down with a hammer, tape it on the outer edges and leave to dry.

Trim off the ends of the maple strips and use a finely-set block plane to level the inlay without tearing the squares.

Rotate and refit the boards in the jig, but with the long grain direction facing you. You'll need to adjust the strips holding them. Repeat the machining procedure and once again glue the inlay into the grooves and let dry. Trim and level the inlay, belt sanding with the grain. The board is complete.

Moulding

Make up some classical section moulding in a contrast wood to place around the base edges, covering up the hardboard and around the edges of the playing boards.

Cut neat mitres and glue and tape them in place. Treat both boards as one with a gap in

▼*Rout a guide bush slot in a piece of plywood which will become the jig for routing*

▼*Saw the thin pieces of wood into strips for inlaying into the top*

▲ *Rout the grooves and insert the strips*

▲ *Cut and fit the edge moulding*

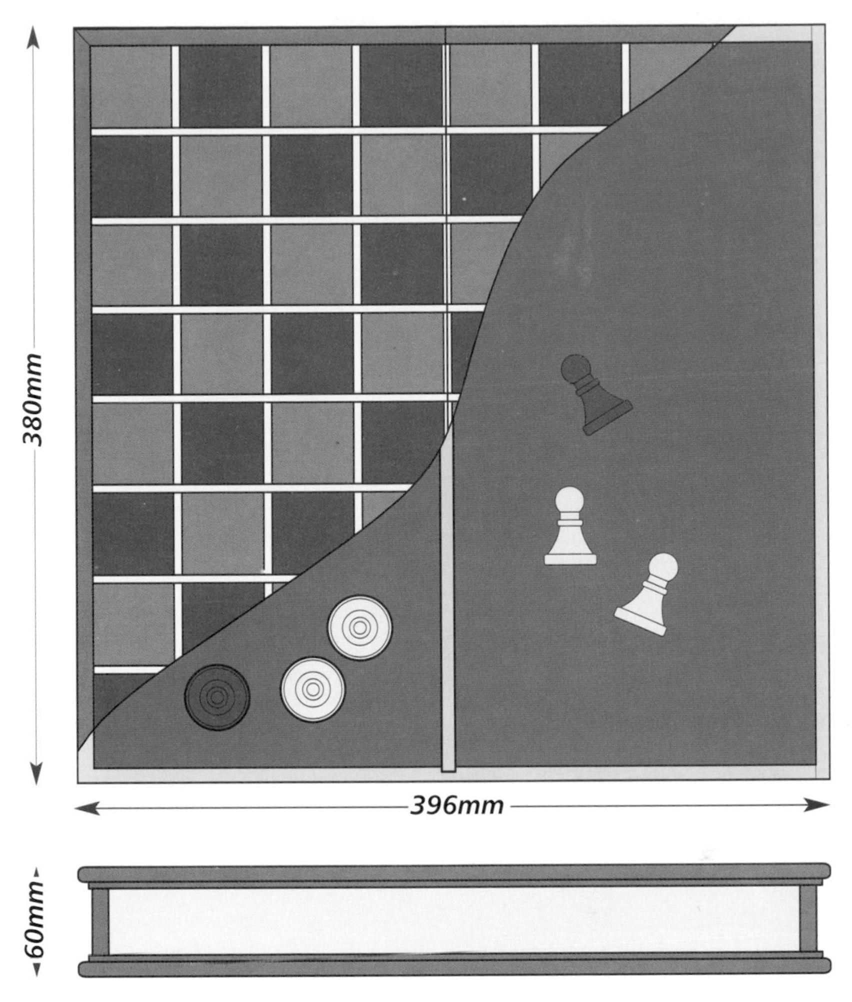

▲ *Basic dimensions*

between so the mouldings line up, and to cover the ends of any infill strip needed to make up the width of the top.

The top moulding should hang down about 1mm more than the top thickness. I found the mouldings projected over the box sides enough for the loss of a saw kerf width not to be noticcable. At the corners of the box glue some strips of thin sawn or knife-cut veneer to cover the birch end grain. They also are an added feature.

Hinges and finish

The hinge recesses could be routed with a jig, but this seems a bit heavy handed as the hinges are so small.

Instead, fit a 3.2mm straight cutter and fence, knife-mark around a hinge to give an accurate shape, and gently machine out to the depth of half a folded hinge. The hinges can't be recessed into the lid, but the hang down of the moulding will cover them.

Fill any defects and sand the playing surface with an orbital sander. Hand sand all other seen surfaces using 220-grit or finer. Apply sanding sealer in several ragged-on coats and rub down between coats using 400-grit lubricating paper.

Apply a good wax, but not on the lid underside, the base or the inside base which will all be covered in baize.

Use an adhesive like Copydex to glue the baize or felt neatly onto these surfaces. Use some tiny screws to fix the hinges in place and some small strips of Velcro on the box edges to keep the lid closed.

It doesn't matter if you aren't a master craftsman, because now is the chance to imagine you're a chess Grand Master instead!

▼*The finished chess box...*

▼*...opens to reveal its dual purpose*

Fantastic filing

Tidy away your paperwork with a compact filing cabinet

DO you keep all your vital papers in one of those steel or plastic lock-up cases designed for domestic paperwork? Not very big is it? A two-drawer full-size filing cabinet would be ideal, so do as I've done and make a neat compact unit which can fit under a desk or stand by itself.

Measurements

Like any piece of furniture with a specialised containing function, the internal measurements are the critical ones, if you can't fit your suspension files then it isn't any use at all!

So, take a standard-width suspension file (there are some sub-size ones designed to save space), the critical dimensions are the 390mm centre-to-centre distance of the cutouts that slide on the rails in the drawer, the height of the file from the bottom to the cutout (237mm), and the height from this point to the top of the ID tab clipped on top (about 22mm). Everything else is determined by these sizes.

A fairly deep unit of 570mm means that with one drawer out it is unlikely to tip over. If this unit is fitted under a desk you can make it shallower to suit. Because it's freestanding there is an overhang with an ovolo moulded edge; for under-desk use the top can be flush.

The overall height of 690mm should just fit under a desk and give enough height for two drawers. If it is a bit tight you could reduce the plinth height of 70mm slightly, or block up the desk.

The width of 500mm is about 19mm wider than that needed to accommodate the files in their drawers, and the 12mm plus 12mm thickness of the runners. Any difference is made up with packers and a bead edge moulding is applied to the inside carcass faces to cover the packers.

A wooden filing cabinet is the perfect addition to any home office

The timber must first be made up to size, use a glue joint cutter and remember to allow for waste

Rout a tongue on the sides and ends of the side panel strips

All stock is standard 150mm by 25mm prepared softwood, which gives a finished thickness of about 20mm. Cut all carcass parts overlength and overwidth.

"A fairly deep unit means that with one drawer out it is unlikely to tip over"

Base, panels, sides

Start with the internal base, top and back panels and drawer front panels which are jointed together. You need to allow for the overlap in the joints. Set up a glue joint cutter in the router table, do some test cuts to ensure it is properly centred, then machine all edges to be joined.

Do one edge then flip the board over to do the other edge. Glue, assemble and cramp all pieces. Any misalignment shows

With a slotting cutter, rout the biscuit jointing slots in the edges of the bottom

Tooling up

- *Slotting cutter*
- *Profile and scribe cutters*
- *Rebate cutter*
- *Panel raising cutter*
- *Straight cutter*
- *Glue joint cutter*

Hafele runners and furniture fittings are obtainable in small quantities to order, or ex-stock, from Brighton Tools & Fixings, Tel 01273 562020.

As the biscuit slots are set a way in from the edge, matching slots for the bottom must be cut in the sides, using a straight cutter

Rout a groove in the carcass sides for the back and machine a groove on the back so it is flush when fitted together

Rout the grooves in the drawer box sides for the back and bottom

and will need thorough belt sanding to level it once dry.

Next tackle the sides. Use a tongue-and-groove or variable groove set to make the frame, leaving a slot of 6mm to 9mm width, and a depth of 10mm to 13mm, with tongues on the rail ends to match.

The centre boards are the same thickness and need a bevel machined on all long edges to give a V-groove effect when assembled. First machine all the tongue-and-grooves, except those around the outside edges.

Instead, assemble all the boards and then cut to the right size before machining a tongue all round the outside. Do this before V-grooving to avoid breakout. Set up a V-point cutter in the table; the bevel should not be too deep or it will affect the tongue-and-groove.

Rout the V-grooves, including the outer edges, then assemble together and glue the frame around the centre boards. Cramp up, check for square and leave to dry on a flat surface.

Cut all panels to size except the back panel, place together in a lying down attitude, and make some strike marks at 150mm to 200mm intervals for biscuit jointing. Use a biscuit cutter with the correct bearing for No. 20 biscuits and machine the slots.

Run a groove all around the back of the carcass to tongue the back panel in place. Cut the back panel to the internal size, plus the tongue on all edges.

All internal surfaces should now be thoroughly sanded, though not to a fine finish as they will not be very visible. Apply glue to the biscuits but leave the back panel loose to allow for shrinkage. Cramp up the carcass, check for square and make sure it is not 'in wind'.

Wipe off excess glue and leave to dry. The plinth strip is also biscuited to the bottom panel. You now have a box.

Belt sand the exterior surfaces with the grain and orbital sand with a medium grit, leaving the fine sanding till later on. To complete the carcass, run a moulding around the top edge (this can be done earlier on using the router table).

"The bevel should not be too deep or it will affect the tongue and groove"

Drawers

Measure the inside of the carcass to check the dimensions will be adequate to hold the two drawers. Two drawer boxes are needed, to which decorative front panels will be fixed. Make the drawer depth less by the thickness of the applied front panel and then another 5mm, so there is no danger of the fronts sticking out proud when installed.

The drawer height will allow both drawers and the overhanging fronts to clear each other when pulled out. The sides are full depth and overlap the front and back to resist the stress of drawer opening.

Tongue-and-groove the drawers' sides, fronts and backs and also the bases. Run a groove around all the inside faces. The top of the groove should be 21mm up from the bottom so the bases with their offset tongue will be flush on the underside when fitted.

Use the panel raising cutter to create the drawer fronts

The components of the filing cabinet ready to fit together

Pack the drawers apart and mark where the runner's packing pieces will be needed

Fit the packing pieces and screw on the runners

Dry assemble and measure the size of the bases allowing for the tongues. Cut to size and rout a tongue all round.

Sand internal surfaces to a finish, glue and cramp the drawers together, leaving the base loose, check for square and leave to set. Sand each drawer to a finish on the outside.

I used Tonk strip (library strip) for the files to hang on. To position them, refer to an actual file and mark groove positions on the long top edges of each drawer.

Use a 2mm groover on an arbor with a bearing giving a 9.5mm cut depth in a ¼in router. Sit a drawer on its side, set the cutter depth and carefully run right along the edge. Cut the Tonk strip to length and use small countersunk screws to fit it.

Drawer fronts

The drawer fronts have two raised panels. Cut and plane the frame pieces to width and also to length. The object is to make the fronts to fit the carcass opening tightly, they will be trimmed for a running fit later.

The rails need to be 19mm overlength as they are scribed into the stiles. Do the scribing cuts first on the router table, ensuring there is a backing piece to prevent breakout.

Fit the profile cutter, exchanging cutter and bearing positions if it is a reversible set, or raise the height if you have a combination set. Do test cuts to get a flush joint and machine one edge of each piece.

Dry fit the frames and measure the panel sizes, which should be 2mm less in each direction for an easy fit, and cut to size. Fit a panel raiser in the table, a through fence will give continuous support for a smooth, straight-edged cut.

Machine the panel in several passes so the router isn't overstressed, starting with the cross-grain passes each time so the long passes remove any tearout.

Dry assemble each panel to check how well they fit together.

Take the front panel apart then sand all the mouldings and the front and back of each panel. Then glue up and reassemble, check-

"If the stiles have been left overlength trim off the horns"

Drill holes in the drawer box fronts, screw through until the sharp points show, and mark the applied drawer fronts ready to fit

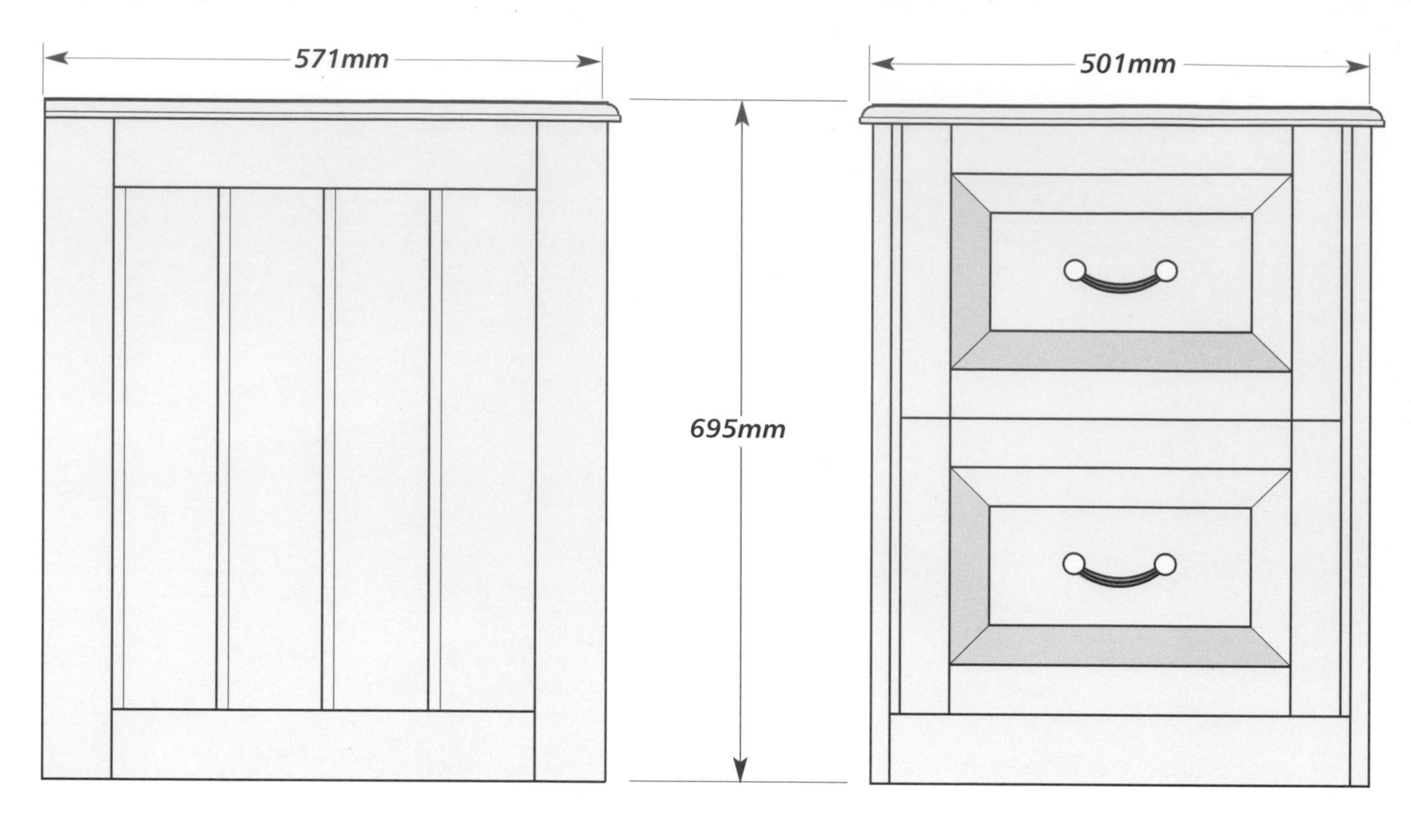

▲ *Approximate dimensions of a filing cabinet, these can be adjusted to suit*

ing for square. Once the glue is dry the frame's faces can be sanded. If the stiles have been left overlength trim off the 'horns'.

Finally, use some slim packers to position each drawer front in place, one above the other, using the saw to trim them until they are a comfortable fit with a 1.5mm to 2mm gap all round.

Runners

Take the filing cabinet runners and fix them inside the carcass with short twinfast screws. Use packing strips, (I found 9.5mm ply was perfect), so that each drawer will be centred in the carcass. The actual height position isn't critical, though midway up each drawer would be about right, although they have to be level and the same height on both sides of course.

Make a template on a piece of hardboard the internal height of the carcass with the runner positions and the drawers and the drawer fronts, so you can get the positioning just right to allow the drawers to clear each other.

By opening and closing each runner it is possible to find the fixing holes. The Hafele Accuride runners I used are particularly good in this respect, being very easy to fit. Ensure the screws are the right size and go in square so the heads don't protrude and catch on the moving sections of runner. Note that there is a plastic receiver at the back of each runner which holds the drawer closed.

Rest the lower drawer on some blocks at the right height and fix the runners to it flush with the front. Repeat the operation on the upper drawer using higher supports, referring to your template so the positioning is correct.

Fit the handles to the panelled drawer fronts with the bolts or nuts recessed in on the back. Then drill four holes in each drawer-box front at the pilot diameter of the screws that will be used to fix the fronts on; make sure the screws will run through where the fatter raised section of panel will be!

Run the screws in so the sharp tips are just exposed and press each drawer front in place, ensuring they have even gapping all round. The marks left by the screw points can be drilled and the fronts screwed on. Any slight misalignment can be straightened with a tap from a hammer; use a block of softwood to protect the drawer front.

Finishing

You can go for a natural pine finish using varnish flatted between coats, or put a stain on first to give it a bit of colour, maybe to match existing furniture. If you do, make sure the carcass is well sanded with no cross-grain scratches, as the stain will show these up. It is easier to remove the drawer boxes and fronts before applying a finish, in particular you can wipe a band of dye down the inside faces of the carcass so it doesn't look too bare inside.

Push the filing unit into position and add files and paperwork – it won't take long to fill!

▼ *Fit on the Tonk strip for the files to suspend from*

▼ *The finished filing cabinet, ready to fill*

BLACK&DECKER
KW780E 600W
A1 230V~ 50Hz 2.7A
no 8000-30000/min
BD 2
Made in Italy

INSPIRATION

This Mechanics of Making mini-series looks at how to change a great concept into a great piece of work

This is the first in a short series aimed at the novice or intermediate level woodworker, giving my own idiosyncratic views and I hope, some useful hints and tips on how to plan and execute those slightly more difficult commissions and maybe avoid some of the problems I have encountered over many years.

INSPIRATION

There are two ways of creating a work of art or craft, be it wood or any other material. One is the 'dash-it-off' stream of consciousness method, where little apparent thought takes place. Instead you literally take what is in front of you and make it into something. Performance art or simply whittling a stick into a particular shape are two examples of how something can be created that is unique and almost unbidden. Because it has not been preceded by endless premeditation, the results simply appear because brain and hand have been able to work together unfettered by 'mental blocks'. For most people this seems to be a bit of a struggle while for a few, this sort of 'off-the-cuff' art or craft is quite a natural thing to do.

The other more pedestrian method which is better suited to us woodworkers, is to design a solution in response to a problem, albeit sometimes more an aesthetic one than a necessity. You get a request – "I need a chest of drawers" – OK, so you design a chest of drawers. It can be more-or-less straightforward in appearance. It could be quite fancy or plain. It could be contemporary or traditional in design and it could incorporate materials other than just wood.

THE ART OF COMPROMISE

So, first of all we have the basic requirement followed by an overlay of a desire to create both an attractive and functional object. At the concept stage there may not be much more than a rather rosy conception of what it will look like and quite possibly some lively discussion with the person who has commissioned the piece – your partner for instance!

The first step in transforming the idea in your head into a work of art is to start with a sketch. Some people even have the skill to add a bit of colour, thus giving it more life (Fig. 1). However, be aware that reality can get in the way a bit. Freestanding furniture or other items tend to be easier because they merely sit on the floor or a table or hang off a wall. Fitted furniture and any other fixtures have to conform to their surroundings or they simply won't fit in properly or look right, or in some more extreme cases, even function properly. I have mentioned all this early on because I'm always aware when I design something that it will have to be compromised in some way to meet the client's needs.

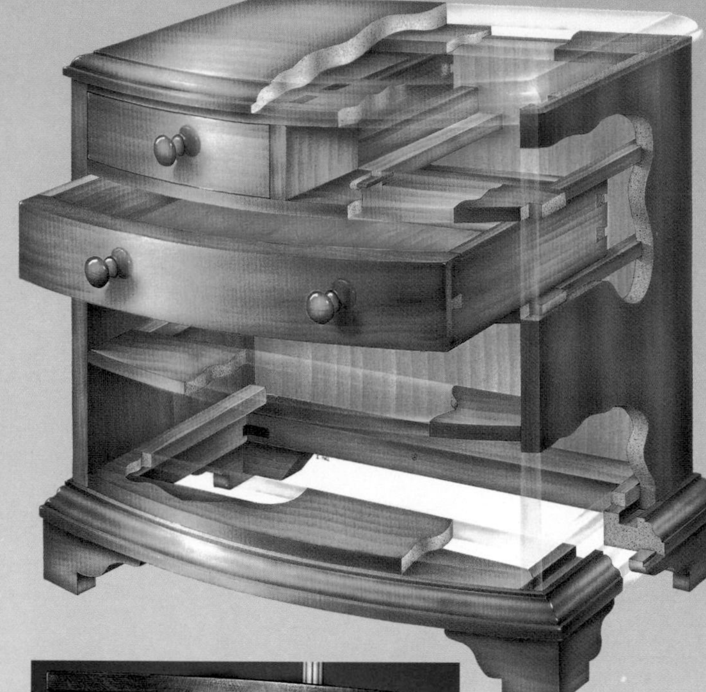

Figure 1 **Few of us can hope to achieve a superb informative drawing such as this one by Ian Hall**

Photo 1 **This beautiful one of a pair of walnut corner cupboards on stand by John Cadney shows how different plain and burr timbers can be.**

Photo 2 **A superb example of a mahogany broken pediment surmounting a breakfront bookcase by Paul Richardson**

MATERIAL THINGS

Then there's the actual material – wood is funny stuff, two pieces of the same timber can be quite different in appearance and behaviour (photo 1). You have to respect wild grain that tears easily and short grain that is likely to shatter if the component is too thin. Some timber looks good but isn't practical for certain situations. Untreated maple, for example, looks good and is safe with food, but punishing on cutters when machining. Mahogany, on the other hand, is more toxic but is great in appearance for a dining table or bookcase (photo 2).

Quite a lot of woodwork also needs screws or fittings of some sort, such as hinges or handles. There are now some quite stylish fittings available as well as the more traditional brassware or black iron. I usually give brass hinges, and even screws, a light rubbing on fine abrasive paper to give them a better look. Things like handles don't just have to look good, an elderly person may need a shape they can grip to open doors, so ergonomics is a factor (photo 3).

BACK TO RAW BEGINNINGS

I don't want to make a big deal about all this but my own experience has been of nice designs tempered with a hefty dose of reality. As a cabinetmaker I suppose the whole process of creating a workable design that people will actually pay me for, is a mixture of inspiration, perspiration and desperation!

Seriously though, I wouldn't want to put anybody off creating their own unique pieces in wood, but you do need to have an eye to the various problems that can arise. So you can see from what I am saying that the 'inspiration' of the title is just the opening part that hopefully allows you and the client or end user to get the job off the ground. So, let's get back to the subject matter of the title.

FORM FOLLOWS FUNCTION?

Taking our chest of drawers as an example, let's see what we can realistically do with it. It could just start off as a rectangular box as has been done since cabinetmaking began (photo 4). It wasn't long before early cabinetmakers started conferring different shapes upon the humble chest, the bow front for example. Interestingly on a traditional chest having the front feet swept in shape seems to work well visually, which is also true on chairs though generally this would be on the back legs where it also gives stability (photo 5). So instantly, an attractive shape is allied to a function (photo 6).

You can take inspiration from a piece of architecture – many modern buildings include some interesting forms and shapes, whatever the critics may say. The natural world is filled with shapes that we can 'borrow' from. Wherever you get your idea from, just remember that while each piece you make is genuinely unique, there is very little that is literally 'new under the sun'. Even great artists have copied each other, even themselves on some occasions, and observed and rendered the world around them. In other words what they have done isn't so original, but it looks it. That's the trick.

The overall shape of any piece of woodwork with secondary decorative function should look good when you stand back from it. The proportions need to look right and it needs to fit in well with its surrouhdings (photo 7). Indeed this is a good starting point for the style of the piece. You need to give reference to it, so that things like plinth and skirtings, dado and mid-height mouldings and the like, don't look odd side-by-side by being slightly out of alignment or with an ill-matched choice of mouldings. Once again this serves as another example of our inspired design getting compromised by the world around it because a beautiful object in wood cannot sit aloof from its surroundings.

It is also of great importance that your piece of treasured work looks good close-up. With great attention paid to the detail in the execution of the work, starting with initial machining, then the moulding work, assembly and finishing will all pay dividends at the end. Thus, it isn't enough to have just a good idea – the trick is to carry it out to the best of your ability. There are various essential steps such as proper technical drawings and organised cutting lists that will ensure the final outcome is a success. See the next exciting instalment for more on these vital issues!

Photo 3 **An unusual handle design which combines style and ease of use**

Photo 4 **A deceptively simple, square modern chest of drawers in Macracapa, made by Roger Smith**

Photo 5 **This Chippendale style carver chair shows the swept back legs that give elegance and stability (picture courtesy of John Lloyd)**

Photo 6 **Back view of an unusual open style of chest design by Duncan Lyall**

Photo 7 **A substantial, well proportioned mahogany Georgian style breakfront bookcase *in situ*, by Paul Richardson**

MATERIALS

The second instalment of this Mechanics of Making mini-series looks at a small selection of timbers that make up the raw materials for furniture-making

Karl Hahn's chest of drawers offers proof that pine doesn't have to be plain and boring

In the first of my discourses on the essentials of creating a complicated piece of woodwork, I talked about the problems that arise during the design process when trying to transform a great idea into a great piece of work. Since the primary material is timber, and it is going to be chosen for a number of reasons, we need to decide on our selection criteria and what sort of woods we can use.

SOFTWOODS

For a start, convenience comes into the equation. Softwoods are generally sold either as sawn carcassing grade or PAR (Prepared All Round) which means that the timber has been sawn oversize and then trued on large scale planing equipment so the faces and edges are flat and parallel to each other and the adjoining faces and edges are at 90 degrees to each other. So we start off with a massive advantage in preparation terms.

Not all softwoods are the same timber species although 'pine' is the generic term we mostly use. Some softwood for the DIY market may have resin pockets and be very pale and soft in appearance. It comes prepacked in random lengths and tends to be in slightly smaller dimensions. It is better to look to various timberyards and go through their stock to see if you can find tougher more attractive softwood and choose pieces with more or less knots depending on what you want. The thumbnail test is good for checking how tough the wood is.

The rear view of an oak chair by Robert Reid shows both quarter sawn ray and straight grain timber

HARDWOODS

This is generally but not exclusively timber other than pine. Oak, ash, elm, cherry and mahogany are just a few of nature's vast catalogue of trees, most of which have some use to woodworkers. I'm not going to bore you with a list of timbers since it would simply be too vast. So let's take a look at a few timbers that are reasonably easy to obtain and what they can be best be used for. Remember that hardwoods are generally sold as sawn boards, although some yards sell a selection of prepared boards or even prepare to order if you know what you want. There is always some waste involved, no matter how it is supplied.

OAK

Oak comes in various species, although English oak is not widely available due to the vast reduction of native trees. The majority that is sold in the UK comes from France, although it has similar characteristics to our native oak. Usually the log is sawn through and through which results in a beautiful silvery figure on the top and bottom boards in the pile. This can be used to great effect on door panels, furniture and high grade joinery. Oak is tough but it can split. It is pale when freshly sawn but turns into a golden colour after a while, especially with a finish on it. Expect a lot of waste due to its wayward growth.

A beautiful example of steam bent ash by David Colwell

ASH

Ash is another lovely timber, being very creamy in colour and turning into a honey-gold colour after time. Its smooth, even nature and fine 'crown' makes it ideal for domestic work. The heartwood has a large dark centre, referred to as olive ash, with the lighter sapwood at the edges of the board. Better behaved than oak, it can be bandsawn, glued and laminated together

This table top shows just how stunning wild grained elm can be

This close-up of an intricate toolcase in yew by Marcus Mindelsohn brings out the warmth and figure perfectly

to form curves, or steam bent using a steam chest and a former. This makes for immensely strong components for chairs etc. It machines a bit more easily than oak although the end grain is almost as tough.

ELM

Another stunning home-grown tree, the elm has a rich, nutty brown colour and unlike oak the whole width of the board can be used without difficulty. It does however have a tendency to wriggle right across the board to give a wavy shape which needs to be flattened on a wide bed planer. Elm is incredibly strong and very attractive when used with more organic, rustic furniture forms. It is also weather resistant and a bit softer than the two previous timbers, making it easier to work with. Some interesting pieces of figured burr or pollarded elm are available, often found at the end of a standard board. This can be used to good effect in door panels or decorative boxes.

The warm and pleasing colour of cherry is ideal for this ladies sewing table

CHERRY

Despite being a native species, English cherry tends to grow in gardens so is not commonly available. American cherry is a more readily available alternative and tends to be paler and a lot less exciting. A good example of English cherry, which is not very large in size, has a strong honey yellow-brown colour with hints of rich dull red and even slight purple with a very light ivory white band of sapwood around the outside of the log. Suitable for small components and thick sawn veneers, it is ideal for use in dining chairs, mirror frames and small fancy cabinets. A nice wood providing you can get hold of it.

YEW

A very English tree, this is in fact a softwood but you can't get it from a builder's yard! It is treated by the trade as a hardwood by default as it is such an unusual timber. Yew trees often grow to great age and have rather wild growth habits. This results in naturally flawed boards that make it very much a decorative rather than a strength timber for most purposes. It has an orangey mildly figured grain with whitish sapwood which is often used with the heartwood rather than just cut off. Odd holes and irregular grain are considered normal. Yew is ideal for smaller components and sawn or knife cut veneers.

MAHOGANY

This is a very generalised and misleading term since there are a variety of different species that are referred to as mahogany although strictly speaking they aren't. In the reproduction furniture trade these woods are often simply called 'brown wood'. These include Cuban, Honduran, African, sapele, utile, to name but a few. The last two are definitely not mahoganies by any stretch of the imagination, but they are often used as substitutes. You won't be able to obtain the Cuban variety as it is all but extinct! The others tend to be more readily available and can be obtained from specialist timber-yards. There are a variety of figured cuts of some species which end up as veneers. All are reasonably easy to machine, although there will occasionally be silica deposits in some woods that can blunt cutting edges. The dust is more toxic and bitter tasting than most. These woods are ideal for domestic furniture and boxes.

Curl mahogany veneer looks superb on this dressing table by Paul Richardson

I hope these timber descriptions are helpful and whet your appetite for trying different varieties, many of which are both beautiful and strong. Remember the right choice of wood can dramatically alter the appearance of your project. The next part of this series goes on to look at the technique of drawing. 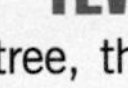

DESIGN

The next stage in the Mechanics of Making series focuses on turning a rough sketch into a proper technical drawing

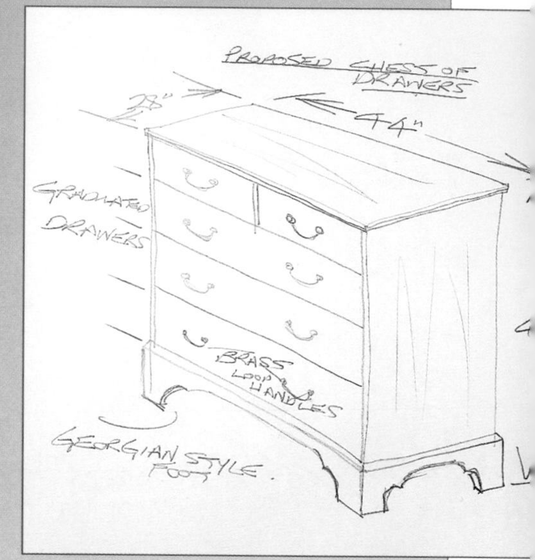

A sketch is just that, a starting point for something more precise

In my first article in this series (pages 92–3) we looked at how to transform an idea into a rough sketch or design and the hurdles we might encounter in doing so. I pointed out that essentially all design is some kind of compromise, albeit a good one that aims to satisfy all our requirements. The previous article (pages 94–5) took things a stage further, looking at the choice of timber. Having got something sketched out that appears to work you now need to make a proper technical drawing.

The first thing to get out of the way is the rather retro discussion about imperial versus metric. I am of course talking about systems of measurement. Many of our readers still prefer imperial because they have been brought up with it and aren't about to change. And let's not forget our readers on the other side of the Atlantic who still use the imperial system.

Personally, while I still only recognise miles as opposed to kilometres, I made the awkward transition from inches and 1/8ths to millimetres and centimetres some time ago. I would even go as far to say that on the whole I find it easier to work in metric, especially when scaling up from 1/10 scale drawings to full size. The only advice I would offer, without hopefully stating the obvious, is to use 1/16, 1/8 and 1/4in as your divisions rather than 1/10ths. That way you will be consistent with remaining imperial cutter and timber sizes.

COMPLETE CADS

The next argument is the CAD (Computer Aided Design) versus paper drawings. Many readers have computers and there are a variety of CAD packages on the market. Once again I have mastered, albeit with some difficulty, how to use 2D CAD as opposed to 3D. While 3D is more complicated, it allows you to 'extrude' a 2D shape to give it a rather spooky 3D appearance that can also allow rendering in fairly realistic textures including wood. You can also use directional lighting effects and even 'walkthroughs' and 'flyovers' that allow the viewer to apparently move around the on-screen image.

This is all well and good so long as you have enough time to learn this pretty complex package. Interestingly most cabinetmaking businesses, even the larger ones, use CAD for its 2D abilities only. This allows them to generate fairly accurate printed-out images with dimensions that can be used by craftsmen on the shop floor. I say reasonably accurate because such drawings aren't always as precise as they are cracked up to be when you apply a ruler to them.

Nevertheless, I have found that a good CAD package allows me to create my designs in a relatively short period of time, much quicker than the traditional method of using a pen, pencil and paper. I would however advise against cheap and cheerful CAD software as it may contain some idiosyncrasies. Its files, for example, may not be fully readable by other CAD programs and it may be prone to unexpectedly 'quit' or 'freeze'. It's well worth spending a bit more money investing in a proper CAD package.

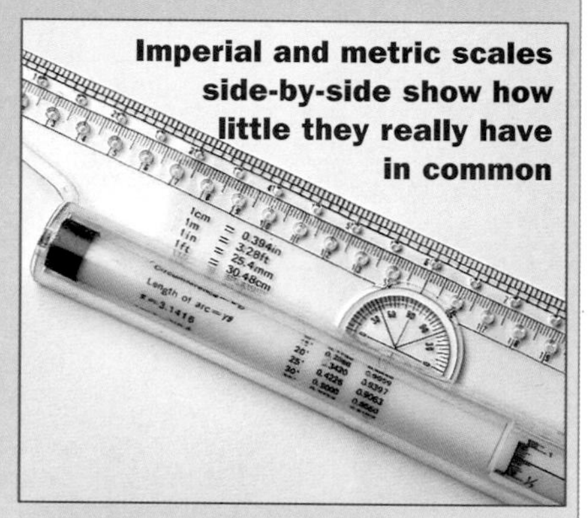

Imperial and metric scales side-by-side show how little they really have in common

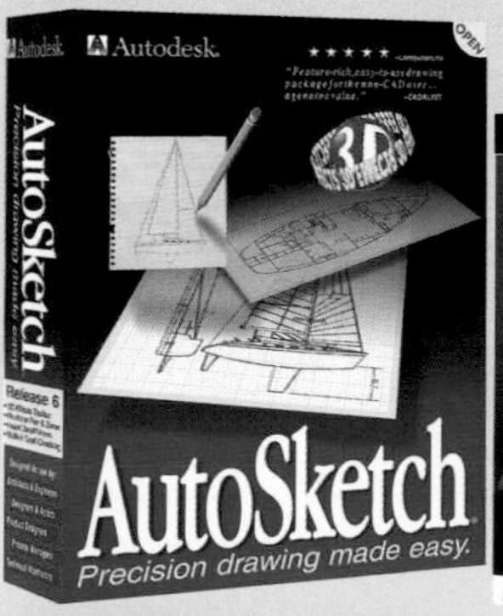

CAD software packages for PCs. Macs have their own CAD software

ALL ABOUT THE PAPER

Many of us will, of course, still use paper drawings which is no easy task. Swotting up on drawing technique from a book on the subject will help you get better, more easily interpretable results. However, here are some of the basics I've adhered to over the years which have served me well.

A non-bleed, ultra white, marker pen

"It is possible to draw any object, however awkward its shape, if you have enough time and skill."

drawing pad in A2 or A3 is ideal as it gives a good bright background to your lines. It's also easy to erase pencil or even technical pen lines using high quality chemical erasers (not the kiddy sort!) where a thin steel erasing shield is used to protect the surrounding lines.

Propelling pencils for technical drawing, in say 0.35mm and 0.50mm thicknesses, allow lines to be accurate without resharpening the points. Several technical pens with disposable ink cartridges are needed for truly clear finished drawings. My usual sizes would be 0.25mm, 0.35mm and 0.5mm. Any thicker and just one line can look like a tarmac road, except that is, on much bigger scaled drawings!

Simple drawing boards fitted with a parallel motion, or all plastic drawing boards with a clip on ruler and drawing head, such as those made by Rotring, are both very easy to use and take up very little space. A flexible curve and several templates with various radii are needed for drawing curved shapes. A scale rule with the most commonly used sizes such as 1:5, 1:10 and 1:25 is also required.

TECHNIQUE

It is possible to draw any object, however awkward its shape, if you have enough time and skill. Most woodworking projects however follow reasonably sensible shapes that shouldn't take too long to put down on paper. The reason for making proper drawings is to develop accurate visual information from which you, or for that matter anyone else, can then make the piece without too much difficulty.

I use the word 'develop' because as you draw one elevation of the piece you can start drawing the other elevations. The result is that any problems in the appearance or construction become evident enabling you to deal with them there and then. It also allows you to apply accurate dimensions to all important parts so that the piece can be correctly made.

The term 'elevation', used commonly in engineering and architecture, refers to one view of an object from a particular direction. Usually you have a front elevation, an end elevation and a plan view enabling you to see the proposed piece from three positions. If there is room to do all this on one piece of paper (A2 being the most likely) by lining the views up, it's possible to transfer critical lines from one view to another, saving time and ensuring that each part of the drawing matches the others in both shape and size.

Firstly set out the outline shape using pencil, remembering not to draw too heavily. You are allowed plenty of criss-cross construction lines that will need to be erased later. Carefully add in all the various components, using the scale rule to place each line or radius accurately. Certain details that are sometimes hidden are shown with dashed lines although this is easier to do at the ink stage. This will not always show enough detail in which case another cross-sectioned view is needed as well as the original elevation.

The next stage is to carefully ink the lines in. Make sure the technical pen is working well before you apply it to the drawing as it could cause a large ink blot which is impossible to remove. It may seem obvious but you should start inking a line from the beginning and stop at the other end. No dawdling, no unnecessary starts and stops, just one neat continuous line.

Always use rulers and templates with proper ink edges. These will have bumps or a rebate underneath to raise the edge off the paper and prevent ink running underneath and making a mess. Always keep a piece of blotting paper handy to wipe the pen tip and ruler clean. Give one line a few seconds to dry before starting on the next as you can easily smudge the first one. Once all the inking in is complete, remove the pencil lines with a 'pencil-only' eraser so as not to affect the ink.

Now add the dimensions using a thinner pen size with arrowhead lines and limit marks. It's no bad thing to add small blocks of text that explain important detail. Finally, title and date your drawing complete with the scale used. Any slight ink overruns can be erased using an ink eraser and a round edged blade fitted to a scalpel. The result should be a perfectly neat, self explanatory drawing from which you can make a cutting list, but I'll save that for next time.

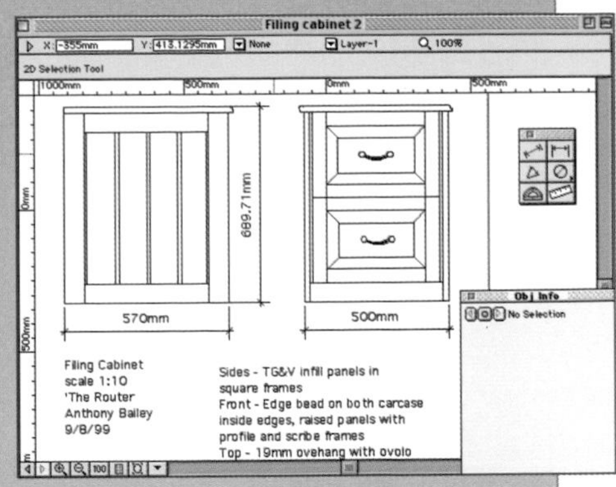

A typical 2D CAD drawing

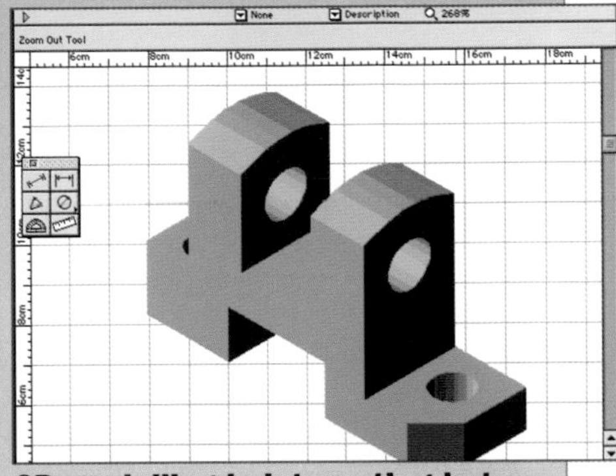

3D modelling is interesting but not strictly necessary for good readable drawings

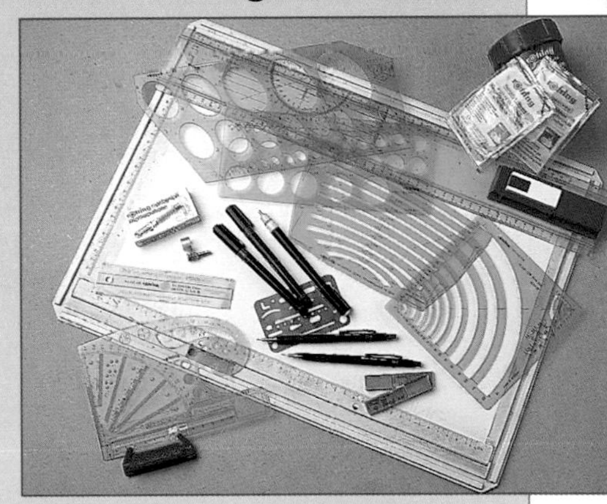

Lightweight drawing board with all the necessary equipment

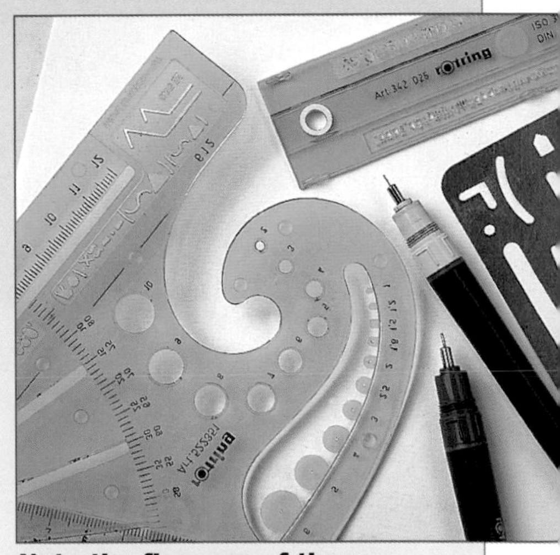

Note the fineness of the pen tips, the bumps on the templates and an erasing shield which prevents unintentional removal of other lines

Prepared timber in a trade timber yard

CUTTING LIST

Mechanics of Making continues with some tips on the best way to devise a cutting list

Marking out and sawing waney edged boards is laborious and time consuming

Some basic information about timber is necessary both at the design stage and as you prepare your cutting list, to ensure that you choose the right stock for each part of the job. I often find that when writing out a cutting list I need to make one or two common sense changes that I failed to take on board at the design stage.

Softwood is generally supplied prepared, in metric dimensions. These tend to vary slightly. Some DIY prepared softwood is finished slightly smaller than trade timber stocks in order to economise on raw material. Such is the nature of mass softwood production, that 'prepared all round' (PAR) stock is remarkably square and ready for use.

Hardwoods are typically supplied as through and through sawn boards. In this form, preparation is essential using a circular saw table followed by a planer thicknesser. I say 'essential' because these machines are used to cut the boards to width and then plane flat and square. Some timberyards offer this as a service, naturally for a charge, which is ideal if you don't possess these machines.

Man-made boards come in the standard 2440 x 1220mm which equates to 8 x 4ft. There is the less common size of 3 x 1.5m (10 x 5ft) and DIY stores often sell small pieces of board. These are expensive for the amount you get but take up less storage space. Choose the right board thicknesses for carcass sides and backs (thinner, lighter boards are quite adequate for back panels).

MATHEMATICS

Make a cutting list of finished sizes showing extra length for joint cutting where necessary. Opinions vary as to the best way to lay out such a list although I always do it this way:-

- **Material - softwood/hardwood/ply/MDF/etc. (specify which)**
- **Name of component**
- **Component size**

If the thickness is constant for most of the list, 19mm (¾in) veneered MDF for example (1mm (1/32in) is the approximate thickness of the veneer added to the 18mm (45/64in) MDF stock), put this before the material so as not to repeat it on every line that follows:-

- **Length (+ any extra for cutting waste) x width x number of pieces**

(If the thickness changes, which might be the case with a list of softwood sizes, then put it at the end of the list.)

An example would be:-

- **Softwood PAR**
- **Rail**
- **1470mm x 90 x 22 x 10off**

Note that I haven't bothered to put millimetres after each figure as this is only necessary if you are giving the list to someone else to work from. I don't use centimetres as I find it less complicated to work without inserting decimal points. At the end of the line I have used the term 'off' to denote the number of components, the standard term within the woodworking-trade. In the previous example above, that number is obviously 10.

Below is a cutting list for the front of a two panel radiator cover:-

- **18mm MDF**
- **Stiles 630mm x 65 x 2off**
- **Top Rail 980mm x 65 x 1off**
- **Bottom Rail 980mm x 80 x 1off**
- **Muntin 504mm x 65 x 1off**

ENGLISH

Firstly, the material of the front panel and the whole radiator cover is constant at 18mm, all being MDF which will be painted, as it can withstand the dry heat of the radiator. Therefore the thickness has been expressed first and is not repeated throughout the list.

The term 'stile' refers to the upright outer component of any door or panel frame. The bottom frame has its own line on the list, being wider than the top rail as visually this will appear more correct. This is true of other subjects such as the amount of frame around a painting. If you look in an art gallery you will see a wider area below each painting, and is a matter of aesthetics.

The last item on the list is called a 'muntin'. This is the centre upright that fits between the top rail and bottom rail. The name derives from the French – *montand* – meaning to mount or sit on, which is exactly what a muntin does. The length has been worked out by subtracting the width of both the top and bottom rail and then adding a very deliberate 19mm, the amount needed by the standard profile and scribe cutter set I used to mould and joint the whole front panel. This 19mm allowance is for the scribe part of the mould to plug into the profile shape on the two rails, (2 x 9.5mm per joint = 19mm). This is how I have arrived at both the sizes and quantities on the list. In other words I have considered the function, material, appearance and resulting sizes and quantities. Therefore this simple cutting list hides a hidden agenda because it was worked out using careful mathematical calculation.

CONCLUSION

If you have a lot of components, their machining needs a well ordered mind. You can make the job less of an ordeal by making a proper cutting list. As you work through the list, tick off what you have cut out and machined. This way you know exactly what is left to do as you approach the stage of being ready for assembly. The next article will look at the mechanics of working out the correct machining order.

Measuring diagonals to check the intended cut line is truly at 90°

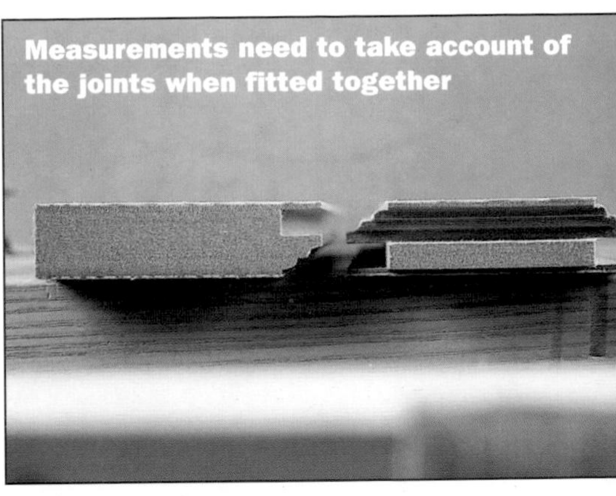

Measurements need to take account of the joints when fitted together

Careful stacking avoids confusion and mistakes

"If you have a lot of components, their machining needs a well ordered mind."

A typical frame with each component named for clarity

The methods are justified by the quality of the results

MACHINING ORDER

Continuing the mini-series on the Mechanics of Making, the focus is on selecting wood, marking out and the correct order of machining

It is important to mark out all defects before trying to cut components out of hardwood

When working with softwood, a calculator and cutting list are often all you need to help you decide how to cut out the components of a piece. There may be a bit of figure or decorative knots which you can use for certain key parts put aside for later. With hardwoods, you need to be a little more creative.

On one occasion I had a stack of oak boards, some with a plain figure and others with silver rays. My calculations revealed that I had enough of the silvery stuff for 14 out of 16 matching door panels! To make matters worse, the extra boards I then bought didn't have the same figure to match the rest.

CUT IT OUT

There is no easy answer when faced with this problem. However, by studying the boards and measuring and marking out prior to sawing, it is possible to detect potential problems before you have gone too far. I use a stick of chalk to mark sawn boards ready to cut. The beauty of a chalk line is that you clip one end of the line to one end of the board, hold the chalk taut along the required line and lift and 'ping' it, leaving a bright clear mark where you want to cut.

All pieces need to be well oversize, allowing for planing and sawing to the exact length later on. With man-made boards, it is possible to sketch out the board size (2440 x 1220mm is standard) on paper and divide it up to simplify the cutting process and minimise waste. This avoids lots of unnecessary 'criss-crossing' lines on the actual board and subsequent mistakes. Once you have worked out the cutting plan, draw it out clearly on the board.

Proceed to cut everything to rough oversize dimensions and use your cutting list as a constant guide, putting a line through each component once cut out. If there are several of each size, I usually put the appropriate number of diagonal slashes across the line of numbers on the list. This allows you to cut just a few of one component and complete the set later, in the hope of finding more suitable size pieces to cut the rest out of.

Try to stack everything in an orderly fashion and mark each sawn piece with an

The chalk line is a very quick, efficient way of marking rough sawn boards

Abbreviated markings help identify all components as they are processed

It is important to know which are the best surfaces in order to maintain the accuracy of components

The luxury of a planer thicknesser pretty much guarantees consistent results

Neat stacks of components avoids mistakes and having to reset the router table unnecessarily

Panel made with a reverse glue joint cutter, one half of the joint is machined from the other face

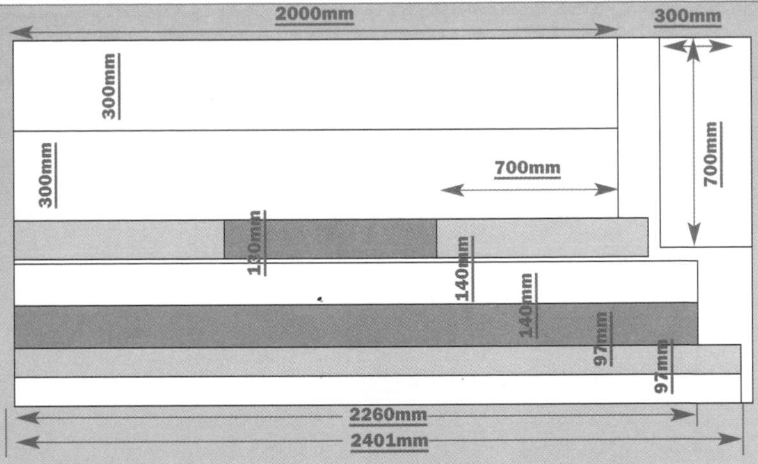

Planning your cuts saves both time and wastage

abbreviation such as FR TOP R, for the front top rail, or LWR BK P for the lower back panel, for example. This is useful as you can identify the components as they go through the planer. It's preferable to do your own planing as it is absolutely essential to get everything accurately sized and square. The conventional way is to plane a face until flat, then make a chosen adjoining edge which needs to be at 90° to the face. This face and edge need special marks to show that they are the reference surfaces from which the other face and edge are thicknessed from.

Thicknessing involves passing the opposite face and edge through the thicknesser part of the planer, taking off no more than 1–3mm at each pass until you have reached the final size. Turning the timber over between passes will ensure that the chosen face and edge are re-machined. This will improve the quality of the finish and so is preferable to 'overhand' planing. Re-mark the components with a soft pencil to avoid damaging the surface.

THE MACHINING FORMULA

Assuming all the parts have been prepared, there will be a succession of machining operations, many of which can be carried out using the router. Choose the most logical order of operations by thinking through how each will be carried out. Do this first when the components need to be cut precisely square and to length before machining. Sometimes joints need to be cut before any decorative moulding work, sometimes vice-versa. Stack the components ready for machining in neat piles according to the sequence of operations. This usually means that identical components will be stacked in one pile unless there is anything different about their machining that needs to be done.

SHOW & PROVE

In the previous article I used a radiator cover as an example, so if we have half a dozen covers to make, let's stack the components correctly. The joints and the main moulding decoration involve using a profile and scribe cutter set. This is one of the few examples where both operations are done in one go. The scribing operation is done first so that any resultant tear-out is machined away on the second pass which is the profile cut. This profile shape is the moulding around the inside edges of each frame of the radiator panel and is done for aesthetic reasons.

So first of all, the components to be scribe-cut are put in one pile. These are the top and bottom rails and the muntin (or centre upright). Since both ends of each piece are to be scribed, it isn't necessary to mark the ends as a reminder. Once the cutter is set and the scribing done, the cutter is reset for the profile cut.

Now we need to create a new stack. As this is such a simple operation, just the one stack will do. However, all components are profiled on one long edge only, with the exception of the muntin which is machined on both long edges. Rather than stack it separately, mark the correct edges on all the components with a pencilled cross. So one cross is pencilled on each component and two crosses on the muntin. There is another reason for marking them – a stile and rail cutter set normally requires that scribing is done from one face and then everything is turned over to profile from the other face.

Marking edges with a cross ensures they are the correct way up and eliminates any obvious mistakes. If the chosen face of the components is much better than the other face, it may be wise to put crosses on the scribe edges at the start. That way you are sure that all the best faces will be facing outwards and will match together nicely. When each set of components has been completely machined, put a pencil line through that part of your cutting list so you know it is complete. Other machining operations may then be needed, in this case, ventilation slots on the top and bottom rails. Again, the same stacking procedure is used to ensure consistency and completeness of the operation. If you are organised and thorough you can avoid unnecessary mistakes when machining.

Next time I will give some useful tips on good machining practice.

MACHINING CARE

The next level of the Mechanics of Making series: machining with the router

Advice is freqently given about how to machine using the router. Rather than reiterate the more obvious points, I am going to look instead at how you can increase your chances of getting a good result, safely. The first thing to decide is whether you will be working freehand or in a table.

OPTION ONE - FREESTYLING

As practised by most of us, basic freestyling involves using the router with a standard fence or a bearing guided cutter. These both carry risks because a relatively short fence or tiny bearing running against the workpiece, combined with the smallish base size of the router, do not ensure a precise or certain result. Fitting an enlarged sub-base, possibly with an extension to the side fitted with a hold-down knob, or even extended fence facings, give a much more acceptable degree of precision.

John Lloyd, an antique restorer and key contributor to *The Router*'s sister magazine, *Furniture & Cabinetmaking*, goes one step further in the search for freehand accuracy. When I was involved in furniture restoration, the router was the last thing I dared to apply to the surface of a valuable antique. John however, has devised a series of jigs for specific tasks that take the danger and scope for error out of such operations.

For example, he uses an MDF jig gently 'spiked' onto the surface of a chair back leg joint. This allows him to machine away the split and shattered area, typically found when the leg joint breaks, using a guide bush with the jig. It is then relatively simple to fit a 'key' of new wood that fills the recess and locks the upper and lower part of the leg together. So, here is an example of precise and controllable routing that gives a guaranteed result. Note that it involves the use of a guide bush, a highly accurate method of working.

OPTION TWO - THE TABLE

The second highly favoured option is to use a router table. Many operations are possible on the table and indeed this is usually more desirable than using the router freehand. A major let down is the quality and features offered by most ready-made tables.

A small table is fine if you are doing small work. Table extensions are alright if they are level and flush to the main table which itself needs to be truly flat and have no 'wind' or twist to the surface. You can check for yourself by using a steel straightedge and sighting carefully along the surface. If the top is out of true, you either need to correct it, if possible, or consider something better. This usually takes the form of making your own table, which is not as difficult as you might think. Birch ply or MDF make good surfaces although they need to be sealed and waxed to give the requisite degree of 'slip'. A key feature is the

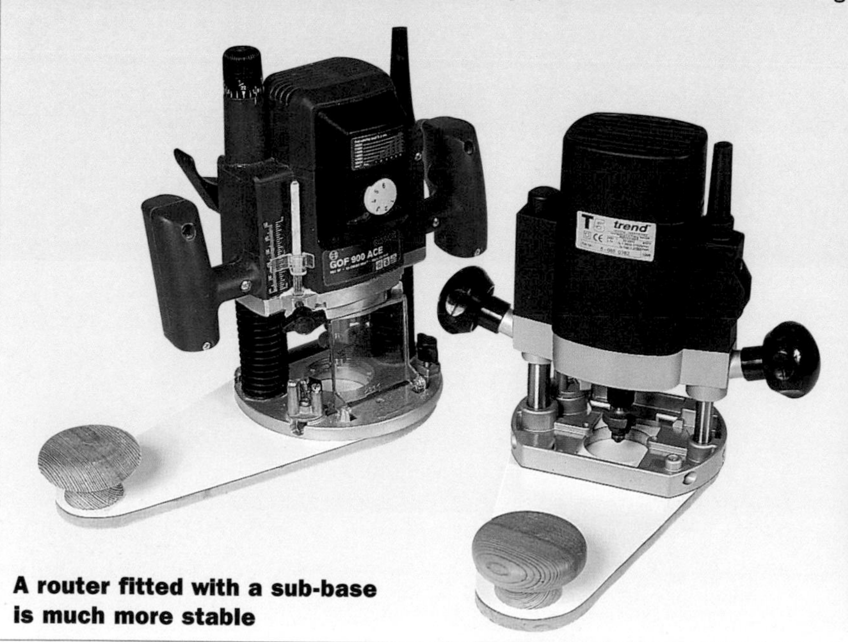

A router fitted with a sub-base is much more stable

John Lloyd's jigs enable safe, accurate repairs of valuable antique furniture

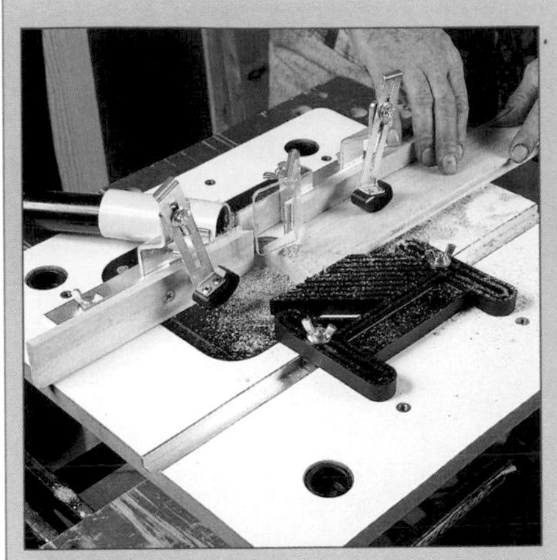

A small table is only really suitable for small work

A big router table allows safe accurate machining of long or large workpieces

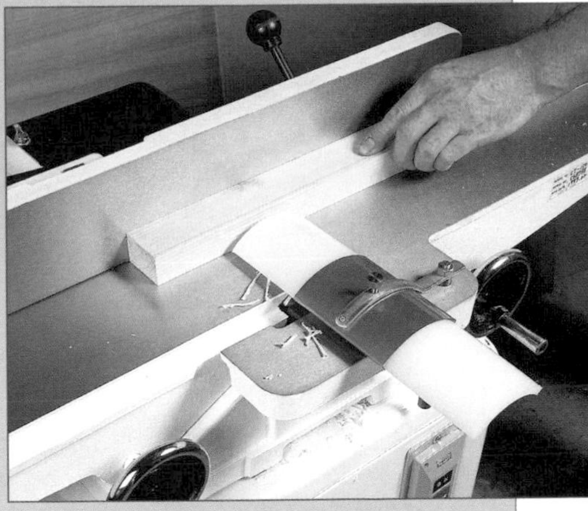

Good timber preparation is an important part of the machining process

need to support adequately underneath so it is kept truly flat. My own preference is for a table as large as a spindle moulder because it allows long sections and even frames to be machined.

It may seem basic but your table should be sitting firmly on a level floor. I have worked in workshops with very uneven floors and it makes precise machining difficult, if not downright impossible. Equally the fence faces need to be level and parallel to each other. Often they are slightly out of true which means that at the very least any moulding may be incompletely formed. A metre long steel rule is a good means for checking the faces. If they are out, it may be possible to use card, paper or veneer tape behind the sub-faces to true them up.

THE WOOD

Of course, none of this stands a chance if the timber itself is not accurately prepared in the first place. A well set-up saw table and planer/thicknesser makes all the difference, although prepared softwoods are generally very accurate in section, if not in length. A bow, concave way round against the table fence will prevent proper machining. If it is a convex side against the fence all the surface will at least get machined, although it may cut too deep which would cause the wood to slip into the gaps between the fences. Short workpieces make this less of a problem as any bow is a shorter section of an arc.

Obviously, none of this is a substitute for well prepared stock. Timber will often move after machining, even overnight. It may be desirable to plane timber oversize, leave to settle and finish planing the day before you unleash the router. This will help prevent the timber going out of shape. Hold-downs will also help control the workpiece. Small same-sized sections can be passed through a 'tunnel' fixed to the fence which will give a safe, efficient workholding and chatter-free finish.

THE CUTTERS

The cutters themselves need to be in good condition. Worn or damaged cutters will not perform well and consequently the cut finish will be poor, possibly with burn marks and tearing. New or well honed TCT or HSS cutters always give a far cleaner cut. With worn collets, there is a risk of the cutter slipping out and causing damage to work, or even worse, yourself. Regular replacement is thus essential.

SUMMING UP

It is down to us router users to ensure that at each stage of the making process every care has been taken. Failure to do so introduces elements of uncertainty that undermine the quality of the result. This is not only disappointing but increases the time taken as corrective filling and sanding may be required. This calls for extra lengths to be cut to cover the level of wastage created. By taking due care and doing things properly, you are, at the end of the day, saving yourself valuable time.

Don't expect precise results without proper hold-downs or spring fingers

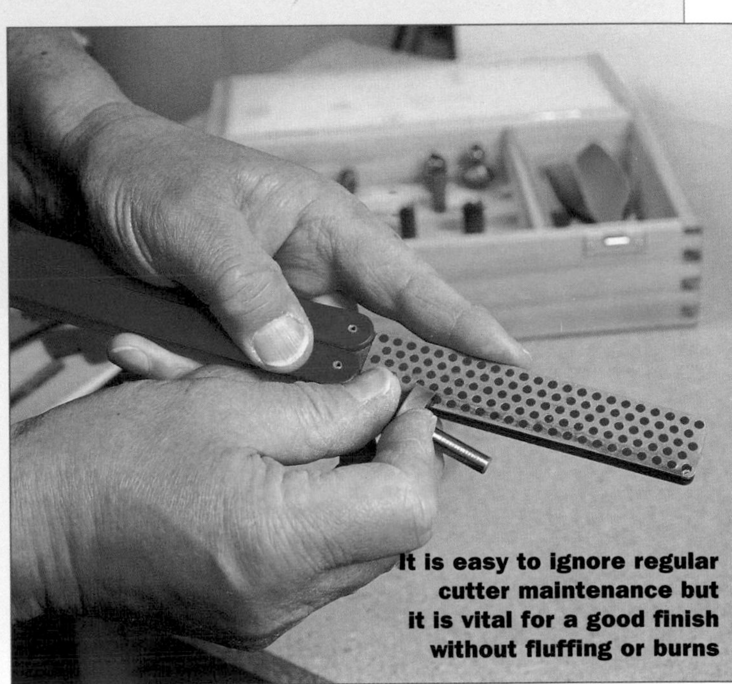

It is easy to ignore regular cutter maintenance but it is vital for a good finish without fluffing or burns

Sanding the inside of this piece would be impossible after assembly

FINISHING

The next instalment in the Mechanics of Making series takes a look at the art of applying a finish to a piece of work

An orbital and random orbital sander

They say that it all starts with the finish. I have looked at all the stages in the making process up to and including machining. Curiously, I have put this before 'Assembly' which forms the next part. You may well ask yourself why?

The answer is that failure to prepare and finish components at an early stage in the proceedings can give a disappointing outcome to say the least. That is not to say that you should be applying French polish, varnish or Danish oil before you put the job together, although this might be the case with intricate components.

This is rather an acknowledgement of the fact that filling, sanding, applying a finish, cutting back and polishing the final coats on the wood, are part of a logical sequence that assembly tends to interrupt. After all, if you are making a chest of drawers, the interior of both the chest and the drawers requires proper attention. You can't, for example, grab it straight off the planer, with glue stains and lumps of filler everywhere.

Internal surfaces must be brought to a finish before final assembly. This doesn't preclude dry fitting to check how it will go together, on the contrary. At this stage your components should be well machined with few defects present. There will be pencil marks and possibly knife marks on critical lines and you will be checking each part fits and is correctly marked to avoid wrong assembly. Now is the time to get out a sharp chisel and a dovetail saw in order to make fine hand adjustments that are not possible on a machine.

Pre-planning the whole construction helps to show the logical order of assembly. All internal surfaces should be sanded while disassembled, although external surfaces should generally be left. Choose good quality aluminium oxide papers available by the sheet or roll. Never use a grade coarser than 150 grit, unless doing initial belt sanding, as this would indicate your work is not good enough to start with. Machine sanding is easier on separate components and is generally better than hand-sanding. Try to use the correct amount of glue, and make sure that any overspill is removed while wet. Otherwise you will have to chisel it off very carefully when dry.

Flat or wide, joined boards may need belt sanding with the grain. Sand to 80 grit if it is very uneven, although 120 grit is better and can be used on newly veneered boards with care (a sanding frame helps).

The next step is to move on to finer sanding using an orbital or random orbital sander. Although it's more expensive, the latter gives a superior result. Velcro abrasive discs make the changing of coarse grades quick and hassle free. Start with no coarser than 150 grit, preferably 220 grit or 240 – even 320 is a good grade for the fine finishing of veneers. Use circular or figure-of-eight motions to even out the sanding pattern left by the disc. In the case of a plain orbital sander this isn't necessary but you should keep the sander moving. Be prepared to throw away worn or gummed up abrasive as the latter can mark the surface. Only mouldings and small sections need hand-sanding, which is best done before they are cut to length to avoid rounding over the pre-cut ends.

Above **Hand-sanding an edge – there are times when machine sanding isn't possible**

Right **A random orbital sander will give very good results**

Don't sand joint areas as these need to fit tightly together. Once each sub-assembly or full assembly is together you can turn your attention to the outside. If you have exposed joints, belt sanding may be necessary to level the surfaces. This might be too difficult with a plane or trimming cutter in the router. Proceed as before, using a random or plain orbital sander. Any applied mouldings should be left off as they interfere with machine sanding. Use a protected surface to place your work on – carpet can be useful but it may hide dangers such as screws or hard lumps of glue. Underlay is much smoother and hazards are more apparent. A large piece could sit on a couple of smooth battens. Getting help to turn it over will also avoid damage.

On a complex piece such as a wine rack for example, where various small components fit together, full finishing may be necessary. This means taping over all joints to exact lines or to the shoulders on tenons, etc. These areas stay completely bare of polish or varnish and can still be glued together afterwards. Any applied moulding should be put on last. The mitres need to be accurate and the use of filler should be kept to a minimum. Be careful when sanding mitred junctions of mouldings on an otherwise flat surface, as cross-grain scratches can easily occur. This becomes a serious problem if you intend staining the piece. The stain can do several things. It will absorb heavily into the endgrain, fail to absorb into plastic-type fillers or absorb differently to the surrounding wood and finally, show up any glue marks. This is where your earlier efforts in taking care pay off.

Whatever finish you apply, care is obviously needed. Use good quality applicators, such as brushes or French polishing rubbers that don't leave bits on the surface. Use 'friable' abrasives to flat off each coat. A friable abrasive breaks down and crumbles, so no deep persistent scratches occur. Proper finishing paper is coated with white coloured stearate wax powder that prevents the paper or particles of the sanded-off finish to stick to the surface of the work. The final top coats of any finish need to be with the grain and very evenly applied. Any further treatment should consist of nothing more than ultra fine 0000 wire-wool, a burnishing cream or a similar substance. At this stage abrasives have no part to play as even the finest grade will mark the surface.

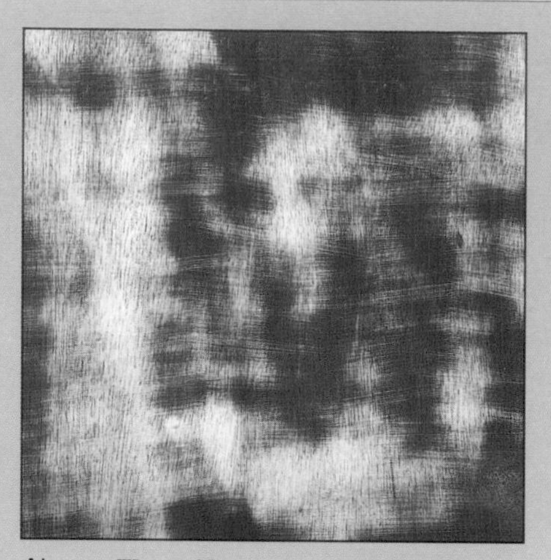

Above **The effect of cross-grain scratching has been exaggerated but it shows just how bad it can look**

Left **A taped joint with dye on it**

Above **A high finish like this takes time and trouble but is worth it**

Below **A selection of typical finishing materials**

ROUGHED UP

The science of abrasives is a complex and interesting one. Sadly, I lack the depth of knowledge to claim to be an expert. Nevertheless, I have done plenty of sanding in my time. The basic principle of abrasives is basically to rough something up to make it smooth again! Yes, it really is that simple if you think about it.

You start with a coarse abrasive and work through the grades, finer and finer until you get a surface that passes for finished. All the carefully graded but still irregular lumps of abrasive grit tear viciously at the surface of the wood and the combined scarification makes us believe that what we see and touch is actually smooth!

In the old days hand scrapers were used much more than they are now as well as materials such as shark skin with its naturally rough, abrasive surface. Antique furniture restorers sometimes use carefully cut pieces of glass as scrapers, on very hard short grained woods that can tear easily.

As a schoolboy I was in charge of the woodwork teacher's office/store, and what a treasure trove it was, containing everything that excited my interest as a would-be-woodworker. Among the pearl glue granules and all kinds of brass screws, there was some flint paper with its slightly greenish colour and softish nature, now no longer available. You can still obtain glass paper but it tends to be rather crumbly and not as relevant as modern aluminium oxide papers.

During my phase as a restorer I used quite a lot of garnet paper which is orange in colour and friable i.e. it crumbles after a while and thus avoids vicious lasting scratches. There is an abrasive for every situation and different ways of using it.

A great variety of abrasives are available for every task

ASSEMBLY

Mechanics of Making: careful assembly is all-important for the success of your furniture project

True to what I said in the previous part of this series, I am looking at 'assembly' after 'finishing'. This is because you have to consider how much you will be able to sand and finish a piece of furniture once it has been put together. Interior areas, joints and complex constructions can all pose a problem if they are not sanded carefully first.

Let's assume that you have been sensible and done what I have suggested – your masterpiece now has to be assembled carefully. Firstly, although everything except external surfaces may be sanded to a finish, you still need to be able to identify and fit the correct pieces together. A small table with identical legs will have the same joints but they may only fit well with particular components. Down the ages craftsmen have marked joints to overcome this problem, thus a leg may be marked A or 1 (traditionally Roman numerals have been used) and its matching rail marked the same. Where two rails fit into the leg, it may be better to have unique pencil or knife marks running across the assembled joint parts so it is obvious that they must fit when reassembled and glued together. When sanding these parts, it is possible to rub the pencil marks out unless they are underneath, in which case they will be hidden from the eye once assembled. I would recommend marking up the pieces with a knife as these marks are difficult to accidentally sand away.

Another point is that even before sanding you must do a dry assembly. This will tell you whether there are any problems that would be difficult to deal with later on. All joints ought to be a good fit and there should be no need for the excessive use of a hammer and block to get them in place.

GLUE

Although this is going back to the beginning, an important part of the design is your choice of glue. There are a variety of types and they all have different properties. PVA glue is cheap and dries at a reasonable rate. It is elastic by nature and not intended for filling joint gaps. In comparison, Cascamite powder needs to be carefully mixed to the right consistency, can cause dermatitis, fills gaps, is water resistant and has to be used within a certain time limit to prevent it expiring and going hard. There are various other examples with different characteristics that should influence your choice.

From an assembly point of view, making the right choice is essential. To get the best drying rate from any glue you need to warm up a workshop in winter and try and work in cool conditions in summer. In the latter case, slight things that may seem insignificant, such as opening doors and windows or gluing up early in the morning or late at night, really do make a difference. Laminating a curved shape from thin strips of wood using PVA is not a good idea because it is a flexible glue. Cascamite on the other hand, sets hard and fills any tiny gaps, making it ideal for this purpose.

ACCESSORIES & ORDER

The next thing is your assembly area. You need a clear working space and a flat surface big enough for the job in hand. Certain pieces like dining chairs or small tables can be stood on a saw table in order to ensure they stand level without any wobble. Once the glue has dried you won't be able to bend a frame to correct such a defect and all you can do is trim the legs until it stands rock steady.

Clamps and cramps are very important – you must have the right amount for the project in hand and they need to be dependable. Broken or poor quality cramps won't do what you need them to. Sash cramps are needed for carcass work, although strap clamps may be suitable on certain occasions. A good selection of G-clamps, mastic gun clamps and F-clamps will always come in handy.

On certain occasions, it can make sense to do several sub-assemblies. For example, the pieces for a table top can be cramped as one, as can the legs and underframe. In such a case the top would not be glued to the underframe as this would prevent it from moving. Screws and blocks would be much more suitable. Breaking down the assembly into several stages gives you better control of the process and prevents the glue from drying too quickly as the assembly time is shorter.

THE IMPORTANCE OF ACCURACY

Great attention needs to be paid to the accuracy. Correct marking out and machining will pay dividends as the

Unique pencil marked joint

From left to right – Aliphatic Resin, PVA & Cascamite

"From an assembly point of view, making the right choice is essential"

Knife-marked joint using Roman numerals

There is plenty of choice on the market

"Clamps and cramps are very important — you must have the right amount for the project in hand and they need to be dependable"

The two steel squares are more reliable than the rosewood square

tolerances will be finer and it should be easier to get the whole thing square. I never use ordinary carpenter's squares for checking as they are never accurate. Instead I use a couple of engineer's squares and a large roofing square which has been corrected with a punch and hammer, to spread the arms until they match one of the largest of my engineer's squares.

Cramps need to be placed right over joints rather than off to one side, which can cause bowing or distortion. Having said that, if an assembly is out of square you need to make an exception and do exactly what I have just told you not to – in order to bring things into line! Another way to check for square is by holding a steel tape rule across the diagonals. In theory this should be exactly the same measurement although in practice it seldom is. You need to get a good average of squareness in both directions.

It's a good idea to clean up the glue quickly, before it marks the work or becomes too difficult to remove. The use of a 'second best' chisel without any rough edges to it and a damp cloth usually does the trick. With oak, great care is needed as water can activate dark staining of the wood. It may be better to let the glue congeal slightly and then scrape it off. In this case a damp cloth is not needed.

Note that some operations such as hinge-recess cutting may be easier before assembly.

So there we have it, every part of the making process described in this series, from concept to finished article – now you can put this into practise!

RIP-OFF

Delta tablesaw

A tablesaw allows us to quickly cut timber both to width and length, provided some form of mitre fence or dimensioning carriage is fitted. Since giving up full-time professional woodworking, I have found myself in need of a cheap and compact tablesaw. I looked at what models were on the market and after careful consideration opted for the Delta machine.

This is a variant of the 'Made in Taiwan' model, available everywhere. It doesn't take up a lot of room, but has an extension to its extruded alloy top, a long, straight fence that is locked back and front, and takes a mitre fence. This model sounds fine, you may think, and if you make some slight allowances for performance, you'd be right. Naturally, these are better machines but they are heavier, may have cast tables, and cost rather a lot. I would hazard a guess that most readers are not using such machines.

CRUCIAL CUTTING

The saw's depth of cut is important – less than 50mm (2in) won't be much use on solid timber but it will tackle sheet material. The blade kerf or slot width will be narrower on a cheap table which is acceptable on lighter work, although thicker blades are preferable for heavy work. It needs to be TCT rather than steel plate, which will be very poor quality. The number of teeth will be adequate for general work although you may want to supplement it later on with a finer tooth blade for fine work and crosscutting. The blade may have a tilt-arbor for bevel cutting.

FENCING AND OTHER FEATURES

The fence needs to run the full length of the table and clamp at both ends so it won't flex or move out of alignment. The table itself may flex slightly if it is an extrusion like mine, but what wouldn't be acceptable on a professional machine is tolerable here. Guarding must be adequate and prevent timber lifting off the table if the saw tries to kick-back. A no-volt release (NVR) switch near the operator ensures you can knock it 'off' in a hurry if you need to. Finally, the mitre fence needs to be 'running', but not loose, fit in its groove and is better if it is 'trapped' so it cannot just lift out when you don't want it to. You need a table or roller stand at the out-feed side or another pair of hands, to catch the work. Some form of extraction, a mask and protective gloves are all essential for handling rough timber.

IN USE

That covers the essentials of a home tablesaw setup, but what about using it? Firstly, your chosen material needs to be suitable to put on a static saw. If you have 200 x 100mm (8 x 4in) panels that

In the first part of this Machining series, we start off by looking at the process of ripsawing and crosscutting

Above **Wood under crown guard**
Below **Fence set for ripping**

require cutting, you will need to use sawhorses, a portable electric saw and a straightedge first, in order to reduce the boards to manageable sizes. It isn't often that such boards are used at full size anyway. If your straightedge is straight and your saw has a fine blade, you should be able to do finished cuts without recourse to the tablesaw. You do need to remember the blade to baseplate offset each time, so your finished sizes are not hopelessly wrong.

When using the tablesaw it is the fence-to-blade distance which is critical for rip cuts. I don't rely on fitted scales, instead I use a good quality steel metre rule. Always switch off the saw and hold the rule against the blade, touching the fence squarcly in order to get the correct size, and recheck once the fence is locked. Make sure the fence is parallel to the blade or at least 'toeing-out' slightly to the rear. If it 'toes-in', wood will become trapped as you saw and may even kick back at you. For board sawing, a full-length fence surface is appropriate, but for ripping solid wood, a sub-fence that starts at the fence front and stops just past the blade's leading edge, ensures that if the wood warps on sawing apart, it won't become trapped.

When crosscutting small sections, the mitre fence comes into its own. Short pieces should be clamped to it and if a length stop is fitted you can use that for accurate repeat cutting to length. Failing that, clamp a large block to the rip fence at the very front, butt each piece against that and push onto the saw. The cut-off section will not then get dangerously trapped between blade and fence once it passes the block.

Wide pieces of sheet can be cut using the rip fence as a length-stop, but it cannot then be used as a mitre fence. The important thing is that the workpiece is neither too long nor likely to swing about on the table and the amount to be cut off is either a square or narrower piece. A piece that is longer than it is wide may get trapped at a slight angle and kick back with surprising force!

As using the router is our aim, sawing should be used to take this into account. It is possible to rip down quite small sections and mould them, but unless they are done using a device called a 'tunnel', the results may be rough and have burn and chatter marks. It is better to mould the edge of a wide board and saw each section off. A quick pass over a planer table will clean and straighten each new edge you wish to mould. Panels for frame and panel doors can be ripped and trimmed to size on the saw and then moulded. The edges don't really need planing as they will be hidden in a frame.

CROSSCUTTING

Crosscut saws fall into two main categories – those for the professional market and those for the DIY market. The professional models include radial arm saws, pull-over saws, where the saw blade is pulled or pushed across the wood, and compound mitre saws. The lighter DIY chopsaws typically have most of the functions of a compound mitre saw but with less power and a smaller capacity. If you only need to cut small sections, the latter type are fine, although the professional models fare better for standard carcassing and joinery sections.

THE RANGE

I have a professional crosscut saw which can do compound mitres, although I mostly use it for plain mitres. It has a powerful motor and a general purpose TCT blade that comes with it. This is acceptable most of the time but the more desirable fine-tooth blades cost quite a lot more. They leave a smoother, more chip-free cut finish. The turntable bed is quite large but there is a limit to the crosscut capacity compared to the more expensive machines.

It is hard to justify shelling out for a top-of-the-range saw unless you are working in a professional capacity. If the saw is well made and set up properly, it may be possible to do quite tolerable crosscutting of wider boards, provided the stock is properly prepared. A radial arm saw may seem like a panacea for all saw needs but it performs far less well as a ripsaw, compared to a separate tablesaw.

Small chopsaws are at home in the shed or garage and may even have a top rip-table for small work, but they can be quite limiting, capacity wise. Personally I would recommend buying a mid-range machine like the one I use. Top of the range models tend to be too expensive while those at the other end of the market are not really good enough for long and sustained use.

SETTING UP

Once you have bought your machine, it will need to be set up and checked. The factory settings for all positions may be correct but don't bank on it, always check. The use of an engineer's square, either Allen keys or screwdrivers and strips of timber for test cuts will allow you to adjust all the functions according to the manual. The blade needs to be truly upright and at 90° to the fence. These are the key settings for accurate cutting. After prolonged use you may need to recheck them.

Making scribing cuts on the router table relies on having good, squarely-prepared, stock to work with. For the router-user, cutting to length is essential. The question

Sub-fence fitted to main fence

Main fence and block used as length stop

Crosscut saw

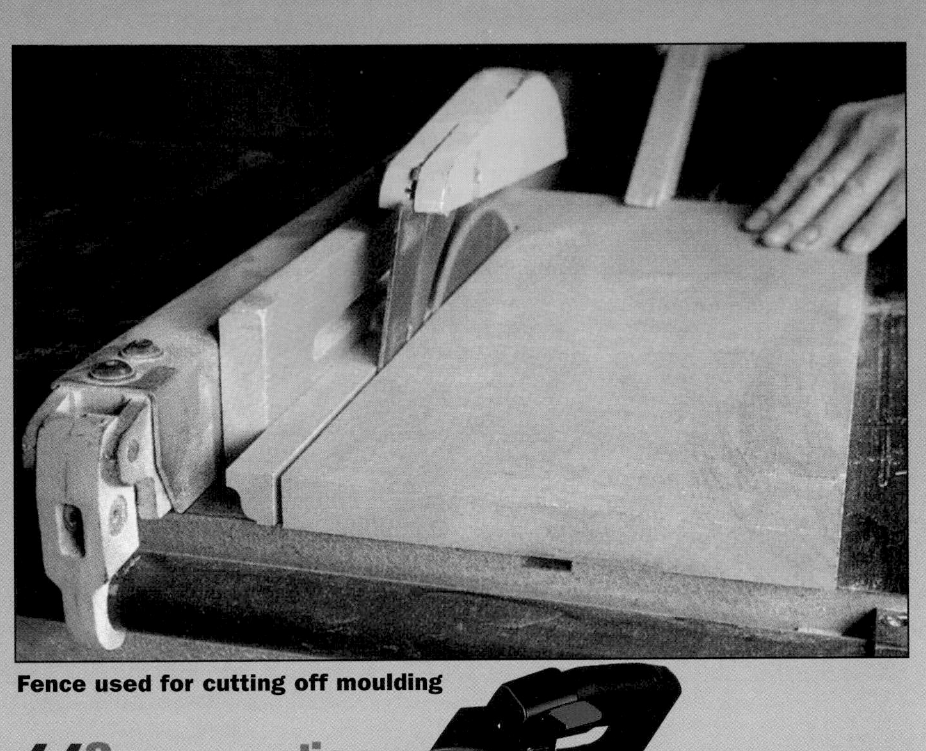

Fence used for cutting off moulding

“One operation that can defeat us, is cutting mitres ready for jointing”

Radial arm saw

Checking saw for square

is, at what stage? During ripcutting it becomes necessary to cut roughly to length so you end up with manageable sections. Precise cutting to length should only take place after planing to size (which is covered in the next article).

It makes sense to machine several short sections as one long piece. It speeds up operations, ensures more consistent moulding on the router, and allows us to choose which bits to use, thus avoiding any defects. A moulding on one face or edge may be neatly cut to length afterwards, so long as the blade enters the wood on that side. This is because ‘breakout’ will occur on the exit face where the teeth leave the wood. If you have a groove in one edge, it doesn’t matter what direction the blade attacks from as any exit face will be torn, which may be visible on assembly.

Common sense and experience dictate when to cut. Whether this occurs before or after routing depends on the components to be routed and how they are to be used. The problem of breakout occurs mostly when crosscutting, where the wood fibres are cut through, as opposed to ripsawing, where the blade cuts between the fibres.

TENONS AND MITRES

Where you are forming tenons to go in mortices and the like, the dimension of the end of the tenon is not that critical. In other words, the overall length of these components is far less important than the position of the tenon shoulder. It is still important to crosscut to a reasonably consistent length but the cut finish is not important as the tenon still has to be formed.

One operation that can defeat us, is cutting mitres ready for jointing. Cutting one mitre is easy but cutting four sets to form a frame or box is a little tricky as they may well not be at 45°. This inevitably means there will be gaps when assembled. Apart from the proper setting up of your saw, doing a test frame first will show the type of result you can get. Having matching pairs of components is essential. Most crosscut saws have a length stop which can be put to good effect for repeat length cutting. The work cramps fitted on a crosscut saw often aren’t up to the job and you need to be sure when you buy a saw that work-holding is just that and not likely to let the work move around.

A key advantage of a crosscut saw is its mobility. While it is great as a site tool, for routing you need to do as many operations in the workshop as possible. Routing on site, as well as crosscut sawing, is not only messy. It can lead to great inaccuracies that would be avoided if you were in the workshop. Extraction is always a must for a crosscut saw as dust output is substantial.

PLANE & SIMPLE

WHAT TO LOOK FOR

You need to look for certain things when choosing a machine:

- A flat table
- A fairly large flat fence that can be fixed accurately at 90° to the tables
- Plenty of power to cope with large workpieces
- If a thicknessing bed is fitted, it must be parallel to the cutter block
- Stability – no waggle when in use
- A good cut finish

With regard to the last part, this will generally be better when thicknessing because the work is being firmly held down by the feed rollers and the feed rate is constant. This compares favourably to planing on the top tables by hand. It is usual practice to thickness all surfaces after initial planing, as it will remove any ripples and tears caused on the hand-planed passes. The machine's manual will show you how to change and adjust the cutters in the cutter block. It looks simple but it needs care and re-checking before use as even a slight variation in cutter projection will affect the accuracy of the cut.

The next stage in the Machining series looks at the process of planing

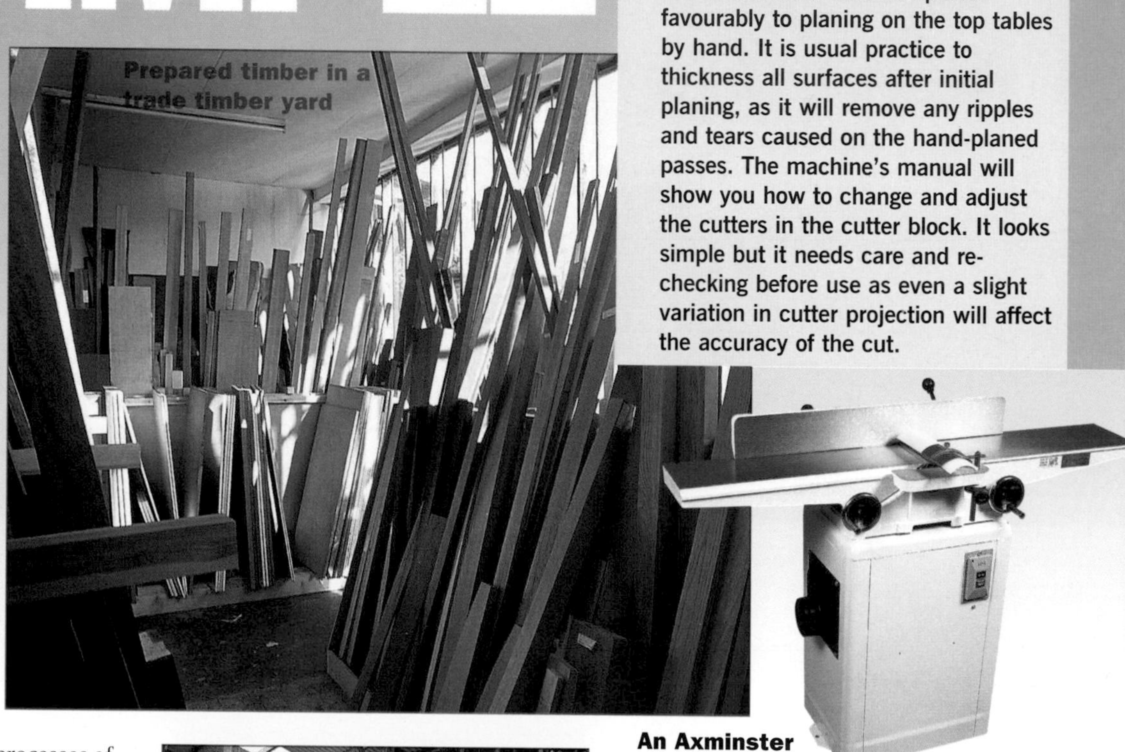

Prepared timber in a trade timber yard

An Axminster jointer

Somewhere between the processes of ripsawing and cross-cutting is where most surface planing takes place. The use of a saw alone is not enough to give us good, accurately-prepared pieces of wood, unless we are engaged in structural carpentry where precision isn't a factor. The electric planer, with its slicing blades and accurate bed surfaces, allows us to improve the state of the wood to the point where we can start machining with the router in earnest.

As with all other woodworking machines, there are choices to be made.

A full-blown professional planer/thicknesser is very heavy and costs a lot of money, but it will work day-in, day-out without complaint. At the other end of the spectrum there are hand-held electric planers. Lightweight, static machines come somewhere in between.

THE PLANER

If you use only softwoods, you may be able to avoid buying a planer. Softwood

An extensive range of high-quality softwood

bought from a decent timber yard, as opposed to a DIY superstore, is usually well prepared to accurate sizes. If you ask to select before you buy, you can choose straight, unwarped planks without resin or undue knots. However, if you need non-standard sizes or use hardwoods, a planer is required.

Starting with hand-held planers, we need to recognise that they are a good way of removing wood at an alarming rate, and as a result shower chippings everywhere. Accurate they are not! Some have inversion stands or even a special thicknessing base attachment. This gives us an expensive, yet very small facility that cannot give accurate results with long pieces of wood.

WHICH ONE?

The starting point must be some sort of small static machine. One of the most compact is the Axminster Perform surface planer model which is ideal for smaller sections. It is easy to move and will sit on a bench or table. It doesn't cost too much either. However, it lacks any means of thicknessing. Thicknessing is where a piece of wood, already planed on an adjacent face and edge, is re-run through the thicknessing part of the machine, making the other face and edge both flat and parallel to the first one.

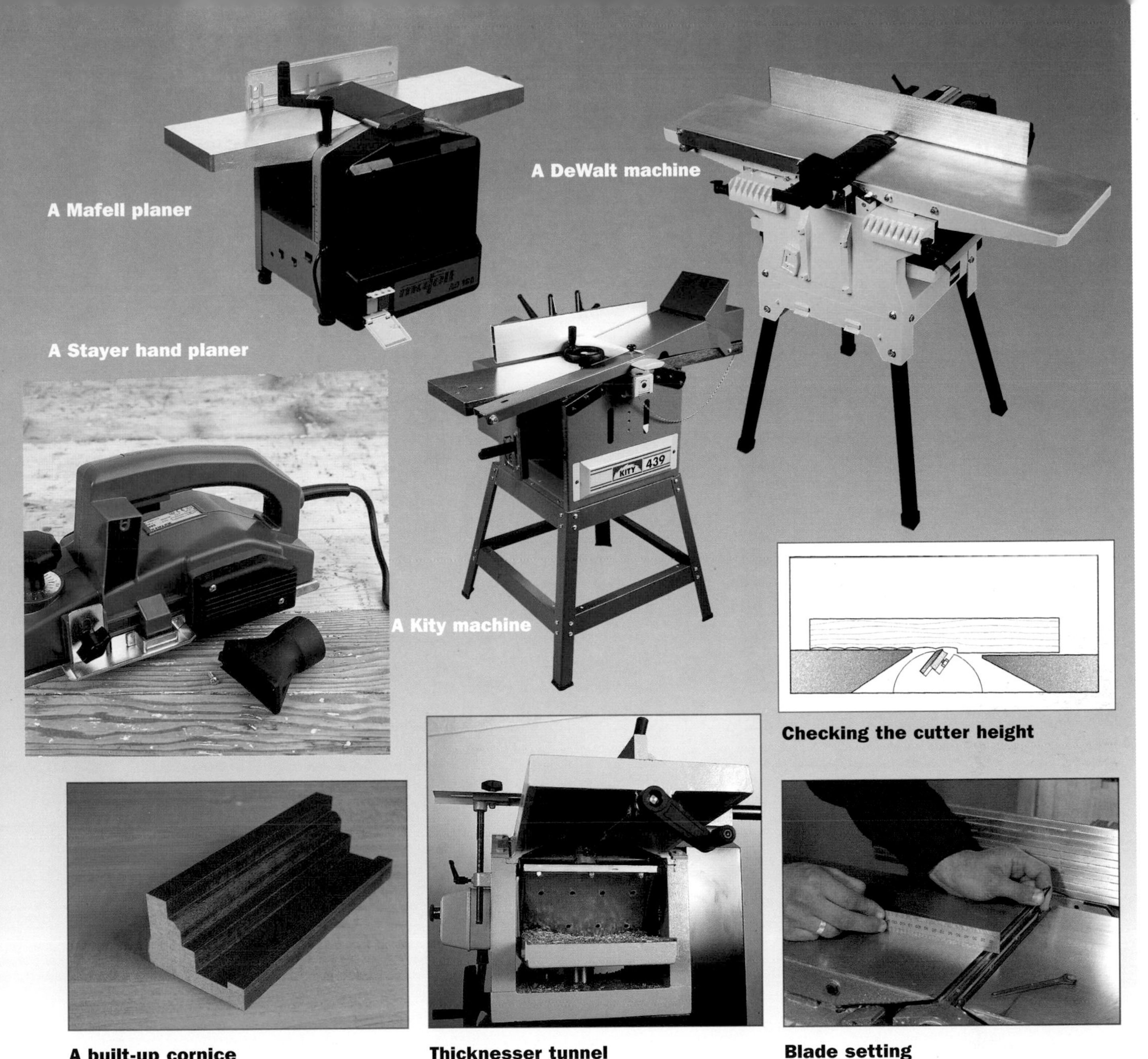

A Mafell planer

A DeWalt machine

A Stayer hand planer

A Kity machine

Checking the cutter height

A built-up cornice

Thicknesser tunnel

Blade setting

A step up might be the 'baby' Mafell. This does have a thicknessing ability making it more of a useful all-rounder. Next in line are the larger Kity and DeWalt models. The Kity does a reasonable job but the bigger DeWalt is better still. At this size there are competing models, all in a similar price range, which are well worth paying for, provided you are serious about wood. Anything above this and you are into the professional league.

UNLEASH THE ROUTER

Planing before routing is invaluable. Suppose you want to make up panels for frame and panel doors. Usually each panel will be made from two or more boards of the same thickness. This is especially true if you use reversible glue-joint cutters. Any inaccuracy at the thicknessing stage will result in a stepped joint which is difficult, if not impossible, to plane or sand smooth. To do this the thicknessing bed scale needs to be accurately adjusted so you can achieve consistent thicknessing easily.

Another example would be using a 'tunnel' to mould identical components. A tunnel is just that – made of ply or MDF it clamps to the fence of the router table, perching on top. It is accurately made and allows identically-sized small sections to be moulded safely and precisely in quantity and without 'chatter marks'. One workpiece is used to push the first piece through and so on. If you prepare the parts on the saw only, there will be size differences and surface roughness which will give poor results. Square, thicknessed stock will take care of this.

MOULDINGS

Built-up mouldings such as a cornice will benefit from proper preparation. Indeed, a cornice often has one or more separate unmoulded stages which a planer will do perfectly. Using a router is neither practical nor necessary. If you make a moulding, and even with your best efforts the cutter still tears the edge of the wood, it may be possible to run the moulded stock through the thicknesser and clean off the roughness, without substantially reducing the wood.

Once you have a planer, it proves its usefulness through the course of a job. Suppose you need a quick piece of moulding to finish something. You have the option of either going several miles down the road to the nearest DIY store, or preparing your own good, square stock and applying the desired moulding.

By the end of this series it becomes apparent that while a saw table is essential, so too is the trusty planer.

In the next part of the series we look at whether the router really is the most versatile power tool in the workshop and suitable for any job.

In the third and final part of the Machining series, find out about the machinery options available to the router user

WORK AIDS

Many home-based woodworkers use very little in the way of machines except for the router, drill and orbital sander. If you work on a small scale that's fine and through the artful buying of materials you can avoid some of the initial preparation work. Many woodworkers, however, have various machines, only some of which will be routers.

THE BIGGER PICTURE

In previous articles I have looked at tablesaws, crosscut saws and planers. But what about machines like morticers, spindle moulders, slot morticers, and dado heads on radial arm saws? It is foolish to pretend that the router can do everything with equal facility, so perhaps it is a case of choosing the right tool for the right job. That is, of course, provided we have the space and the money.

Some improvements to the workshop don't involve more machines. A bigger workbench, more assembly space or extra clamps may make life easier and productivity better. If you hanker after other machines, they may just take up valuable room and prevent you working efficiently. The router scores here of course, because it is so compact and portable.

CENTRES OF EXCELLENCE?

With this in mind, you may opt for an all-in-one workcentre like the Triton 2000, that is capable of sawing, routing, biscuit jointing and inverted jigsawing. A radial arm saw may be able to take a router mounted on a bracket for overhead working, thus providing a greater amount of facilities in the same amount of space. It may also be able to take a dado head and guard in place of the standard blade. This allows you to do wide housings (grooves) quickly. However, you need to set it up carefully each time and it may be easier and quicker to just use a straight cutter in the router table, especially for a one-off job.

The Triton workcentre

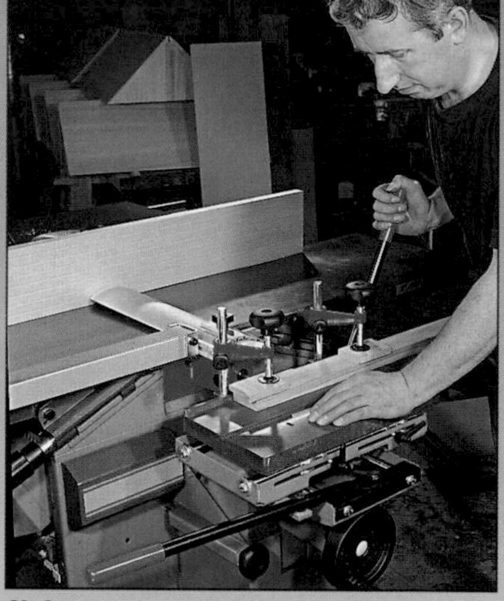

Using a slot morticer on a planer

PLANER/THICKNESSERS

In the previous article I discussed the planer and thicknessers. The medium to large models can usually take a slot morticer on the side. This allows morticing with workpieces clamped on a movable bed which is pulled across the special cutter mounted in a chuck on the end of the planer's cutter block. This sounds fine, but the chisels give a rough finish and quite a bit of effort is needed to pull the wood over the cutter. The slots are rounded at the ends just like a routed mortice. The slot morticer projects from the planer's side and makes quite an obstruction in a small workshop space.

CHISEL MORTICER

Next is the chisel morticer. This uses hollow, square chisels in different sizes with a matching boring bit in the middle. Small machines lack the facilities, capacity and efficient work-holding of

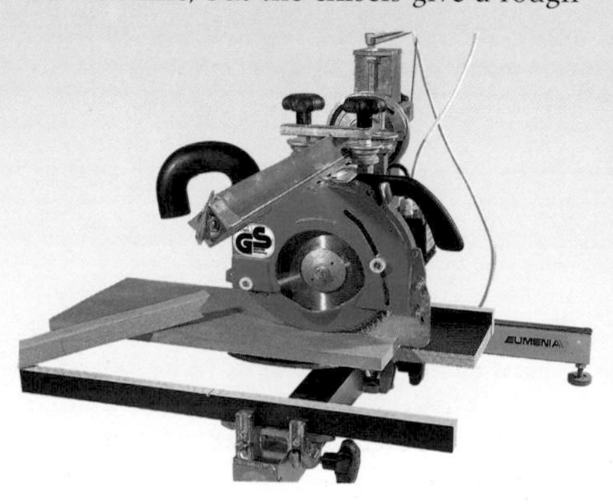

The Eumenia radial arm saw

Chisel morticer

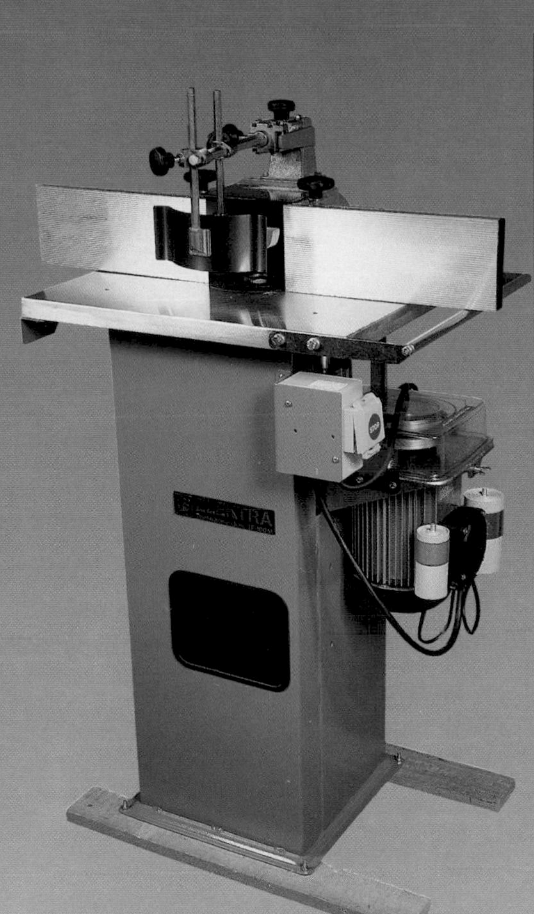

A spindle moulder from Elektra Beckum

Spindle moulding tooling

An Axminster shaper

the larger machines. However, they are still useful, with the capacity to do square mortices of any reasonable length or width and they can often go deeper than the longest straight router bit. A very useful machine if you can afford it, with the bonus that space isn't a problem due to the compact footprint.

MAKING MORTICES

If you don't need to do loads of mortices, the router will do a pretty good job instead. Except for very small mortices, a ½in big router is essential. It is easy to make up a mortice 'box' in which you can place the workpiece with the router sitting overhead, guided by the fence.

There are various extra long, straight cutters on the market which will do mortices of reasonable depth. These include the 'pocket' and 'stagger-tooth' cutters which are optimised for this sort of work. The stagger-tooth pattern lacks a bottom cutting insert and needs to be 'ramped' downwards as the router travels along, in order to get to proper depth. The pocket type may have a rather short cutting section, but can still plunge deep in passes, with the shank entering the hole to allow the cutter to reach deep. Round-ended mortices can be squared with a chisel, but it may be easier to round the tenons by hand. You can cheat by having square tenons that are simply a tight fit from end to end, so they bite slightly into the rounded ends of the mortice, with glue applied only to the faces or 'cheeks' of the tenon, not to the narrow edges.

SPINDLE MOULDER

The last most contentious machine is the spindle moulder. I have used a number professionally and to be honest, I have enjoyed working with them. Although they have a bad reputation for safety, any accidents that have occurred are more often than not down to the operator being careless. A number of settings and safety checks are required before switching on. Having done all that, they are remarkably easy to use. Modern safety pattern cutter blocks and electronic braking all contribute to this. There are some small spindle moulders, although the majority are substantial in both size and price. Tooling can be expensive – a set containing a block and a variety of interchangeable profile cutters is the basic requirement. Efficient guarding and hold-downs are vital.

A spindle moulder is perfect for long runs of moulding but it can be tedious setting up just for short lengths. It helps to machine more than you need, to avoid all the resetting required if you run short on a job. The cut finish is generally very good and improves further if an expensive power feed unit is installed. Small spindle moulders use only small diameter blocks, which puts them closer to routers in terms of peripheral speed at

"If you don't need to do loads of mortices, the router will do a pretty good job instead"

the cutting edge. Large machines have equally large cutter blocks and these improve the quality of the cut and finish.

An in-between solution might be the Axminster shaper table which is solid and very spindle moulder-like in appearance, but intended to drive router cutters, albeit at a slower speed than a router. Many users swear by these shaper units, so they could be worth a consideration in place of a router table or having to use spindle tooling, if you are nervous of it.

The pillar drill in use

THE ROUTER TAKES IT ALL

So, we come back to our friend the router. A large one, such as the Freud FT2000E, has plenty of power, takes up little space, is ideal mounted in a table and can be set up quickly for short runs. Spindle moulders are reckoned to give a better cut finish without burns or chattering, but this can be improved on the router table using multiple passes and good hold-downs or spring fingers.

ROVER

About the author

After a long early career as a professional photographer and assistant, Anthony made a clean break and followed up his other passion, which was woodworking.

For ten years he worked as an antique restorer, cabinetmaker, joiner and bespoke kitchen builder. Latterly, Anthony started writing articles for woodworking magazines and after many years' effort now finds himself in the lucky position of being the GMC in-house photographer shooting many woodworking subjects with which he is extremely familiar.

For authors and magazine contributors it is reassuring to discover that Anthony is very much on their wavelength and good at bringing out the best in his subjects when they come before his lens.

Anthony lives in a delightful cottage in East Sussex with Patsy his wife and four lovely children Francis (8), Amber (10), Lucy (12) and Alexander (14). They all have creative and artistic leanings which suggests they are very much 'a chip off the old block'!

Left:
Anthony seen here loading up his chunky, vintage Land Rover. For the Land Rover cognoscenti, it is a 1972 Series III short wheelbase 2.25 litre petrol engine model fitted with an unleaded cylinder head. It has been handed down to him by his father who bought it new and Anthony maintains it in tiptop condition. His children have christened it 'Poison Ivy' (naming of Land Rovers is a common practice in the UK).

Conversion table: inches to millimetres

inch		mm
1/64	0.0565	0.3969
1/32	0.03125	0.7938
3/64	0.046875	1.1906
1/16	0.0625	1.5875
5/64	0.078125	1.9844
3/32	0.09375	2.3812
7/64	0.109375	2.7781
1/8	0.125	3.1750
9/64	0.140625	3.5719
5/32	0.15625	3.9688
11/64	0.171875	4.3656
3/16	0.1875	4.7625
13/64	0.203125	5.1594
7/32	0.21875	5.5562
15/64	0.234375	5.9531
1/4	0.250	6.3500
17/64	0.265625	6.7469
9/32	0.28125	7.5406
5/16	0.3125	7.9375
21/64	0.1328125	8.3344
11/32	0.34375	8.7312
23/64	0.359375	9.1281
3/8	0.375	9.5250
25/64	0.390625	9.9219
13/32	0.40625	10.3188
27/64	0.421875	10.7156
7/16	0.4375	11.1125
29/64	0.453125	11.5094
15/32	0.46875	11.9062
31/64	0.484375	12.3031

inch		mm
1/2	0.500	12.700
33/64	0.515625	13.0969
17/32	0.53125	13.4938
35/64	0.546875	13.8906
9/16	0.5625	14.2875
37/64	0.578125	14.6844
19/32	0.59375	15.0812
39/64	0.609375	15.4781
5/8	0.625	15.8750
41/64	0.640625	16.2719
21/32	0.65625	16.6688
43/64	0.671875	17.0656
11/16	0.6875	17.4625
45/64	0.703125	17.8594
23/32	0.71875	18.2562
47/64	0.734375	18.6531
3/4	0.750	19.0500
49/64	0.765625	19.4469
25/32	0.78125	19.8438
51/64	0.796875	20.2406
13/16	0.8125	20.6375
53/64	0.828125	21.0344
27/32	0.84375	21.0344
55/64	0.858375	21.8281
7/8	0.875	22.2250
57/64	0.890625	22.6219
29/32	0.90625	23.0188
59/64	0.921875	23.4156
15/16	0.9375	23.8125
61/64	0.953125	24.2094
31/32	0.96875	24.6062
63/64	0.984375	25.0031
1	1.00	25.4

Index

TITLES AVAILABLE FROM

GMC Publications

BOOKS

Woodcarving

Beginning Woodcarving	*GMC Publications*
Carving Architectural Detail in Wood: The Classical Tradition	*Frederick Wilbur*
Carving Birds & Beasts	*GMC Publications*
Carving the Human Figure: Studies in Wood and Stone	*Dick Onians*
Carving Nature: Wildlife Studies in Wood	*Frank Fox-Wilson*
Carving on Turning	*Chris Pye*
Celtic Carved Lovespoons: 30 Patterns	*Sharon Littley & Clive Griffin*
Decorative Woodcarving (New Edition)	*Jeremy Williams*
Elements of Woodcarving	*Chris Pye*
Essential Woodcarving Techniques	*Dick Onians*
Lettercarving in Wood: A Practical Course	*Chris Pye*
Making & Using Working Drawings for Realistic Model Animals	*Basil F. Fordham*
Power Tools for Woodcarving	*David Tippey*
Relief Carving in Wood: A Practical Introduction	*Chris Pye*
Understanding Woodcarving in the Round	*GMC Publications*
Woodcarving: A Foundation Course	*Zoë Gertner*
Woodcarving for Beginners	*GMC Publications*
Woodcarving Tools, Materials & Equipment (New Edition in 2 vols.)	*Chris Pye*

Woodturning

Adventures in Woodturning	*David Springett*
Bowl Turning Techniques Masterclass	*Tony Boase*
Chris Child's Projects for Woodturners	*Chris Child*
Colouring Techniques for Woodturners	*Jan Sanders*
Contemporary Turned Wood: New Perspectives in a Rich Tradition	*Ray Leier, Jan Peters & Kevin Wallace*
The Craftsman Woodturner	*Peter Child*
Decorating Turned Wood: The Maker's Eye	*Liz & Michael O'Donnell*
Decorative Techniques for Woodturners	*Hilary Bowen*
Green Woodwork	*Mike Abbott*
Illustrated Woodturning Techniques	*John Hunnex*
Intermediate Woodturning Projects	*GMC Publications*
Keith Rowley's Woodturning Projects	*Keith Rowley*
Making Screw Threads in Wood	*Fred Holder*
Turned Boxes: 50 Designs	*Chris Stott*
Turning Green Wood	*Michael O'Donnell*
Turning Pens and Pencils	*Kip Christensen & Rex Burningham*
Useful Woodturning Projects	*GMC Publications*
Woodturning: Bowls, Platters, Hollow Forms, Vases, Vessels, Bottles, Flasks, Tankards, Plates	*GMC Publications*
Woodturning: A Foundation Course (New Edition)	*Keith Rowley*
Woodturning: A Fresh Approach	*Robert Chapman*
Woodturning: An Individual Approach	*Dave Regester*
Woodturning: A Source Book of Shapes	*John Hunnex*
Woodturning Masterclass	*Tony Boase*
Woodturning Techniques	*GMC Publications*

Woodworking

Advanced Scrollsaw Projects	*GMC Publications*
Beginning Picture Marquetry	*Lawrence Threadgold*
Bird Boxes and Feeders for the Garden	*Dave Mackenzie*
Celtic Carved Lovespoons: 30 Patterns	*Sharon Littley & Clive Griffin*
Celtic Woodcraft	*Glenda Bennett*
Complete Woodfinishing (Revised Edition)	*Ian Hosker*
David Charlesworth's Furniture-Making Techniques	*David Charlesworth*
David Charlesworth's Furniture-Making Techniques – Volume 2	*David Charlesworth*
The Encyclopedia of Joint Making	*Terrie Noll*
Furniture-Making Projects for the Wood Craftsman	*GMC Publications*
Furniture-Making Techniques for the Wood Craftsman	*GMC Publications*
Furniture Projects with the Router	*Kevin Ley*
Furniture Restoration (Practical Crafts)	*Kevin Jan Bonner*
Furniture Restoration: A Professional at Work	*John Lloyd*
Furniture Restoration and Repair for Beginners	*Kevin Jan Bonner*
Furniture Restoration Workshop	*Kevin Jan Bonner*
Green Woodwork	*Mike Abbott*
Intarsia: 30 Patterns for the Scrollsaw	*John Everett*
Kevin Ley's Furniture Projects	*Kevin Ley*
Making Chairs and Tables	*GMC Publications*
Making Chairs and Tables – Volume 2	*GMC Publications*
Making Classic English Furniture	*Paul Richardson*
Making Heirloom Boxes	*Peter Lloyd*
Making Screw Threads in Wood	*Fred Holder*
Making Shaker Furniture	*Barry Jackson*
Making Woodwork Aids and Devices	*Robert Wearing*
Mastering the Router	*Ron Fox*
Pine Furniture Projects for the Home	*Dave Mackenzie*
Practical Scrollsaw Patterns	*John Everett*
Router Magic: Jigs, Fixtures and Tricks to Unleash your Router's Full Potential	*Bill Hylton*
Router Tips & Techniques	*Robert Wearing*
Routing: A Workshop Handbook	*Anthony Bailey*
Routing for Beginners	*Anthony Bailey*
Sharpening: The Complete Guide	*Jim Kingshott*
Sharpening Pocket Reference Book	*Jim Kingshott*
Simple Scrollsaw Projects	*GMC Publications*
Space-Saving Furniture Projects	*Dave Mackenzie*
Stickmaking: A Complete Course	*Andrew Jones & Clive George*
Stickmaking Handbook	*Andrew Jones & Clive George*
Storage Projects for the Router	*GMC Publications*
Test Reports: *The Router* and *Furniture & Cabinetmaking*	*GMC Publications*
Veneering: A Complete Course	*Ian Hosker*
Veneering Handbook	*Ian Hosker*
Woodfinishing Handbook (Practical Crafts)	*Ian Hosker*
Woodworking with the Router: Professional Router Techniques any Woodworker can Use	*Bill Hylton & Fred Matlack*

Upholstery

The Upholsterer's Pocket Reference Book	*David James*
Upholstery: A Complete Course (Revised Edition)	*David James*
Upholstery Restoration	*David James*
Upholstery Techniques & Projects	*David James*
Upholstery Tips and Hints	*David James*

Toymaking

Scrollsaw Toy Projects	*Ivor Carlyle*
Scrollsaw Toys for All Ages	*Ivor Carlyle*

Dolls' Houses and Miniatures

1/12 Scale Character Figures for the Dolls' House	*James Carrington*
Americana in 1/12 Scale: 50 Authentic Projects	*Joanne Ogreenc & Mary Lou Santovec*
Architecture for Dolls' Houses	*Joyce Percival*
The Authentic Georgian Dolls' House	*Brian Long*
A Beginners' Guide to the Dolls' House Hobby	*Jean Nisbett*
Celtic, Medieval and Tudor Wall Hangings in 1/12 Scale Needlepoint	*Sandra Whitehead*
Creating Decorative Fabrics: Projects in 1/12 Scale	*Janet Storey*
The Dolls' House 1/24 Scale: A Complete Introduction	*Jean Nisbett*
Dolls' House Accessories, Fixtures and Fittings	*Andrea Barham*
Dolls' House Furniture: Easy-to-Make Projects in 1/12 Scale	*Freida Gray*
Dolls' House Makeovers	*Jean Nisbett*
Dolls' House Window Treatments	*Eve Harwood*
Easy to Make Dolls' House Accessories	*Andrea Barham*
Edwardian-Style Hand-Knitted Fashion for 1/12 Scale Dolls	*Yvonne Wakefield*
How to Make Your Dolls' House Special: Fresh Ideas for Decorating	*Beryl Armstrong*
Make Your Own Dolls' House Furniture	*Maurice Harper*
Making Dolls' House Furniture	*Patricia King*
Making Georgian Dolls' Houses	*Derek Rowbottom*
Making Miniature Chinese Rugs and Carpets	*Carol Phillipson*
Making Miniature Food and Market Stalls	*Angie Scarr*
Making Miniature Gardens	*Freida Gray*
Making Miniature Oriental Rugs & Carpets	*Meik & Ian McNaughton*
Making Period Dolls' House Accessories	*Andrea Barham*
Making Tudor Dolls' Houses	*Derek Rowbottom*
Making Victorian Dolls' House Furniture	*Patricia King*
Medieval and Tudor Needlecraft: Knights and Ladies in 1/12 Scale	*Sandra Whitehead*
Miniature Bobbin Lace	*Roz Snowden*
Miniature Embroidery for the Georgian Dolls' House	*Pamela Warner*
Miniature Embroidery for the Tudor and Stuart Dolls' House	*Pamela Warner*
Miniature Embroidery for the Victorian Dolls' House	*Pamela Warner*
Miniature Needlepoint Carpets	*Janet Granger*
More Miniature Oriental Rugs & Carpets	*Meik & Ian McNaughton*
Needlepoint 1/12 Scale: Design Collections for the Dolls' House	*Felicity Price*
New Ideas for Miniature Bobbin Lace	*Roz Snowden*
Patchwork Quilts for the Dolls' House: 20 Projects in 1/12 Scale	*Sarah Williams*

Crafts

American Patchwork Designs in Needlepoint	*Melanie Tacon*
Bargello: A Fresh Approach to Florentine Embroidery	*Brenda Day*
Beginning Picture Marquetry	*Lawrence Threadgold*
Blackwork: A New Approach	*Brenda Day*
Celtic Cross Stitch Designs	*Carol Phillipson*
Celtic Knotwork Designs	*Sheila Sturrock*
Celtic Knotwork Handbook	*Sheila Sturrock*

Celtic Spirals and Other Designs — *Sheila Sturrock*
Complete Pyrography — *Stephen Poole*
Creating Made-to-Measure Knitwear: A Revolutionary Approach to Knitwear Design — *Sylvia Wynn*
Creative Backstitch — *Helen Hall*
Creative Embroidery Techniques Using Colour Through Gold — *Daphne J. Ashby & Jackie Woolsey*
The Creative Quilter: Techniques and Projects — *Pauline Brown*
Cross-Stitch Designs from China — *Carol Phillipson*
Decoration on Fabric: A Sourcebook of Ideas — *Pauline Brown*
Decorative Beaded Purses — *Enid Taylor*
Designing and Making Cards — *Glennis Gilruth*
Glass Engraving Pattern Book — *John Everett*
Glass Painting — *Emma Sedman*
Handcrafted Rugs — *Sandra Hardy*
How to Arrange Flowers: A Japanese Approach to English Design — *Taeko Marvelly*
How to Make First-Class Cards — *Debbie Brown*
An Introduction to Crewel Embroidery — *Mave Glenny*
Making and Using Working Drawings for Realistic Model Animals — *Basil F. Fordham*
Making Character Bears — *Valerie Tyler*
Making Decorative Screens — *Amanda Howes*
Making Fabergé-Style Eggs — *Denise Hopper*
Making Fairies and Fantastical Creatures — *Julie Sharp*
Making Greetings Cards for Beginners — *Pat Sutherland*
Making Hand-Sewn Boxes: Techniques and Projects — *Jackie Woolsey*
Making Mini Cards, Gift Tags & Invitations — *Glennis Gilruth*
Making Soft-Bodied Dough Characters — *Patricia Hughes*
Natural Ideas for Christmas: Fantastic Decorations to Make — *Josie Cameron-Ashcroft & Carol Cox*
New Ideas for Crochet: Stylish Projects for the Home — *Darsha Capaldi*
Papercraft Projects for Special Occasions — *Sine Chesterman*
Patchwork for Beginners — *Pauline Brown*
Pyrography Designs — *Norma Gregory*
Pyrography Handbook (Practical Crafts) — *Stephen Poole*
Rose Windows for Quilters — *Angela Besley*
Rubber Stamping with Other Crafts — *Lynne Garner*
Silk Painting — *Jill Clay*
Sponge Painting — *Ann Rooney*
Stained Glass: Techniques and Projects — *Mary Shanahan*
Step-by-Step Pyrography Projects for the Solid Point Machine — *Norma Gregory*
Tassel Making for Beginners — *Enid Taylor*
Tatting Collage — *Lindsay Rogers*
Tatting Patterns — *Lyn Morton*
Temari: A Traditional Japanese Embroidery Technique — *Margaret Ludlow*
Trip Around the World: 25 Patchwork, Quilting and Appliqué Projects — *Gail Lawther*
Trompe l'Oeil: Techniques and Projects — *Jan Lee Johnson*
Tudor Treasures to Embroider — *Pamela Warner*
Wax Art — *Hazel Marsh*

Gardening

Alpine Gardening — *Chris & Valerie Wheeler*
Auriculas for Everyone: How to Grow and Show Perfect Plants — *Mary Robinson*
Beginners' Guide to Herb Gardening — *Yvonne Cuthbertson*
Beginners' Guide to Water Gardening — *Graham Clarke*
Bird Boxes and Feeders for the Garden — *Dave Mackenzie*
The Birdwatcher's Garden — *Hazel & Pamela Johnson*
Broad-Leaved Evergreens — *Stephen G. Haw*
Companions to Clematis: Growing Clematis with Other Plants — *Marigold Badcock*
Creating Contrast with Dark Plants — *Freya Martin*
Creating Small Habitats for Wildlife in your Garden — *Josie Briggs*
Exotics are Easy — *GMC Publications*
Gardening with Hebes — *Chris & Valerie Wheeler*
Gardening with Wild Plants — *Julian Slatcher*
Growing Cacti and Other Succulents in the Conservatory and Indoors — *Shirley-Anne Bell*
Growing Cacti and Other Succulents in the Garden — *Shirley-Anne Bell*
Hardy Palms and Palm-Like Plants — *Martyn Graham*
Hardy Perennials: A Beginner's Guide — *Eric Sawford*
Hedges: Creating Screens and Edges — *Averil Bedrich*
The Living Tropical Greenhouse: Creating a Haven for Butterflies — *John & Maureen Tampion*
Marginal Plants — *Bernard Sleeman*
Orchids are Easy: A Beginner's Guide to their Care and Cultivation — *Tom Gilland*
Plant Alert: A Garden Guide for Parents — *Catherine Collins*
Planting Plans for Your Garden — *Jenny Shukman*
Plants that Span the Seasons — *Roger Wilson*
Sink and Container Gardening Using Dwarf Hardy Plants — *Chris & Valerie Wheeler*
The Successful Conservatory and Growing Exotic Plants — *Joan Phelan*
Success with Orchids in the Greenhouse and Conservatory — *Mark Issac-Williams*
Tropical Garden Style with Hardy Plants — *Alan Hemsley*
Water Garden Projects: From Groundwork to Planting — *Roger Sweetinburgh*

Photography

Close-Up on Insects — *Robert Thompson*
Double Vision — *Chris Weston & Nigel Hicks*
An Essential Guide to Bird Photography — *Steve Young*
Field Guide to Bird Photography — *Steve Young*
Field Guide to Landscape Photography — *Peter Watson*
How to Photograph Pets — *Nick Ridley*
In my Mind's Eye: Seeing in Black and White — *Charlie Waite*
Life in the Wild: A Photographer's Year — *Andy Rouse*
Light in the Landscape: A Photographer's Year — *Peter Watson*
Outdoor Photography Portfolio — *GMC Publications*
Photographing Fungi in the Field — *George McCarthy*
Photography for the Naturalist — *Mark Lucock*
Viewpoints from *Outdoor Photography* — *GMC Publications*
Where and How to Photograph Wildlife — *Peter Evans*

Art Techniques

Oil Paintings from your Garden: A Guide for Beginners — *Rachel Shirley*

VIDEOS

Drop-in and Pinstuffed Seats — *David James*
Stuffover Upholstery — *David James*
Elliptical Turning — *David Springett*
Woodturning Wizardry — *David Springett*
Turning Between Centres: The Basics — *Dennis White*
Turning Bowls — *Dennis White*
Boxes, Goblets and Screw Threads — *Dennis White*
Novelties and Projects — *Dennis White*
Classic Profiles — *Dennis White*
Twists and Advanced Turning — *Dennis White*
Sharpening the Professional Way — *Jim Kingshott*
Sharpening Turning & Carving Tools — *Jim Kingshott*
Bowl Turning — *John Jordan*
Hollow Turning — *John Jordan*
Woodturning: A Foundation Course — *Keith Rowley*
Carving a Figure: The Female Form — *Ray Gonzalez*
The Router: A Beginner's Guide — *Alan Goodsell*
The Scroll Saw: A Beginner's Guide — *John Burke*

MAGAZINES

Woodturning ◆ Woodcarving ◆ Furniture & Cabinetmaking ◆ The Router ◆ New Woodworking
The Dolls' House Magazine ◆ Outdoor Photography ◆ Black & White Photography ◆ Travel Photography
Machine Knitting News ◆ BusinessMatters

The above represents a full list of all titles currently published or scheduled to be published. All are available direct from the Publishers or through bookshops, newsagents and specialist retailers. To place an order, or to obtain a complete catalogue, contact:

GMC Publications, Castle Place, 166 High Street, Lewes, East Sussex BN7 1XU, United Kingdom
Tel: 01273 488005 Fax: 01273 478606 E-mail: pubs@thegmcgroup.com

Orders by credit card are accepted